RUDRANEIL SENGUPTA is the deputy editor of 'Lounge', the weekly feature section of *Mint*. He lives in New Delhi with his wife and five dogs. He holds a master's degree in English from Jadavpur University, Kolkata, and worked as a sports journalist for TV news channels till 2010. In 2008, he was awarded the Ramnath Goenka Award for Excellence in Journalism for a documentary on river rafting in India (Best Sports Journalist, TV). In 2015, he won the Society of Publishers of Asia (SOPA) award for excellence in reporting on human rights issues for a story he co-wrote with Dhamini Ratnam on gender testing of female athletes.

ENTER THE DANGAL

*Travels through
India's Wrestling Landscape*

Rudraneil Sengupta

Harper
Sport

First published in India in 2016 by Harper Sport
An imprint of HarperCollins *Publishers* India

Copyright © Rudraneil Sengupta 2016

P-ISBN: 978-93-5029-769-8
E-ISBN: 978-93-5029-770-4

2 4 6 8 10 9 7 5 3 1

HarperCollins *Publishers*

A-75, Sector 57, Noida, Uttar Pradesh 201301, India
1 London Bridge Street, London, SE1 9GF, United Kingdom
Hazelton Lanes, 55 Avenue Road, Suite 2900, Toronto, Ontario M5R 3L2
and 1995 Markham Road, Scarborough, Ontario M1B 5M8, Canada
25 Ryde Road, Pymble, Sydney, NSW 2073, Australia
195 Broadway, New York, NY 10007, USA

Typeset in 10.5/13.5 Minion Pro at
SÜRYA, New Delhi

Printed and bound at
Replika Press Pvt. Ltd.

For Mandakini Gupta

CONTENTS

PREFACE

IN THE BEGINNING there was the Great Gama. He was India's first sporting superstar. From Peshawar to Patna, from Junagadh to Jamshedpur, in Calcutta or Dhaka or Srinagar or Madras—there was no place where the Great Gama did not draw magnificent crowds.

He was not a big man. There were other wrestlers of legendary heft, but this compact tempest of muscle had blown them all off the ground.

More than half a century after his death, Gama remains a powerful memory, wrapped in a myth: an oral legend passed from wrestler to wrestler in every wrestling school in India.

An old wrestler told me: 'When I am ill, I look at a portrait of Gama that hangs in my akhada. I feel the illness leave me, I feel my strength surging back.'

Who really was the Great Gama?

This is a book that explores wrestling as it is practised now in India; the men, women and events that have shaped its history from Gama to Sushil Kumar; whose two Olympic medals yanked the sport out of its rural obscurity and on to TV screens. It is a journey through the wrestling landscape of India, both past and present.

From behind the scenes with India's Olympic wrestlers to akhadas quietly defying urbanization. From dangal to dangal in villages and small towns to the intrepid women who dared to break the barriers in this 'manly' sport. From Gama's journey to becoming a 'world champion' to the man who became one of the first Asians to foray into staged American pro wrestling, what we now know popularly as World Wrestling Entertainment (WWE).

Through the voyage, an observation: wrestling is not obscure, and never has been. It has only been hidden from those who have never tilled land. Kushti rules the farmlands. It has done so for centuries. It has had pride of place in the courts of Chalukya kings and Mughal emperors. It was embraced by Hinduism and Islam, and has led its own gentle revolution against the caste system, rejecting its fundamental underpinnings.

The British loved it when they first came to the country, and understood immediately its importance to India's martial tradition. Then they turned against it during the freedom movement.

Nonetheless, this is not a book of history, nor is it a scholarly investigation.

The focus of this book is to tease out the lived experience of Indian wrestlers now, to share their daily life (for wrestling is not a sport, as every wrestler told me, but a way of life), their struggles and beliefs and their oral tradition. The historical references are used as a storytelling tool, to give context and depth—when needed—to the stories and beliefs that are an integral part of the wrestling philosophy.

Since wrestling in India now is dominated by the northern states—Haryana, Delhi, Punjab, Uttar Pradesh and Maharashtra— the book too stays largely within these geographical boundaries.

The southern states of India, as well as places like Bihar and Gujarat, can claim a rich history of the sport, but in the present times, wrestling has all but disappeared from these places, surviving only in little pockets. No international wrestlers come out of these areas, nor do they form a part of the local 'dangal' circuit. I have had to leave those pockets out.

The most glaring omission here, a question I can't shake off, is the puzzling decline of a Muslim wrestling culture. As the importance of Gama—Ghulam Muhammad—attests, there was once, not so long ago, a thriving and vibrant community of Muslim wrestlers. Much of the lexicon of Indian wrestling, for example, consists of Persian and Arabic words, and contemporary wrestlers and coaches are well versed with the exalted importance of wrestling in the Mughal court, and the contribution of the Mughal Empire in spreading the culture of wrestling through patronage. Now, a Muslim wrestler is as rare as an Indian Olympic champion. This loss deserves a book of its own, and is far beyond the scope of this one.

The names of two people in this book have been changed on their request—Satbir and Billu Singh.

THE TALE OF THE TWO-TON WRESTLER

There was once a two-ton wrestler who was undefeated. Restless to meet someone who could truly challenge him, the giant went in search of a certain three-ton wrestler he had heard of. He did not have to go far. The two wrestlers met at a farmer's field, and began wrestling immediately. It was a furious match and the earth shook as they grappled. There was a herd of fifty goats nearby, but the wrestlers, consumed by their fight, did not notice them, and crushed six goats to death.

The goats belonged to an old woman. When she saw what happened, and that the wrestlers had gone on wrestling without any heed, she gathered both the dead and living goats and put them in a bag, and slung the bag over her back. Then she picked up the two-ton wrestler and put him on one shoulder. She picked up the three-ton wrestler and put him on her other shoulder, and started walking home. The wrestlers were still too much in the heat of battle to notice.

As she walked, a black vulture got a sniff of the dead goats in her bag and circled down towards her. It grabbed the old woman and flew off. As the bird flew over the king's palace, the woman slipped from its talons, and landed in the eye of the princess, who was sitting on the palace roof. The princess rubbed and scratched frantically, but could not dislodge the thing that had gone into her eye. She called her courtiers, she called the royal doctor, but no one could help. Finally, the king had to call a high council to figure out what to do. The council agreed that a fisherman renowned for his skills must be called in to cast a net into the princess's eye and drag out whatever it was that caused her such discomfort.

The fisherman came with his family and cast the net. Then they pulled and pulled. Days went by. The fisherfolk grew more and more tired. Finally, they pulled the net all the way through the eye, and there, in the net, was the old woman, her bag of goats, and the two wrestlers—still grappling on her back, as if nothing had happened.[1]

Section I

The Olympic Wrestler

1

ENTER THE DANGAL

Finally, silence. The man selling boiled eggs has snuffed out his hissing burner and rattled off, his wobbly cart stacked high with empty egg trays. The sweet-lime-juice man followed soon after, leaving a wake of fragrant citrus peel. The akhada courtyard is now empty, except for two men noiselessly plastering posters on the walls of the wrestling hall in the middle of the square. They are working by the light leaking out from the row of rooms that form the periphery, thin veins of pale yellow against the dark.

'The biggest wrestling competition in Haryana,' the posters say. 'The biggest prize money ever', in supersized lettering, above a row of photographs of politicians too smudged to recognize in the dark. The two men litter some handbills outside the row of rooms for good measure and leave.

One by one, the lights in the rooms start going off. The wrestlers will sleep now. Only in the outhouse, where Mehr Singh reclines in front of the television, is there a light on. This small room has three single beds laid out parallel to each other, like in military barracks, and the TV is tuned to a music show. Mehr Singh's eyes are heavily glazed, and more bloodshot than usual, the result of three hours of steady drinking and smoking. He had started smoking his hookah soon after he woke up at four in the morning, drawing on the cool, long pipe all day long.

Since sundown, he has also drunk his way through half a litre of cheap whisky. The room smells sharply of tobacco. Mehr Singh looks at me uncomprehendingly for a moment, then follows my gaze to his glass which is perched precariously on the bed, some whisky still left in it.

'It's not good for a wrestler,' he says a little apologetically. 'When I was young, even the smell of this,' he points to the glass, 'even the smell bothered me. But now it's like water.' As if to prove this, he picks up the glass and empties it in one gulp. He leans towards me, like a giant fish swimming up through water, and says, 'You are all set? You will go to the dangal tomorrow?'

He smiles slowly when I say yes, nods a couple of times in approval. 'It will be a good one,' he says. 'It's an old competition; I have fought there many times, once got a bad injury there. Of course, back then, we used to walk to these dangals. When the season came, it was walk, walk, walk. We would walk ten miles, fifteen miles, to reach a dangal. We would get there, wash ourselves at a pond, or a river if there was one, and go to sleep under a tree till the competition begun. That was the life. You needed nothing. A tree to sleep under, and food, and that's it.'

He becomes wistful. His dark head tilts towards his chest, the heavy-lidded eyes close. The prickly jowl collapses into his neck. Then he wakes up again.

'Old scars ache in this weather,' he says, his voice the deep rumble of a heavy engine in low gear. He lifts his pyjamas to the knees and rubs one and then the other in slow circles. 'All wrestlers have bad knees. It is the curse of the sport.'

Mehr Singh's house, a sprawling bungalow, is just a couple of steps away from his wrestling school—the akhada. The house has large balconies, a massive ornate gate topped with sharp spikes, two large, happy dogs who run out of those gates at every opportunity, and windows everywhere.

Every day of the week bar one, Mehr Singh sneaks out of those gates in the predawn light, dressed in sparkling white kurta-pyjamas, shuffles to the akhada compound and walks around watching his coaches bawl out the late-risers. The wrestlers all come and touch Mehr Singh's feet before beginning their daily routine. He inspects the rooms, and then the two wrestling halls. One hall stands in the centre of the akhada. It boasts a glass façade. Inside, there is just enough space for a single Olympic-sized wrestling mat. The more accomplished senior wrestlers practise here. The other hall is a detached structure at one end of the main akhada building. It is large, with three mats, and weights stacked in one corner. Climbing ropes dangle down from its high roof. There are homilies scrawled on the walls in bold lettering.

Between the large hall and the main building is the earthen wrestling pit. Mehr Singh stops here, bends to touch the earth, lets it run through his fingers, and touches a finger to his forehead. Then he settles down on a plastic chair under the shade of a young banyan tree outside, his hookah fired up. He spends his entire day here; smoking, watching. For lunch he moves to the outhouse, where food is brought out to him. When training resumes in the evening, he occupies his chair once more. Coaches, senior wrestlers, neighbours and friends drop by all day. In the evening, when the workday is over, Mehr Singh holes himself up in the outhouse with the TV and his whisky.

Now it's late, and the akhada is asleep. He switches off the TV, struggles to his feet and shuffles out. The room is plunged into silence, and then faint noises outside begin reasserting themselves: the distant throb of highway traffic, the dopplered faraway swoons of truck horns, a tap dripping somewhere close by.

Finally, like an outcast sneaking back into a place where he is not allowed, Mehr Singh makes his way back home. But home is not for him. If he could, Mehr Singh would never leave the akhada he built.

It is the season for dangals. Winter is on the ebb. The harvest festivals are only just round the corner.

Satbir pahalwan—one of Mehr Singh's favourite students—wants to make as much money as he can fighting in village tournaments over the next sixty days. His itinerary is loosely defined; the biggest dangals of the season are marked out: one in Haryana this week, Delhi in three weeks' time, a big fight in Punjab, somewhere near Chandigarh, just four days after Delhi, then to Rajasthan, and finally, when the heat has settled and winter well forgotten, a major tournament in Uttar Pradesh. In between the big ones, there are numerous small dangals to choose from; but those decisions will be taken on the fly. Satbir and I do a rough calculation: if all goes to plan, he would have covered around 3,500 km by the end of the season.

He is eighteen, and this is his first serious foray into the circuit. But Satbir has been fighting dangals since he was twelve years old; as part of a youthful akhada team, he has fought in hundreds of tournaments in the immediate vicinity of Rohtak.

Anyway, that was not for money. Now he must build his own reputation, learn where he stands as a wrestler, and try to make his living off it. If things go well, next year he plans to go as far as Maharashtra, where the dangals offer three times more money, he says, than in Haryana or Punjab, or even Delhi.

As long as the season lasts, the pahalwan will be on the road, sleeping when he can and where he can. He will make his home in cars, buses, trains and railway stations.

He will expect the villages where he goes to fight to provide food. Good food, the food of the pahalwans, with plenty of ghee, milk and thick rotis.

The pahalwan will do all the things that his guru himself had done more than thirty years ago.

Mehr Singh had graduated, briefly, from a village wrestler to a national-level athlete, winning medals at top competitions. He even won a medal at the Asian level, before a torn knee ligament, left largely untreated, curtailed his career. Before him, his father had worked the village circuit with considerable success. Before that, his grandfather and his great-grandfather, and perhaps even further back, though Mehr Singh cannot reach that far into the past with any certainty. The travelling wrestler is an ancient figure in India, he tells me—it is a tradition thousands of years old. He is just one of the uncountable many who have walked across the vast plains, looking for fame and money through the art of wrestling.

'The difference between me and my grandfather is that he could walk to Pakistan—even Afghanistan!—if he wanted to. There were no borders in his time,' Mehr Singh says. 'I was bound by what is India now.

'And the difference between me and Satbir...' Mehr Singh stops, thinks about it, smiles. '...is that he doesn't really have to walk anywhere.'

At noon, as the akhada is about to plunge into a siesta, Satbir's brother comes to pick him up for the first of this season's tournaments, being held in a village called Ritauli, a little less than 25 km from Rohtak.

Satbir is late—standard, I'm told, for the travelling wrestler—and his brother drives beyond all reason or sense. He floors the accelerator at the tiniest window of opportunity, and brakes very late, throwing everything he has on the pedal. The car lurches forward like a raging bull. Through the congested town roads, with his palm flat against the horn, he manoeuvres like a man out to kill and maim. On the highway, the speed makes it worse. When he brakes, it feels like the car will flip on its front wheels. When he swerves, it is a miracle that the car doesn't keel over on its side. Every few kilometres, traffic from both sides of the highway gets abruptly and dangerously squeezed on to a single lane because of construction work on the other side. Even this does not deter the frantic driver, who misses oncoming trucks by reckless inches.

The pahalwan manages to sleep through all this, reclining on his seat, even as his solid head bounces brutally. The brother, a lean man with light grey, twinkling eyes with crow's feet around them, has nothing about him that suggests he is a homicidal maniac—except for the thin-lipped, wry smile that stays fixed on his face through the drive.

When we finally get off the highway, and careen through a muddy dirt road into the village, he starts slowing down. Then Satbir's brother speaks for the first time since we met. He turns around with that same wry smile, and says, 'Satbir will become an international pahalwan, bhai, but I'm already an international driver.'

Up ahead, there is a large gathering at the edges of the village, smothered in a cloud of dust. The dangal has begun already. Next to where Satbir's brother has parked the car, wrestlers are using a water tanker to shower down after their muddy bouts. A wrestler holds the attached pipe above his head, lets the water gush over him. He is wearing a red langot. As the dust washes off his skin, the beautiful trained muscles of his arms, shoulders and chest, and the long slabs of muscle on his thighs glisten in the sun. Satbir is stocky—his muscles bulge but don't separate into symmetrical sections—but this man here is a vision of pure athleticism. The ancient Greeks could have used him for a model of the perfect Olympian. A boy of about eight or nine is staring at him too, mouth agape.

A few feet away, in a large clearing between the last line of houses and the rolling wheatfields of the village, wrestlers are kicking up dust as they scuffle. Four fights are on simultaneously, watched by a widening circle of men six to seven rings deep, the last of those concentric circles formed by cars and tractors. Most of the cars belong to the wrestlers, and there is a constant bustle as they step in and out of them to change, eat, drink, fight, or sleep. People have gathered on the roofs of the bigger cars. The tractors have been parked expressly for the purpose of giving people in the last circle a raised viewing platform. Beyond this, carts selling sugar cane juice, sweet lime juice, chickpeas, peanuts, iced lollies and golgappas are doing brisk business.

A man yells incessantly into a loudspeaker, announcing the names of wrestlers, the villages they come from, their gurus and akhadas, and commenting on the skills and techniques on display. He lets forth fawning harangues on VIP guests—local politicians, bureaucrats and businessmen—who, it is announced, are great philanthropes donating money not just for the dangal, but for a new temple in the village as well. He shifts seamlessly to a harsh, reproving tone for the misbehaving crowd, who are engaged in a constant and low-key battle of pushing and shoving, which turns intermittently into proper scuffles. The action on the field is equally riotous. Fights spill out of the arena and are taken up by partisan supporters. Villagers wielding long sticks swish around with unhinged menace to keep spectators away from the wrestling area. Flying dust makes the fights impossible to follow.

Satbir pahalwan waits patiently. He takes his time fixing his red langot, then his brother massages some oil on him. As his fight—one of the prime slots for the evening—approaches, he begins to limber up next to his car. He jackknifes into push-ups. He does a few rapid squats. He jerks his thick neck muscles left and right to warm them up. Finally, his name is announced. It's the last fight of the day, a heavyweight bout, and a local giant will take on Satbir. Satbir is a foot shorter than his opponent, but has enough bulk to make up for that difference.

The two fighters, now only in their langots, stand in the centre of the arena. As tradition demands, they smear handfuls of earth on each other before they begin their bout.

The crowd is now quiet, attentive. Even the food carts have stopped business. The two heavyweights crash into each other. For the first few minutes, they push and pull to gauge each other's strength. Satbir's opponent drops down to get a hold of his legs, but Satbir is quicker, and sidesteps the challenge. Now he's had the chance of moving behind his opponent and locking arms around his waist. The local boy drops to his hands and knees, trying to shake Satbir off. The outsider heaves and twists, straining all his muscles to try and torque his rival on to his back. He fails. The referee separates them. Now it's Satbir who shoots for the legs, and gets them. His opponent goes down in a heap, but manages to rotate mid-air, so that he lands on his chest and elbows. According to dangal rules, if the back of both shoulders of a fighter touches the ground, he loses. There are no points here, no handouts for technical nuances or superiority. Pin your opponent down, 'show him the sky'—that's the only way to win a bout. Realizing that he's out of his depth, the local boy starts back-pedalling to avoid Satbir's advances. More than once, he back-pedals straight out of the wrestling circle. The crowd gets aggressive, curses fly through the air. Better to be thrown and defeated than this shameful retreat.

Satbir gets more and more frustrated with his opponent's clumsy evasions. Covered in earth and eyes glazed over in aggression, he is unrecognizable. Every time his opponent runs outside the bounds of the wrestling pit, he fumes and remonstrates with the referee. Why is he not being disqualified, Satbir wants to know. Why continue this farce? Finally, Satbir gives up the ghost of rules and regulations, chases his opponent into the crowd, and takes him down in a horrible mess of limbs and dust. Brawls break out immediately, spectators rush into the wrestling area, the stick-wielding peacekeepers enter the fray with war cries, the commentator screams at fever pitch and, somewhere in that dust-blind limbo, others try to separate the wrestlers and guide them outside the melee. Satbir's brother looks on with his droll smile. The pahalwan is brought to his car and we make a quick exit. The fight was, after all, with a local boy, and there's no telling who in the crowd might pull a knife or a gun for revenge.

Satbir is sullen and silent at the best of times; now he's got murder on his baby face. He sits in the car in his langot, caked in dirt and drying mud, only his thick lips and eyes showing through. The brother drives safely, a different man now, and after a while, breaks the silence.

'Those idiots can go fuck their mothers,' he says. 'Why did they pair you with a fool like that?'

'I knew there was something wrong the moment the fight started,' Satbir says. 'I could see he was scared. What a waste.'

'Oh no, it's not a waste,' the brother says. 'You will get the prize money. That's not bad.'

'No, it's not. Not at all,' Satbir says drowsily. 'I just hope they hand over all of it, otherwise they've got another battle coming up.'

Satbir does not come from a family of wrestlers, but wrestling is a revered sport in his village, which lies between Delhi and Rohtak. On balmy afternoons, when the children come out to play and the village elders gather in small groups for hookah and conversation, the older men often call the children to them, match one boy with another, and tell them to start grappling. There's always a gift at the end—perhaps a rupee or two, or some sweets—and the children are only too happy to tussle in the dirt. Here, from the time they are five or six years old, the boys get their first schooling in biomechanics, the wonderful ways to manipulate the human body without breaking it, and the concept of a fair fight, where the aim is not to hit or hurt your playmate, but to dominate him with skill and cunning. 'Let's see who is the strongest,' the old men say, and nothing could be more tempting for the children.

When Satbir was ten, he was already spending more time wrestling than anything else. If he was nowhere to be found, his parents knew he was at the village akhada—a square patch of loose, clean soil next to a small shrine to Hanuman, the patron god of kushti.

'My father was very happy that I was wrestling all the time,' Satbir says. 'In the village it is a matter of great honour to be a good wrestler, and my family had no wrestlers.'

A family without a pahalwan—there is something incomplete about it, something almost impotent, as if the family did not have enough to eat, or there was a genetic defect, or they were not connected to the soil they tilled in a meaningful way. So it was with relief that Satbir's father brought his ten-year-old son to

Mehr Singh's akhada and handed him over to the guru. From that day on, Satbir's life was dictated by the wrestling school. Home visits were limited to special occasions or emergencies. Once a week, Satbir's father would come to the akhada with milk, ghee and almonds for his son.

'And then it goes into your bloodstream, this wrestling,' Satbir says. 'It's our sport, right? The sport of the earth, the sport of the villages. It is deep in our culture. It is the oldest sport in the world, and it started here, you understand?'

I didn't understand.

It was the summer of 2008. Back then, I was working for a television news channel. The Olympics were on.

'What's repêchage?' my editor had asked me.

'What charge?'

'Not charge, *chage*—RAY-PAY-SHAJ,' he said. 'Look here, it says that Sushil Kumar from India is in the bronze medal bout via repêchage. Who's Sushil Kumar?'

I didn't have the answer to either question. Nor did anyone else on the sports team. Google had the answer to the first: 'Repêchage, "fishing out, rescuing" is a practice in series competitions that allows participants who failed to meet qualifying standards by a small margin to continue to the next round.'

But who was Sushil Kumar? What did he look like? Did anyone have his number? Did we have any old footage of him? Where was he from? Did anyone know where his family lives? Who was his coach?

About a week back, a very strange thing had happened. A man who looked a lot like that high-school maths teacher you dreaded—you know, the eyes of a zealot barely hidden behind dull glasses, a voice that could cure insomnia, an inability to smile even at a moment of historic personal triumph—had won

India its first gold medal in an individual sport at the Olympics. He won it for the 10 metre air rifle event—pretty esoteric stuff.

As if that one gold was not outlandish enough, just a day before the question—who is Sushil Kumar?—went flying around the newsroom, there was another medal for India. To right the balance on the appearances scale, this one was won by a tall, muscular, swaggering man, an athlete from head to toe, a boxer.

What? Indians can fight?

So now here we were, reeling under the carpet-bombing of medals, and there was a man we did not even recognize being fished out and sent back into the battlefield. Yes, this man was in a fighting sport too. He was a wrestler.

We were still confused and floundering when Sushil won. For a few moments after that, the newsroom was engulfed in euphoria. Never mind that no one knew anything about him, or wrestling. It was an Olympic medal.

I watched the footage of his fight in the edit room. Played it back over and over. Played it in slow motion. It was strangely uplifting. Having never watched wrestling, I had this idea that it was an ugly, ungainly sport. But this was beautiful: Sushil Kumar, with his unfashionable, upturned-bowl hair cut, was graceful, powerful, supple. There was a curious and fascinating combination of violence and harmony in the movements of the two wrestlers.

A few weeks later, after his return to India, I went to meet the wrestler. It turned out that he lived and trained right here, in Delhi.

That day, it felt like the door to a secret world had opened for me.

In my ignorance, I thought wrestling was a niche sport, like most games in India are apart from cricket, and that witnessing a match would be a difficult proposition. It was a bit of a shock then to find out that there are close to a hundred wrestling tournaments that take place just in Delhi every year. The wrestlers and coaches I met did not speak or behave like ordinary sportsmen; they spoke invariably of wrestling as a way of life, not a sport. They claimed that once you gave yourself to wrestling, you were in it for life, that you were a pahalwan as long as you lived. They insisted that wrestling's history in India was older and deeper than in any other country in the world—and indeed that wrestling was invented here. They stressed its religious and spiritual side: how the sport plays an important part in both the Mahabharata and the Ramayana; how Krishna was a wrestler, how Hanuman was the greatest wrestler of them all.

'Go and spend some time at some of the akhadas of Delhi,' Sushil told me.

I had never seen or heard of an akhada before, but once I began to ask around, I realized they were everywhere: tucked away behind markets and cemeteries, hidden behind high-rises and office blocks, flanked by wheat fields and citrus groves, along the reedy banks of the Yamuna, or in dim halls inside decaying stadia. All these akhadas had two things in common: from the outside, there was no way of knowing that there was a wrestling school located there; and once inside, it felt like you were out of the city and on a farm in some rural area.

Is this the reason why I had been blind to kushti? Because I lived all my life in a city? Pahalwans invariably told me that 'there is an akhada in every village'.

So it takes a village. But what did this rural pastime with its stories of gods and demons and mysticism and lifelong devotion have to do with the Olympics?

2

THIS IS AN AKHADA

It is simple to set up an akhada—you need little more than a parcel of land 20 feet by 20 feet, a clean source of water, and a couple of shady trees. Though international wrestling is conducted on synthetic mats, traditional kushti needs only an earthen pit. The akhadas that can afford it will have both mats and pits.

Akhadas can be inside sports complexes, or at the back of one's house. They can be at the corner of a cattle shed or on the banks of a river where the wheat fields end and the reeds begin. Fathers can set up an akhada for their sons, or indeed, in increasingly bold opposition to kushti's traditional maleness, for their daughters.

In larger villages and suburban towns, successful former pahalwans like Mehr Singh are given land and money by the villagers to establish their own wrestling schools. Akhadas are almost always set up by former pahalwans, and bear their name. That pahalwan becomes the guru—the one and only point of authority in the akhada, whose word and judgement must be obeyed unconditionally.

Akhadas also don't charge students for the training, for the use of its equipment, or for living quarters. They are free, egalitarian and idealistic. Students pay, if they do at all, a small fee, anything in the range of Rs 200–500 a month, to cover some of the electricity, water and maintenance costs. Pahalwans, though, have to provide for their own food—a practical move, since wrestling demands prodigious amounts of nutrition. Satbir, for example, eats his way through roughly a quarter of a kilo each of almonds, dal and paneer, half a kilo each of fruits and vegetables, a kilo of milk, and expensive US-made protein and vitamin supplements in a single day. By his own account, it works out to almost Rs 20,000 a month, half of what his family earns in the same period. But even here, there is a sense of equitability. Pahalwans who share a room are expected to share the cost and labour of buying and making their food, and senior pahalwans who have made a fair bit of money from dangals underwrite the dietary costs of young wrestlers from poorer families. Though there are no written rules for this (as there are none for anything in an akhada), it is difficult to find an akhada where these informal systems are not strongly rooted. A small cut of a pahalwan's dangal earnings is also voluntarily donated to the akhada, and this often is what pays the salary of the coaches, or covers the cost of new equipment or infrastructure.

Satbir made Rs 21 lakh in the dangal circuit in those two months of almost non-stop competitions, which is what the average mid-level wrestler can expect to earn if he has chosen his dangals well. His family will make that amount, if they are lucky, in about five years of farming. Satbir donated nearly a lakh to his akhada.

There are other, more opportunistic financers: politicians fishing for votes and influence, businessmen looking for purchase, temple committees or religious organizations seeking goodwill, and also to promote kushti as a peculiarly Hindu phenomenon, the origins of which can be traced back many millennia and to religious texts and epics. This is an idea that was given shape and weight during the first decades of the twentieth century, as part of a growing current of militant nationalistic movements in British India. But more on that later.

Life at the akhada reflects its spartan design, and follows a well-established model that varies little from school to school.

At 4.30 a.m., before the sun is out, the wrestlers begin their day with a short, light run. They gather in a circle to warm up with a series of limbering exercises. The neck and the back get special attention. The wrestlers lie on their backs, bend their knees and plant their feet firmly on the ground. They lift their bodies off the ground so that the only points of contact are their feet and the top of their skull. Then they twist and turn in this position, with their necks as the pivot.

Thus warmed up, they go through an hour and a half of furious workouts. They do dands—Indian push-ups—repeated in sets of hundreds. Wrestlers as young as twelve do a hundred of these each day, the more experienced ones go through 500. They'll do a similar number of baithaks—deep squats—with a brutal, sweat-dripping rhythm. Then they climb thick ropes hanging from trees using just their upper bodies.

Their muscles swell and their veins stand out like the roots of an old tree. The body turns into something taut and hard, agile and explosive, like a thick rubber band stretched to its limit and waiting to snap back.

This is followed by a couple of hours on the mat in akhadas that have one, or in the earthen pit, or both. The tempo continues to be frenetic, ferocious. Bodies collide, twist painfully. Arms and legs and torsos get entangled in excruciating ways. The sound is percussive, like a series of unending gunshots, as bodies get slammed on the mat.

Then the morning training session is over. The exhausted wrestlers move with deliberate slowness as they bathe and cook their meals. After lunch, they sleep for two hours. The evening training session is spent honing technique on the mat or the pit, with some weight training thrown in, a few more rounds of rope climbing and pull-ups, and a game of football or volleyball to cool down. Then it's back to cooking, eating and finally, utterly spent, sleeping.

The akhada life is all-consuming. It leaves room for little else but the training.

Though the younger pahalwans have a much lighter training schedule, and mostly attend school during the day, formal learning is usually eschewed by the time they are fifteen or sixteen and ready for serious competition.

The Akhada Chand Roop, on the edges of Delhi, has produced numerous Olympians, including Ramesh Kumar, who won a bronze at the 2009 Wrestling World Championship, India's first medal in forty-two years. It is a lane away from Azadpur Mandi, Asia's largest wholesale fruit and vegetable market, tucked away behind a petrol pump and a mechanic's shop for truckers. A highway the size of a landing strip, and the Delhi metro line atop tall pillars, sweep past it.

The akhada's layout is much the same as Mehr Singh's, except it's slowly crumbling to dust. The walls and the buildings are made of exposed brick coated in layers of grime. The tin shed that covers the tattered wrestling mat is riddled with holes. Even the trees inside the akhada, weighed down by years of highway soot, wear a grey, helpless look. 'Captain' Chand Roop is eighty-seven years old and every day he sits, like he has done for thirty-five years, hidden deep in one corner of the shaded wrestling area. He is called the captain on account of the rank he held in the army, where he was the equivalent of a drill sergeant.

Swathed in layers of blankets, he looks like an ancient, shapeless behemoth. His swollen legs are being massaged by Ashok Garg, a former Olympian who coaches voluntarily here (Ashok also coaches, for a salary, at Mehr Singh's akhada). Ashok was one of the first students at Chand Roop's, plucked from his village by the captain when he was twelve. A small, soft-spoken man, there is nothing about Ashok that suggests he was once one of India's finest wrestlers. He has gentle eyes and a neatly trimmed moustache.

'There was nothing here then, except for the earthen wr   _
pit, trees, the boundary wall and a well in that corner,' Ashok says
of the time when he first came to the Akhada Chand Roop. 'There
was nothing outside either, just scrubland and jungle all around,
and the mandi.'

There were eight or ten other students apart from Ashok in
that first year, and one famous senior wrestler, Rohtas Dahiya, who
was both a student and a coach. In 1980, a year after the akhada
opened, Rohtas went to the Olympics and finished fourth, fighting
on a mat despite never having trained on one. Back then, all the
wrestlers had to make their own living arrangements inside the
akhada and they built little squatter huts around the perimeter,
with plastic sheets for roofs.

'We had no protection from heat, cold, or rain,' Ashok says.
'If it got too hot, we would get wet and roll around in the akhada
earth to cool down…just like buffaloes. And in winter, sometimes
it would get so cold here that Saab-ji—that's what I call the
captain—he would make us practise at night, or make us dig the
pit, just to keep us warmed up.'

The captain had no money, and used his own savings and
his meagre army pension to keep the akhada going, hoping his
students would make it big and take over the finances; or the
government, taking note of his success, would send funds his way.
He disliked politicians, whom he blamed for every ill in India,
so it was out of the question that there would be any deal with
them. In fact, he was too proud to go asking for any funding at all.
He firmly believed that good work comes with its own rewards.
The captain's students did bring in some money, but it was never
enough. Most of them came from poor families, and needed to
build their own lives. No help came from the government.

'But we never felt that we did not have anything, or that we
could not be the best in the world,' Ashok says, still sitting at the
feet of the comatose captain. 'Now we know that to go from these
conditions to an Olympic medal…well…it can only happen in a

story. But back then, under Saab-ji's command, the thought never crossed our mind. Saab-ji was a god to us. A foul-mouthed and violent god. But also kind, caring. If there was a shortage of food, Saab-ji would go without meals secretly, but he would never let us feel hunger.

'He did let us feel his stick though. Only if you deserved it! He could hit you till you bled. It felt like a lynching. Sometimes we would climb that tree over there and stay up in the branches to escape,' Ashok says, laughing a little. 'Saab-ji would stand under the tree waiting for us for hours.'

At this, the captain looks up with hooded eyes. He smiles thinly. 'And now look how my sins have come back to visit me,' he says. 'I can't take a step without the help of these sticks.'

The captain has a wife, but he never really sees her. He hasn't left his akhada in years. He had three sons, all of whom are now dead (cancer, tuberculosis, heart attack), but he says his real sons are in the wrestling pit. But even they are leaving now, looking for a place that can give them more and ask for less. The captain will stay. When the time comes, the akhada and he will go down together.

In cities and towns, where akhadas are seen as some kind of a rural anomaly intruding into an urban reality, and where it has to compete with countless other pursuits and diversions, money is always out of reach. The city akhada is always struggling to survive.

But occasionally, almost accidentally, no matter how humble the beginnings, this largely informal system throws up a world champion or an Olympic medallist. Someone who cuts through the obscurity of the rural and the local to become something more.

3

AT THE OLYMPICS

Tomorrow. No, it's one in the morning, so it's today, technically, and just seven hours to go. Sushil Kumar, for a moment, is hit by a wave of self-pity, by regret, and he forgets that he's sworn off swear words. Four years, and almost every single day building up to this. Every minute of training, every moment of pain, every thought, each competition he has been to, what was it for? To find himself here, in a toilet in the Olympic village in London, vomiting up even the electrolytes he has been given. Worse: shitting water, muscles cramping and spasming up and down his body. It's just too cruel. It seems impossible to fight his body, so he fights his mind. He unleashes a feverish tirade against it—every curse word he knows to keep himself afloat.

And then he's somewhere else, a space he likes. He feels calm and aggressive at the same time. If he has to vomit, he will. If his muscles cramp, let them. If he shits blood, it won't change a thing. There is only so much that the doctor can do—just three doctors for the fifty-nine athletes in the Indian contingent, and a single physiotherapist, who is not even available right now. The doctor has come and gone, given him some electrolytes, which he has promptly thrown up.

He knows, of course, why this is happening. For the last ten days, he has been on a starvation diet, coupled with endless cardio sessions of slow running with heavy, warm clothing. He had to lose six kilos in ten days to fit into his weight class at the Olympics. This is the standard practice for combat athletes, and Sushil is used to doing this. But things can go wrong when you push the body in such extreme ways, and it has today.

His fellow wrestlers are awake with him. Yogeshwar Dutt, with whom he has trained since they were both little boys, massages him even though he is fit to collapse himself. Dutt had won a medal earlier in the day, five hellish matches in the space of a few hours for a bronze medal—India's third bronze in wrestling in Olympic history, after Sushil's win in 2008 and K.D. Jadhav in 1956. Dutt's right eye is swollen shut, and yet he is here. Coach Yashvir steps in to massage when Yogeshwar tires, his lips a thin, stoic line under his salt-and-pepper stubble. Amit Kumar and Narsingh Yadav, the two other wrestlers in the men's team, take their turns as well.

Sushil finally manages to go to sleep at two, six hours from his first match at the 2012 London Games. He wakes up at five. A miracle: he feels good. His mind is calm and sharp, and it tells him, unbidden, 'you will win'. He feels—and this is incredible even to him—happy.

There is Hanuman to thank for this. Jai Bajrangbali.

The weight class in which Sushil fights, 66 kg, offers one of the toughest competitions in Olympic wrestling. There is Mehdi Taghavi, the reigning world champion from Iran, an elegant wrestler whose exceptional skills are matched perfectly by the speed at which his mind works. Tatsuhiro Yonemitsu, the Japanese whom Taghavi had beaten at the World Championships, had avenged that loss at the World Cup just a month before the Olympics. There is the explosive Cuban Livan Lopez, bronze at the World Championship. There is Russia's Alan Gogaev, whom Taghavi had beaten in the final for his world title, and Turkey's Ramazan Sahin, the 2008 Olympic gold medallist. Every one a champion.

As Sushil tightly wraps his red langot in the changing room at the stadium, the names mean nothing to him. He thinks of them as no more extraordinary than his training partner back at Chhatrasal Stadium in Delhi, ready for a lesson or two. He is happy. He will win.

In Baprola, a packed neighbourhood of housing colonies on the outskirts of Delhi, which was a proper village barely a decade ago, a two-storey house is crammed to bursting. Outside, there is a poster of Sushil Kumar kissing his Olympic bronze medal from 2008.

Kamala, Sushil's mother, and some of the other women of the family rush around inside, making tea and ripping open packets of biscuits for the great number of relatives, neighbours and yet others whom no one has seen before. Kamala is a squat, powerfully built woman, with a radiant smile and impish eyes. Unlike her husband Diwan, who prefers wearing clothes in shades of grey or white (faded by years of use), she is always in colourful attire. Sushil not only looks like her, but is also built like her.

She is also agile, fast. Hello, Olympian gene, nice to meet you! She leaps on to the waist-high kitchen counter in a single bound to reach for more packets of biscuits from the high shelves. She passes on plates of dry fruits and glasses of milk to be taken out of the kitchen. All the TVs in the house are tuned to the Olympics. Outside the house, behind the high gates, a scrum of journalists is making a din. Broadcast vans are lined up on the thin strip of highway outside, and traffic is at a crawl. Tea and biscuits are sent out for the reporters too. Other onlookers gather; there is now a thick swarm outside. Only Diwan looks unmoved, a bemused half smile on his face. He is lean, with a stiff grey stubble and piercing eyes. He seeks out his nephew Sandeep's baby boy, and starts tussling with him playfully. It is the only time he smiles broadly. Here's another boy from the family who's got the makings of a wrestler. He reminds Diwan of Sushil when he was a baby.

A roar goes through the house, and is taken up by the crowd outside. On the TV, Sushil has walked out into the Olympic arena. Kamala, heart in her mouth, quickly exits the room, goes to the kitchen. She can't bear to watch Sushil fight. She'll stay in the kitchen till it's all over. Sushil struts straight up to the mat, jaw set, psyched-up, a man in a hurry; and even before the people in the house have had time to gather themselves around the TV, it has begun.

The stadium is packed. Ramazan Sahin, the defending Olympic champion, steps up. The Turkish supporters are loud, louder than the Indians. Sahin makes the first attacking move, sweeps for Sushil's legs, but Sushil twists out of it. Sahin stays low, makes another sweep, Sushil pushes him away, steps back, his eyes on the rival's.

'Apna kaam, apna kaam,' team coach Vinod screams out—stay focused on what you have to do, don't let him dictate the fight. But here's Sahin, and he's got a solid grip from in front. He's slipped his arms under Sushil's armpit and swivelled around, and Sushil has no option but to go down on his knees. Point to Sahin. Sushil gets a leg lock on, tries to turn Sahin on his back with the lock in position, but Sahin counters, breaks the lock, and manages to get himself behind and on top of Sushil. Sahin 2, Sushil 0, and the first period is Sahin's. Sushil's younger brother Amarjeet is in the crowd; he can't believe what he is seeing. He is edgy and annoyed. This should have been over in two periods. Now it's all up in the air, and oh god, oh no, Sushil looks a little less springy on his feet as he goes to the mat for the second period. Amarjeet recalls the night Sushil has endured and prays, don't let this be over, not here, not in the first match.

Sahin gets rapid instructions from his coaches, Sushil's side is silent. Both wrestlers are a little more cautious now, and neither manage a point at the end of the two-minute period. The ball draw. Now it's all luck. Sushil gets to pick the ball. If it comes out red, he gets to apply a hold on Sahin without opposition, and then Sahin has to try and prevent him from converting it into a point. If the ball comes out blue, the advantage is Sahin's and he can finish the match right here, right now, no third period needed. Amarjeet drops his head, closes his eyes. Sushil picks red: finally, some luck. He converts the advantage, a point to claim the second round.

Third period, and now the fight goes into overdrive. Both wrestlers attack incessantly, a blur of hands and legs and rotating torsos. The noise from the crowd is ear-splitting. Thirty seconds in, Sushil feigns an attack to the upper body, but in a flash reaches down and has a hold of Sahin's legs. Sahin tries to defend desperately, but Sushil's behind him now, and takes him down. One more point. Muscles on fire now, the pain oppressive, heavy, weighing Sushil down. He has to stand back up, withstand Sahin's frantic attacks.

'Nineteen seconds, 19 seconds,' Sushil's coach bellows out to him. 'Stay on your feet.' Sahin gets a leg hold, but somehow, on his hands and feet and scrambling, Sushil slips away. He's through to the quarters.

Sushil barely makes it to the changing room, where he collapses in a heap on the floor. The entire team is there— Yogeshwar, Amit, Narsingh, the two coaches and Amarjeet. He is now cramping and spasming badly, his body feels like stone, his fingers have become bent and fixed at weird angles; he needs Yogeshwar just to straighten his fingers. Everyone is massaging him together now, one has a leg, another an arm; the coach makes him sip some electrolyte, a slice of apple, half a banana, a few sips of a protein shake. Amarjeet's wiping away his sweat, fanning him with a towel. 'How do you feel? Is it better? Clench and unclench your fingers.' Slowly, his body starts to loosen. It's a relief. One step at a time, he thinks. Every step is good. He can stand now. Assisted, he can stretch. Then he swings his arms briskly. Good, he's happy. It's happening again.

'Shabash,' Yogeshwar says. The others repeat the cry.

'You will win, you are the best, you can't lose,' Amarjeet says.

'Be calm, do your thing,' coach Yashvir tells him.

'Be defensive,' Yogeshwar says. 'Wait for your chance, conserve your energy, keep things easy. This guy is all about speed, he'll lose his patience, and he'll rush at you. You play with him, okay?'

Okay. He's happy. He can feel the electricity running through him. He is tingling.

Quarter-final. Uzbekistan's Ikhtyor Navruzov. Be patient. Let him rush.

Diwan watches the action unfolding on TV without moving. There is something wrong. He can see it plainly. He has rarely seen Sushil so defensive. He looks a bit stiff too. Manjeet, Sushil's youngest brother, has told Kamala in the kitchen that Sushil has won his first fight. Diwan can hear Kamala say: 'Ah good. Now that the Bhainswaliya Manish (Manish from Bhainswal village— Yogeshwar) has got a medal, my son will also get one.'

'I saw all this in a dream last night,' Sushil's aunt, who speaks a lot, says. 'I saw Manish win his medal, and then I saw Sushil win a medal.'

Kamala laughs. She starts cleaning the kitchen counter.

Diwan's throat feels like it's been baked in an oven. He hollers for Manjeet to get some water, but it comes out feebly. He wishes he could smoke a bidi right now. But he can't. Ever since the cancer and the chemo, no way. The house is stuffed with sofas and beds, but he sits on the floor. He can never get comfortable on a sofa. Now it begins again. Diwan straightens, forgets everything else. Uzbekistan. Who is this wrestler? He's not bad, but Sushil is not moving in for the kill. That's fine. As long as he gets the points. But what is wrong with him? And now Sushil's gone to the physio, he's getting something done to his hands. Diwan wishes he could just call Amarjeet and ask him, but he refrains. A series of moves from Sushil now—he's shot for the legs, he's dropped the Uzbek by his ankles, but he can't move fast enough to get on top of him. The Uzbek's slipped out, but only just, Sushil's got his grip still, and YES! He's lifted Ikhtyor across his shoulders, this will be the pin… but no, a strange lack of strength from Sushil, so uncharacteristic, and the Uzbek escapes a straight defeat. Diwan reminds himself to breathe. He tunes out the noise in the house, the noise outside. Sushil wins the fight. He's in the semi-final, but Diwan is unhappy. He looks around him, looks at all the people, but he's alone in his own world. There is something very wrong with Sushil, there is no doubt about it. How long can he keep going?

'I saw all this in a dream last night,' Sushil's aunt comes and tells Diwan. 'I saw Manish win his medal…'

Diwan walks away without waiting for her to finish.

What are the Olympics like for a competing athlete?

It's a fortnight of tuning out the outside world—blanking out noise, emails, text messages, phone calls, unsolicited advice, fan talk, alien food, foreign music, other athletes—anything that can cause the slightest deviation in the mind. As long as the athlete is in competition, the Olympic village is his or her prison.

Sushil has seen nothing of the Olympics. This is his third time at what is perhaps the modern world's most extravagant spectacle, certainly its most expensive sporting event, and a medal here is undoubtedly the most coveted sporting prize on the planet. He has memories only of dull rooms, gyms, dim corridors where he ran for hours to lose the last few kilos before the weigh-in, and the bright lights of stadiums. They were different rooms, different corridors, different arenas—in Athens, Beijing, London—but they have all dissolved into one uniform mass of grey carpets and white lights and sweat stinging the eyes. He has never been a spectator at a single event. He has not seen Michael Phelps cut through the pool like an improbable sea monster, or Usain Bolt push the human speed limit to a place just beyond logic. He has met Bolt briefly this time around, as he was entering the gym a couple of days back and the lanky Jamaican was coming out of it. He took a picture on his phone as Yogeshwar posed with Bolt.

The Olympian's burden is an extraordinary one. Their chance to truly shine, to become more than just an athlete, comes only once every four years, and when it does, that opportunity can last a few minutes, or a few seconds. A lifetime has to be spent to get to those hours. So the prison is self-made, self-administered; a prison to bide your time and be ready when it comes.

He is ready. He can feel the rhythm in his body, and for the first time in the day, that extreme focus takes over him where he is not even conscious of his thoughts, but everything seems very clear and bright. He does not have to fight his weakness, his urge to vomit has disappeared. Every muscle in his body is twitching to go, and his mind is working smoothly and rapidly as he makes the first contact with his opponent in the semi-final—Kazakhstan's Akzhurekh Tanatarov.

This is where he wants to be, where his mind makes decisions without even telling him and his body executes them, and the decisions are all correct, they all fall into place. The noise inside the stadium is deafening, but Sushil can only hear the sticky sound of Tanatarov and his body against the mat.

Seconds into the opening round, Sushil gets a leg lock in place. But somehow, from that most precarious of positions, Tanatarov slips out of the lock. Now Sushil backs away as the other man tries to get a grip. He comes in low, and Sushil springs forward with startling speed, one hand pushing at Tanatarov's face, the other pulling on his knee, shoulders driving forward towards the Kazakh's hips. The best that anyone can do in this situation, and Tanatarov has trained all his life to do just this so it's reflexive, is to turn as he falls, land on his chest and not his back, to not let the shoulders touch the mat. Sushil is all over him—a leg lock, a cross-body lock, searching for his head and neck, his ankle—he wants to turn Tanatarov flat on his back. Tanatarov twists and turns, tucks his legs in, spreads his arms wide, and pushes towards the zone outside the playing area, to concede a point but not three, which is what will happen if he gets turned on his back. Sushil manages to turn him just in time, millimetres from the safe zone. Three points. Good. This is exactly what he wants—one hold, and then keep pressing, apply technique after technique, don't let the man get away.

The first period is his, but in the second, Tanatarov neatly reverses an attack, the two wrestlers go down in a frenzy of torsos and limbs, and now it's the Kazakh's turn to score. A round each. A world hinges on the last round, the final two minutes.

Sushil attacks without delay. Tanatarov counters swiftly, and gets on top of Sushil. Unfazed, Sushil continues attacking from his vulnerable position. Tanatarov almost gets a pin, but no, Sushil turns out of that, and finds himself flat on his stomach with Tanatarov on top yet again. Three points to the Kazakh. Tanatarov in control. A minute and a half left in the match. They re-engage, Sushil attacks immediately, but Tanatarov's defence is strong. Sushil attacks again and gets a grip around the Kazakh's waist, and propels himself into the man without delay. Tanatarov goes down. In a flash, Sushil puts a leg lock in place. He tries to twist Tanatarov to the right, but can't, so he tries left, then right again. Now he's got a leg lock and a head lock in place, and Tanatarov writhes in pain. He gets flipped. Five points for Sushil. One move, five points.

Tanatarov points to his ear—it's bleeding. He gestures to the referee that Sushil bit him. A serious allegation. Sushil can be disqualified. But the Kazakh's two coaches, who can call for a review here, decide not to do anything. They know that Tanatarov's ear had a bruise before the match had even begun.

With thirty seconds left in the match, Tanatarov frantically gets hold of Sushil's leg. But no joy, the defence is rock-solid. Sushil, on his knees, turns the situation around, grabs Tanatarov by the waist from the back. Now Tanatarov, desperate, rash, pivots and gets his arms around Sushil's waist. Yes. This is what he was waiting for. Sushil drops his hands from the waist to Tanatarov's thighs, and in one, swift, explosive move, lifts the Kazakh over his shoulders like a sack of flour. It's done. He's in the final.

Diwan is so happy he doesn't know what to do with himself. Everyone around him is shouting, congratulating him, rushing around. He smiles self-consciously. They are bringing a beaming Kamala out of the kitchen. She is teary-eyed. There are firecrackers bursting outside. Reporters are shoving mics through their gate. Some are trying to clamber in. On the TV, Sushil is acknowledging the crowds at the stadium for the first time, raising both hands in the air. The camera zooms in on Tanatarov, lying on the mat and crying. Diwan sees Sushil walk up towards the stand where Satpal and his daughter—Sushil's wife—are standing. What is this now? Sushil is suddenly swamped by spectators, they are pushing and shoving, they are trying to drape a flag around him, they are dancing. Diwan's joy turns to anger and anxiety.

'Let him go,' he mutters to no one. 'Let him go. He's weak. It's not over. Why are you celebrating like this? There's a gold medal match to be fought still! Someone get him out of there. Where's his coach? Where's Amarjeet?'

His arms are stiff and mapped with bruises. His eyes have sunk into their sockets. His knees are buckling. But his mind is blank. He has twenty minutes, and the first thing to do is to get to the toilet. It seems like ages before he can come out of there. Then immediately he needs to go back again. If he takes even a sip of water, he throws up. The doctor has nothing to offer. But he is surrounded by well-wishers. The US team is here. The Indian wrestlers had trained with the Americans at their Olympic training centre in Colorado just before the Games. They feel a kinship. The American coaches offer some advice too. The Azerbaijan wrestler in his weight class, who has just lost to the man Sushil will meet in the final, is here to help as well. Amarjeet is struggling to keep himself positive and calm. His hands and legs tremble, he feels sick to his stomach. No Indian wrestler has ever reached an Olympic final. In every way, Sushil is making history. When Sushil won the bronze at the 2008 Games, it was the first wrestling medal at the Olympics for a wrestling-crazy country in 56 years, and it had changed the face of the sport in India. And now he is doing it again. This may well be his last chance. Everyone knows this. That's why they are all here, they all want a slice of history, they all want to see this man, fighting to even stand, go up on the mat and make miracles happen. The physio puts kinesio-tapes on Sushil's spasming neck and shoulders. One of the Indian coaches tells Sushil, 'Let it go, you don't have to fight, you're in no state.' Sushil blanks out a sadness he feels coming, ignores the comment.

The Azerbaijan wrestler offers to warm Sushil up by grappling lightly with him. Just go through the motions and set up a rhythm—move, countermove—start slowly, then build it up, let the body and the training take over. This helps Sushil more than anything anyone can say to him. This intimate somatic language of his sport, better than words.

'Keep yourself loose,' he can hear Yogeshwar. 'You can do it. Just one more fight. It's nothing. It's nothing. You can take on five more. Let's get serious. No compromise now. Play your game. Attack, attack, and get three points out of every attack. Don't let him go when you get a grip. Keep him down.'

It doesn't work out that way. In the first round of the final, both wrestlers are cautious and weary: the Japanese, Tatsuhiro

Yonemitsu, scores a single point. In the second round, when both wrestlers show more urgency, Yonemitsu does something that has never been done before to Sushil—he picks him up—up over his shoulders, and down on to the mat. Sushil never recovers from it. He blindly gropes for the Japanese, but doesn't find his mark. It's the end.

Soon, Sushil is collapsed on his bed in the Olympic village, buffeted by ice packs.

The first-ever Olympic silver medallist in wrestling from India. Only the third Olympic silver medallist from India in any individual discipline. Yet it is not enough.

It's a relief to fall asleep. He sleeps right through the grand closing ceremony, till late the next day. In the afternoon, he is still so dehydrated that the World Anti Doping Agency, that most draconian of all sports bodies, gives him an extra hour to submit his urine sample.

Then it's back to India.

4

A BAND OF BROTHERS

In the afternoon, before the akhada has properly stirred from its deep siesta, an eight-year-old boy who has recently started shadowing Sushil, enters his room all dressed and ready to hit the mat, and announces loudly: 'C'mon, wake up, it's time, you said you will train with me, it's time, c'mon wake up.'

Sushil peers out from beneath his blanket, squinting.

'Oh no. Let me get some sleep also, will you? I trained with you just this morning! How much can I train?'

'No! Yesterday you said you will train with me in the evening, but you went and played football!'

'Please, Ajay, don't shout. You go and start, I will come.'

Later, on the mat, he smiles and says, 'This boy will not let me live in peace.' He tries to fashion Ajay's hair into a mohawk. 'You are more concerned with my training than your own!' And then, to no one in particular, 'Don't let him come into my room before four in the evening.'

Later, Sushil, back in training less than two months after winning his Olympic silver, is lounging in his room in his underwear. An old, tall man with thick glasses, close-cropped hair, and a massive nose comes to discuss his son's career with Sushil, who greets him as 'tau'—the generic word of respect for elderly men, just as the more intimate 'mama' is.

'He is my father's friend, and an old pahalwan,' Sushil tells me, 'and he is very hard of hearing.' He looks slyly at Tau, who stares blankly back.

'…unless you are talking about money…'

The man nods his head slowly like an ancient turtle. 'See,' Sushil says gleefully.

To the man, he says, loudly, 'Tau, it takes time to be a pahalwan, no? Your boy has just started eating ghee and badaam. He's got a good body structure, give him some time to put on some weight, develop himself. I see him sometimes in training, and he's learning technique quickly.'

A glass breaks somewhere in the room.

'Who's breaking what now,' Sushil asks, testily.

Tau does not hear it. 'He's such a big, tall, strong guy, but he has no passion for wrestling,' he says, in his reedy, old voice. 'He has no heart for it.'

'So what can you do about that,' Sushil asks. 'Passion can only come from inside.'

'He's so big, so strong, but he's worthless when he is fighting. He will fight two rounds very well, but in the third (Tau makes vigorous, haphazard gestures) he tries to run away from his opponent! If he really puts his heart in it, even for a month, he will make his breakthrough as a wrestler.'

'I will talk to him,' Sushil says in a placatory voice. 'I will push him in training.'

'He is six feet two,' Tau says. 'So big and strong.'

Sushil is reminded of something. He turns to Pradeep, his training partner, sprawled sweatily on a mattress, 'Arrey, there was this Amriki pahalwan, remember? He looked like a joke—fat, clumsy—bhaunsrikey, thul-thul keh chal raha tha—and then he defeated Aleksandr Karelin…Karelin! At the Sydney Olympics.'[2]

'Yeah, you never know,' Pradeep says. 'Remember that pahalwan from Agroha? Even if he got injured and had to rest for three months, he needed just fifteen days to get back to peak form. Some people are just blessed.'

Pradeep, who also doubles up as Sushil's masseuse and stretching partner, is perhaps the most indispensable man on his personal staff. Small and wordless Dharma is next in order; he supplies Sushil with his daily nutrition—a carefully calibrated sequence of food and drinks, handles his laundry, keeps his room clean (a comparative notion, that) and generally runs about getting things. Sushil is now so used to this constant service that sometimes he just waves his fingers vaguely and gets exactly what he wants. Arvind, a quiet, superbly efficient former international wrestler with a neat moustache and an ice-cool temper, is next. He handles things that need more brainwork; negotiating Sushil's appearances at events, doing paperwork for him and handling his calls. Importantly, he drives Sushil around. He is an exceptional driver, coasting through unruly Delhi roads with soothing ease. Parvesh, a former heavyweight wrestler, is huge and boisterous and likes wearing clothes in peacock colours. He keeps people entertained with constant, grating chatter, and steps in for Arvind when something needs more forceful handling. Rahul, also called Monu, is like Pradeep: an active but fringe international wrestler of the same weight class as Sushil. His presence is less easily explained. He sometimes doubles up as Sushil's partner, but other than that seems to do nothing of note. He is largely silent, but abrasive when he speaks and has a temper that sits on a razor's edge; a rare trait in a wrestler. Sushil's band of brothers all say that they drifted into his circle accidentally, a couple of years before his 2008 Olympic medal, and stayed on.

They do the job his biological brother, Amarjeet, used to do single-handedly before, when Sushil was on the verge of breaking through on the international stage. Now Amarjeet is married and spends less time with Sushil, though he handles the most important of his brother's financial deals and travels with him for international competitions.

Why are we talking about a wrestler who has won one world championship and two Olympic medals? In the annals of international wrestling, Sushil is but a minor footnote. In India, though, he is the great redeemer: an athlete who has led the revival of an ancient glory; who lifted a sport that should have been India's to dominate by some primeval right, but which had sunk under the weight of modern pollution.

We are talking about Sushil because the sporting system he worked his way through should never have led to an Olympic medal or a world championship. It hardly ever does.

Why does this wrestler need a band of brothers to surround him and help him in his training, his daily life? For an answer, we need to visit the national training camp for Indian wrestling, located on a sprawling campus run by the government in Sonepat, Haryana.

The wrestler is most concerned, first and foremost, with his food. You are what you eat. Sushil does not eat the food that's made at the Sonepat campus. He takes me to the kitchen to show me why. The floor is a dark, muddy mess. Vegetables and fruits rot in leaky, rickety refrigerators that have not been cleaned in months. Other vegetables and fruits are piled on top of the rotting ones. Flies sit on everything.

'You see?'

Sushil's friends buy their own produce and cook all their meals in a makeshift kitchen. This is standard practice for athletes with money and resources.

Because of the nature of the sport, injuries are a major part of the wrestler's life. Yet, if they can help it, wrestlers avoid the in-house doctor and physio appointed by the Sports Authority of India (SAI).

Across Olympic training centres in India, these doctors are referred to as 'khasi ka doctor'—someone who can treat only coughs and cold.

So when Sushil is injured, Arvind will put him in a car and take him to a private doctor at one of the best medical facilities in Delhi. Or at the end of his training session, Dharma and the others will take turns to massage him.

Stories are rife of physios who aggravated an injury through mistreatment or negligence. The first priority for non-profit organizations that support Olympic athletes in India is always to appoint a good physio full-time at the training centres, and provide their athletes access to good medical facilities.

Heath Matthews, a South African physio who worked for a couple of years for a non-profit and was stationed at Sonepat, is bemused by the official staff there. 'I would not send a common man with a common injury to these guys. Forget elite athletes,' he says about the SAI doctors and physios. 'The support system is utterly broken, and all the athletes know this.'

The system is not broken; it is just not aimed at the athletes. It is designed, curiously enough, for the political leaders who sit at the helm of India's various sports bodies, and the Indian Administrative Service (IAS) bureaucrats who run the training centres.

The Netaji Subhas National Institute of Sports (NIS) in Patiala is situated on the premises of the erstwhile palace of the maharaja of Patiala. It is a magnificent place, with acres of green fields surrounded by mango orchards. In season, the ground is thick with sweet, tiny mangoes that have fallen from the trees. The palace edifice gleams golden in the sun. Inside, SAI officials spend their days napping amongst dusty files.

Before the 2010 Delhi Commonwealth Games, the gyms, training units and athlete accommodations were in a shambles. They got a major facelift—it would not do to host a spanking international event while your own athletes were rotting. A new gym was built, new tracks laid, new AstroTurfs were put in place, a jacuzzi was built.

In 2012, while working on a series of stories for a newspaper ahead of the London Olympics, I saw a curious sequence of events. Despite a swank new gym, the track-and-field athletes were still using the broken-down old one. It was a disastrous place. The weights were old and rusty. Most of the lights were broken, so athletes worked out by the feeble daylight filtering in through a couple of windows. There was no air conditioning and little ventilation. Worst of all, the floor was so warped that even walking inside the gym could put you in danger of an injury. When I asked the athletes why they did not use the new gym, I was told that they were not allowed. The boxing team was allowed to use the new gym. Vijender Singh from Haryana had won India's first Olympic medal in boxing at the 2008 Games, somewhat lifting the stature of the sport. I was hanging out with the boxers at the new gym, and Vijender was running on the treadmill, when a clerkish man came in and told him something. He looked mildly displeased, but stopped the treadmill and got off it, and began running up and down the room. The administrative head of the Patiala institute came in and began walking, slowly, on the treadmill.

By 2014, the newly laid facilities at Patiala were already in a bad state. Treadmills lay idle, their circuits blown. The running track had bumps the size of footballs. The AstroTurf was so wobbly that the coach of the women's hockey team refused to train his girls on it.

Déjà vu?

In 1994, a leading Indian news magazine published a cover story on India's poor athletic performance two months before the Hiroshima Asian Games.[3]

'[T]he story of Indian sport and the farcical preparations for the games could only have one title—The Great Indian Sports Scandal,' the article begins, before listing a few of those scandals, including mismanagement of funds, training halls that were not ready and the purchase of defective equipment.

'Quite simply, SAI is a failure,' the article continues, with more details of glaring accounting discrepancies, broken infrastructure. Just for added humour, it mentions the team report from the manager of the Indian hockey team, which finished seventh out of twelve teams, a disastrous result considering India had won eleven medals (eight of them gold) in eleven consecutive Olympics in men's hockey starting from 1928.

'He offers no technical specifics on why India lost,' the article says, 'and in the end lists a player-evaluation which a 13-year-old could have compiled. It reads: Ashish Ballal: Total failure; Pargat Singh: Not up to mark; Mukesh Kumar: Average; Dhanraj Pillaiy: Not (sic) team spirit and indisciplined etc etc.

'In most nations, an athlete is accorded a certain measure of respect; he must perform, nothing else. In India, the system works the other way round—mocking the possible hero, tripping him with obstacles.

'Today, almost every Indian sportsperson hesitates to speak the truth. The reason is simple. As one boxer says: "If you print what I just told you, I won't go to Hiroshima." He is not exaggerating. When some federation officials visit their camps, athletes actually touch their feet. One federation secretary even admitted: "I can destroy the career of a champion athlete and nothing will happen. The question is, should I be given such powers?"'

More than twenty years later, little has changed.

'Indian athletes grow up and live in an atmosphere of fear,' Viren Rasquinha, a former captain of the Indian hockey team, told me. 'The administrators make sure that the athletes are always under their thumb. They live with no dignity. No self-respect. They have to beg to get their visas done if they have to compete outside India. If they have a problem, they are shunted about from one clerk to another till they give up in frustration and get the message. If they have to meet the top officials for anything, you can be sure that they will be made to wait for hours, just to make a point.'

Viren is now the CEO of Olympic Gold Quest (OGQ), India's most prolific non-profit organization that supports athletes with funding and expertise. 'The ten years I played hockey for India, I was always frustrated,' Viren said. 'No one helped, no one came and asked us what we needed; we got poor training, poor food and god forbid if any of us got injured!'

OGQ's physios now work permanently at the SAI training centres. If any of their athletes get injured, they are immediately pulled out of the camp and taken to specialist doctors for treatment and rehabilitation. Nutritionists tailor the diets of their athletes, supply them with supplements, and follow up with them to ensure that they are managing to get the required nutrition.

In a startlingly honest admission, Jiji Thomson, who was director general of SAI from 2013 to 2015, told me that the rot in the Indian sports system is so deep, that 'it must start from scratch'.

Let's play that déjà vu game again.

Here's another magazine story, this time written in the run-up to the 1988 Seoul Olympics: 'Once again the Indian Olympic challenge had run into the numerous insurmountable hurdles that have perpetually been the bane of Indian sport. There were the usual shenanigans, jockeying for junkets, meddling with qualifying standards and training and the humiliation of sportsmen as if the Olympics were an occasion for the officials, not the athletes.'[4] It goes on to talk about how an injury that P.T. Usha, then Asia's top sprinter, suffered had been ignored till the athlete was unable to even run, and how the women of the relay team had to appeal directly to the prime minister before they could leave for Seoul after officials bungled their travel plans. 'What happened to the relay girls was yet another example of an old disease, in which Indian athletes are reduced to fighting for trips rather than medals. Perhaps because the officials treat these meets as junkets for themselves, they find it difficult to treat the sportspersons any differently.'

Twenty-six years later, Jiji Thomson swivelled his laptop around to show me a mail from the Paralympic Committee of India naming the contingent they wanted to send for the 2014 Asian Games.

'Here we have someone listed as "office boy",' Thomson said. 'Here is someone described simply as "supplier" for something called "Mahadev Gas Agency". This man is a real estate broker.

Here's a "driver". Who are these people? The Indian Olympic Association and Paralympic Committee expect us to clear these names with no questions asked and the strategy is to send this list at the last possible second so no one has time to verify anything.'

Before 2008, in over a hundred years of Olympic competitions, India had won just four individual medals, none of them gold. In 2008, Indian won its first gold medal, as well as Sushil and Vijender's bronze medals.

The gold was won by the rifle shooter Abhinav Bindra, who trained in a custom-built shooting range at home, found his own coach, funded his own training, and prepared for the Games almost entirely on his own initiative and money, spending on long training-cum-competition stints in Europe. A chapter in his memoirs[5] is entitled 'Mr Indian Official: Thanks for Nothing'.

Just a few days after Abhinav won the medal, the then president of the Indian Olympic Association (IOA), at a function to felicitate the shooter, called him Abhi...er...Abhilav...er... Avinash!' Soon after, the home page of the Indian Olympic Association's website opened with a banner which proclaimed: 'We are proud of Mr Suresh Kalmadi, honourable president of the Indian Olympic Association, for bringing India's first Olympic gold medal.'

The medallist's name can be easily forgotten, because really, the man responsible for the medal was the politician who headed the IOA.

Two years later, after the 2010 Commonwealth Games, which was organized under the leadership of Kalmadi, the long-serving president faced an avalanche of corruption charges, and was arrested and then released on bail after a few months in prison. He lost his post only after a protracted battle, and then tried to attend the 2012 Olympics on government money.

Compared to the national sports federations under the Olympic association, the Sports Authority of India actually begins to look good. The national federations are headed by politicians, who quickly work to establish their own power. Most federation heads remain in place for two decades or more with no performance-related accountability. The record is perhaps held by the political leader V.K. Malhotra, who has now spent forty-one years as head of the Archery Association of India.

Consider the Indian Boxing Federation. In 2012, just four years after Vijender Singh won India's first medal in boxing at the Olympics, and two years after the Indian contingent picked up their richest haul of medals at the Asian Games, the federation was banned by the sport's international body after a blatant move at rigging elections, aimed at allowing its long-serving president to be elected as president of the Indian Olympic Association. The IOA, in turn, was banned by the International Olympic Committee for electing a president who was an accused in a criminal case.

The boxing administration in India plunged into sectarian chaos. There was a sense of inevitability to what followed: The private company that sponsored the boxing body stopped funding it, and all competitions for boxers came to a halt. It was the death of a sport. Four years later, as the 2016 Olympics in Rio loomed closer, the situation remained exactly the same as before.

In 2015, Vijender Singh left India to try his luck as a professional boxer in England. When I asked him if he felt lucky to have escaped the Indian system, he said, 'No, not at all. I started from zero, from a village which had no exposure to the sport, and worked my way up here. But when I look at all the boxers I grew up with, all the boxers I went to tournaments with, junior boxers who have become the best in India now, and I see what they have to go through, I am not happy at all. It's all sadness. Sadness because no one cares for them, no one cares for the sport.'

There is no mystery to why India does not do well in international sports.

It's not the lack of money. Even though the economic might of a nation has a pretty direct correlation with the number of medals it wins, there are enough exceptions to this rule (medals in Olympics 2012: Cuba, 15; Iran, 12; Ethiopia, 7; Kenya, 11; Azerbaijan, 10). India won more medals at the 2012 London Olympics than ever before: two silvers and four bronzes. On the medal table, that translated to the fifty-fifth position among seventy-nine nations. If the medal tally is adjusted for the size of a country's economy, India comes in last. If the tally is adjusted for GDP, India has the lowest ratio of medals to GDP of all participating countries.

It's not entirely about a lack of infrastructure either. Many countries do with much less than what India has, especially after it hosted the 2010 Commonwealth Games.

Dutch marathon coach Hugo van den Broeck, the head coach of a SAI programme to develop long-distance runners, has run in marathons all over the world. He divides his time between India and his family home in Iten, Kenya, a town in the Rift Valley regarded as the epicentre of distance running. Hugo's wife, who is originally from Iten, has represented the Netherlands in the Olympics. Hugo too has run for his country with international distinction. After taking up the Indian assignment in 2015, he was immediately struck by two things. The first, the breadth and depth of the sporting infrastructure in the country.

'Very few countries in the world can boast of so many training centres, so many athletes who live and train and are being paid to do that by the government,' Hugo says. 'The Netherlands doesn't have this kind of structure. Kenya has nothing even close to this.'

The second thing that struck him was the lack of knowledge.

'The training methods were all wrong,' he said. 'The athletes did not know the right way to do the simplest of things: for example, that you stretch after a training session, once your muscles are warm. Instead, everyone stretched before they started warming up.'

Meanwhile, global sports has undergone a performance revolution.

When the US hurdler Lolo Jones was training for the 2012 Olympics, her team would sometimes include as many as twenty-two scientists and technicians. An article in *Wired* describes one such training day: '...they've arrayed 40 motion-capture cameras along the track. She's also being monitored by a system called Optojump, which measures the exact location and duration of Jones' contact with the rubberized surface on every step and after every hurdle. And a high-speed Phantom Flex camera rigged next to the track can zoom alongside Jones and film her...'[6]

That session yielded a rich treasure of information: for example, that Jones was fastest on her fourth or fifth trial (so her coach increased her warm-up time before races); that her left side was not as strong as her right (specific exercises were tailored to address this); and that Jones wasn't kicking down her front leg as soon as she could.

Over the last two decades, science and technology have increasingly become more and more integral to elite athletic training. For that hundredth of a second that separates the winner from the also-rans, athletes rely on a dazzling array of experts: nutritionists, doctors, biomechanists, psychologists, statisticians, video analysts, strength coaches and recovery experts.

There is only one man in India who mapped this path for himself, and he won a gold at the Olympics.

How poor is India's coaching system?

'Can I be brutally honest?' Thomson asks. 'The coaching diploma you get at NIS Patiala has no value and is totally outdated. Our coaches are not given the expertise they need. They know nothing about biomechanics, for example, or sports science. Today if you go to our sports science centres, you will be ashamed. Either it will be a shell with no equipment, or it will be some equipment rotting away because there is no one who knows how to use them.'

In some ways, the wrestlers escape the worst of this systemic indignity. Most athletes in an Olympic discipline in India are permanent residents of the sports authority centres from the time they are ten or twelve years old. The authorities establish their hold on the athletes at just the right, malleable age. A servile and fearful relationship is encouraged. Wrestlers, on the other hand, grow up in akhadas, where their self-worth suffers no early blows. Nonetheless, soon after they make it to the national camp, they realize that they must take steps to protect themselves.

'You can either spend your time fighting the injustice, ranting against the bad training and infrastructure, and trying to change the system, or you can spend your time trying to make a career as an athlete,' Sushil says. 'If we get into this fight, that's the end of our careers. We have to keep our focus on training, so we put in our own systems. What else can you do?'

Sushil admits, reluctantly, that he learns nothing new at the training camps in Sonepat, and frequently rebels against the coach so that he can train according to his own system. He picks up new skills at competitions abroad, or when the wrestling team goes for its annual twenty-day camp to the US Olympic Training Center in Colorado.

'All our learning happens in these places,' he says. 'The coaches break down and explain new techniques. They watch you and understand what your strengths and weaknesses are and work accordingly. If I followed the training method here, all I will do is 1,000 push-ups, 1,000 squats and an hour of mindless wrestling on the mat. Our training is worthless if you want to win at the Olympics.'

This is why we are talking about Sushil Kumar.

5

THE MAKING OF A WRESTLER

Back when Baprola was still a real village, a patchwork of farmlands and scattered forests, Diwan Singh Solanki took his son to his first dangal.

It was a big dangal too, and Diwan could hardly contain his excitement as he grasped his seven-year-old son by the hand and walked towards the neighbouring village of Mundka.

As they walked, Diwan told his son about all the excitement and magic of a dangal: the large crowd he would see there, all the food they could buy, the noise and the buzz, but most of all, the big wrestlers, the magnificent muscled men whose very footsteps would make the ground beneath their feet tremble.

'Will you wrestle too?'

Diwan laughed at the question. No, he said shyly, smiling, pleased that his son had even thought to say such a thing. Diwan had fought in dangals—not in one as big as this—but he was a wrestler, just like his father before him, and his grandfather too.

But Diwan could not make a career out of it, so he had left the world of akhadas and dangals to focus on his family and on farming and cattle. He also got himself a job as a bus driver. He still went to dangals whenever he could manage the time, of course, but this was special.

'We will go to many dangals together, okay?' he told his son.

'And I will not wrestle here, but maybe, when you are a little more grown up, I will come see you wrestle!'

'Yes,' the boy exclaimed.

As they approached Mundka, and the press of people headed for the dangal got thicker and thicker, Diwan swung his boy up on his shoulders. He was small for his age, and sat there dangling his feet and looking around him with wonder.

The wrestling had begun, but before Diwan could shove his way towards the arena, his boy began to cry. It was suddenly too much for him, all those people, the shouting and screaming. His eyes stung from the dust, his throat had dried up so he could not even swallow. Diwan moved away from the centre of the throng, bought the boy sugar cane juice.

'Are you feeling better?'

He nodded. Diwan swung him back up on his shoulders. The boy started to cry again. He felt nauseous, he could not breathe. He needed to get out of there.

With a heavy heart, Diwan realized there was nothing to do but turn back.

The boy and his father walked back home in silence.

A few days later, Diwan stood and stared as his wife Kamala milked the buffaloes in the small cattle shed next to their house.

'What are you looking at,' Kamala asked.

'Right here,' Diwan said, pointing to a bit of ground near the buffaloes. 'If I fix the ground here, this could be a good place to teach him kushti.'

Kamala looked at it and agreed. 'We could move the buffaloes a bit more to this side.'

'It's time I started teaching him, no? He could be good at it.'

'He will be good at it,' Kamala said. 'He will be better than you,' she added, laughing. 'He is faster.'

The couple shared an eight-acre farm and a house with Diwan's two brothers and their families, so space was always a problem. Only the cattle shed belonged to them.

They were not rich. But with a comfortable house, land, an extended family and some cattle, they were not poor either.

Diwan's days were packed. He woke up before dawn to help Kamala with the buffaloes and the farm, then went off to work. Eight hours a day he drove a rickety tin bus, jolting and honking his way through bad roads. But when he got back home in the evening, his son would come rushing up to him and immediately they would start wrestling, laughing. Diwan would pin him down with plenty of force, but the boy would always manage to wriggle and squirm out of the holds.

'How hard can I hold him down without hurting him,' Diwan would wonder. And the answer was always surprising.

'This one must have started wrestling when he was in your womb,' he would sometimes tell Kamala.

'Oh yes,' she would reply, 'he is as fidgety as you are. Kick here, jump there, fall here, make this move, make that move. I live with a family of monkeys.'

Things were good, and Diwan had this premonition that they were going to get better.

His older brother's son, Sandeep, had got a place at Satpal Singh's famous Chhatrasal akhada. Diwan thought that it was not unreasonable to expect that his son too would make it there when he was of age. Kamala and he agreed that their son was a real handful: agile, fast and feisty. He could wrestle, he had it in him.

Diwan got to work fixing a wrestling pit. He dug and hoed, crumbled small clumps of soil with his fingers, rooted around for rocks and pebbles, watered the ground and tilled and raked again, and then levelled it. The earth was now so powdery and soft that it fell like sand through his fingers. He could plant seeds in it to sprout.

He marked the rectangular space off, building a slightly raised boundary of packed earth around it. He showed it to his son. The boy knew immediately what it was. He jumped straight on to the cool akhada earth, delighted. He ran and tumbled on it. Diwan picked him up, twirled him and threw him into the pit. He sprang up and rushed at Diwan's legs. The man went down in a heap, grabbing his son by the arms and lifting him up.

'From tomorrow morning, I will teach you how to wrestle right here, okay?'

'Yes,' the son cried out.

They stood up. Diwan waited for his son to dust the dirt off his clothes. Then he swung him around on his hip and dropped him back on the earth, laughing.

When Sandeep would come visiting, Diwan's son, fascinated by the stories he told of life at Chhatrasal, spent all day with him.

'Send me with Sandeep, Ma, I want to stay with him.'

'You want to leave your family already,' she would ask, laughing. 'And who will cook food for you? Or take you to school? Wash your clothes?'

But that day was coming soon. Diwan had taught the boy everything he knew, and then watched with fascination as the boy started figuring out more complicated moves on his own. He was a natural-born wrestler if ever there was such a thing.

Even Kamala, who had never actually seen a wrestling match, had never attended a dangal, or stepped into an akhada, could see in her son's movements a speed and power that thrilled her.

Yet, when the boy was twelve, and Diwan came to tell her that there was a trial coming up at Chhatrasal, she thought, 'But he is so little!'

The night before the trial was a tense one. Diwan spent it in a state of sleepless anxiety. The boy could not sleep either—his mind raced with the stories Sandeep had told him of Chhatrasal, and he tried to imagine what it would be like to stand in front of Satpal, who was a fearsome giant. The man had ridden an elephant in his langot while people showered him with flowers! His thoughts drifted to tales of another giant, Kikar pahalwan, who was so massive that an entire man could slip through one leg hole of his langot, and who got his name because he had uprooted a kikar tree with his bare hands. What kind of a man can uproot a tree?

Diwan's wife cried quietly all night, and did not speak to her husband.

A new routine set in in the Solanki household. Kamala and Diwan woke up together before sunrise, drank their tea, and headed to the cattle shed. Kamala milked the buffaloes, Diwan did exercises. Then Diwan left for work at five, carrying three litres of milk in a canister, almonds, paneer, ghee and fresh fruits. Sometimes, he was heckled by the neighbours: 'It's the father of the world champion wrestler taking milk to his son!'

They didn't mean any harm, Diwan knew, but the humour was lost on him.

He went to Chhatrasal first, an hour away in a bus, to drop the food off for his boy. By the time he would reach the stadium, the boys would already be in training, and sometimes he lingered for a few minutes before heading to work. At least twice a week, Diwan also visited Chhatrasal after work. Usually, he got there in time to see his son in action—on the tattered mat, on the earthen pit next to it—and he was happiest on those days. On days that he was late and training was over, he sat with his son for half an hour or so, inquiring about his health, if he was practising enough, what new techniques he had learnt, and if he was eating properly. No matter what, Diwan was never satisfied with the amount of work his boy was putting into wrestling. 'You must work harder,' he would tell him sternly at almost every meeting. Soon his boy was so scared of this that he would start doing push-ups and squats if he saw his father coming, even after a full day's practice.

Life at Chhatrasal was everything that the boy had imagined.

There were huge pahalwans there, with muscles like boulders, and the impact of their bodies when they fell on the mat sent currents of excitement through him. Satpal himself was an imposing figure, a giant of a man, with hands the size of shovels. He walked and talked with frightening vigour, as if any moment he would start beating somebody up. He watched everything with cold, keen eyes, and not even the funny little hats he always wore could lessen his fearsome presence.

But what really held the boy's fascination were the ears, the scarred and swollen ears of the wrestlers. When he asked, he was told that it's because of the repeated impact on the ear when you fall on the mat, or when your opponent grabs your neck. It is painful at first, but the pain goes quickly enough, but the ears stay like that forever. He had not fallen enough to have ears like that. When they travelled to dangals together, his father used to point out people with deformed ears and say, 'Look, a pahalwan.' He would stare and follow the ears till the man disappeared. Now those ears were everywhere, and he couldn't get enough of them. He would touch his own earlobes and think, when will this happen to me?

He lived under the shabby stadium, in cramped rooms packed with other boys. No one had more than one bag here, packed with a few T-shirts, a singlet, a langot, a pair of wrestling shoes and a pair of slippers. They lived out of those bags, little gladiators under the rafters, mattresses lined on the floors, the stadium's underbelly their roof; twenty of them in a room which should not have fitted more than ten.

But he did not miss home. There was always something happening—if it wasn't training, it was a competition. He went to dangals with his coaches. Every Sunday, there would be a dangal at Jama Masjid. It was his favourite. The busy markets, the grand old buildings, the press of people. The masjid itself forming a sweeping, dramatic backdrop. Children from all over Delhi would gather at the dangal, and there was always a nice, big crowd, and a bit of money given to them for a performance that stood out. He eagerly waited for Sundays to arrive so that he could test out his training, all the new stuff he had learnt, and gauge for himself his own progress.

Satpal used to do this too, decades ago, at this very dangal, when Guru Hanuman brought his own small band of young boys for their Sunday adventure. He won here almost without exception. Sushil won too—with gleeful ease—but Satpal never praised him, though. Told him, you work and learn and sweat to win. If you lose, you may as well go back home and choose something else to do, don't waste my time or yours. What good is kushti for you if you can't win? This scared Sushil like nothing else. What else could he do if he didn't wrestle?

He dreamt of becoming a great pahalwan one day. A big, hundred-kilo giant. A heavyweight whose very presence in the wrestling circle would make his opponent's knees shake. Like Satpal, like Gama pahalwan, like Kikar. He would be unbeatable. At the stadium, he met a boy who became his closest friend— Yogeshwar. The two of them thought of nothing but kushti.

Then his ears started to change too. When he got slammed on the ground, his ear bent on itself, pressed painfully against his skull, a piercing pain shooting through him, he was pleased. He would grit his teeth and fight the pain, press down even more and slide his head along the ground till he could writhe out of the grip and breathe again. His ears were red and bruised and permanently swollen into a shapeless lump. His ears were turning!

At the end of each day's training, Yogi and he would step out of the shadow of the tin roof over the wrestling mat and walk over to the earthen pit. They would lie down side by side on the cool akhada earth. Their breathing slowed. The pain and the ringing inside their heads subsided. The touch of the soft, fine earth filled them with a happy stillness.

Being inside an airplane was something of a shock to him; a strange, dimly lit space crammed with rows of seats with people in them. And where was his seat? He had prayed for a window, and he got one. Questions raced through his head. He had never felt this nervous, or this excited. Can this thing really lift off into the air? How? What will it feel like? Will the noise deafen him? As the plane gathered speed, so did his chaotic thoughts, until the turmoil was abruptly hushed by a wondrous scene: Delhi, barely recognizable, lit up below like a dazzling dreamscape.

Diwan had to pay for this. The Wrestling Federation of India was not about to send someone just on merit. Your son has qualified, yes, they told him, but so many things can go wrong between now and the tournament. What if the visa does not come on time? What if the doctor says he is not fit to go? Diwan didn't need to hear more. He paid the bribe the federation official asked for. It was a fortune. He had to scrape together most of his savings to come up with it. But it was worth it, his son was going to the World Cadet Games in Poland. Who would have thought? It was 1998, barely two years since he had left the boy at Chhatrasal.

When the young fellow called from Warsaw, the whole family gathered around the phone in Baprola. He told everyone that things were well, the city was more beautiful than anything he had ever seen, and he was doing well, feeling good. To his mother, he complained of the food—just bread (he called it 'double-roti') and boiled vegetables. He couldn't eat meat. The next time he called, it was to tell them that he had won.

This was the second consecutive gold for an Indian boy at the cadet games. In 1997, Ramesh Kumar from Captain Chand Roop's akhada had won there.

For Satpal, it became a weapon. He took the fight to the sports administrators and the Wrestling Federation: give us Olympic mats. He had been doing this for years, and he had powerful backers—legendary former wrestlers and coaches like Chandgi Ram, Guru Hanuman, Captain Chand Roop—but the sports administrators were unmoved. They did not have the money. Even if they had it, they told the coaches, it would be wasted on mats since Indian wrestlers were clearly not cut out for the international stage. It was a curiously self-defeating logic.

Let's not get ahead of ourselves here, Satpal was told. Results come from hard work, not equipment, so aren't your wrestlers working hard enough? First let's see if any of your boys can do anything at an international competition, and then we'll see about a mat.

Now a boy had done just that. Satpal was not going to back down. Even in Baprola, there was a discernible change in the attitude of the villagers. No one laughed when Diwan took milk to Chhatrasal. Now they came to him for advice, asked him about akhadas, about admission to Satpal's school, about the right age for a boy to start wrestling. They spoke of how wrestling was in their blood, its roots in the soil they tilled. Soon, there was a line of fathers up at dawn, carrying milk in steel canisters, travelling to this akhada or that, and Diwan greeted them cheerfully, asked about their sons.

The chief minister of Haryana, a well-known wrestling patron himself, came down to the local school to felicitate Diwan's son on his return from Poland. The boy had earned a bit of fame anyway at the local dangals, largely due to the speed with which he fought. A few months before he left for Poland, he had won twelve matches in quick succession at a village dangal. Now at any dangal in the neighbourhood there were always people asking, 'Is that Baproliya boy here? Will he be fighting today?'

The chief minister called the Baproliya boy up to the stage. He pointed to him and said: 'A village boy, a Haryana boy will bring us an Olympic medal. And it will be this boy. His name… what's your name, son?'

'Sushil.'

'His name is Sushil.'

They are back at the Mundka dangal, their annual pilgrimage, father and son. But this time Diwan does not have to stand jostling with the crowd, straining to see the action from some faraway corner. He is seated on a sofa, uncomfortable no doubt, but the best possible place in the arena, inches away from the wrestling area, and surrounded by 'VIPs'. Sushil can't walk away this time; he is the main attraction.

It is 2006, and Sushil Kumar is a star in the world of kushti. He has won numerous dangals. He has won medals at Asian-level tournaments. After his second gold at the World Cadet Games back in 1999, Satpal had severely limited Sushil's participation in dangals so that he could concentrate on developing his game on the mat. Yet, at dangals, Sushil is known to be able to take on any one and beat them, no matter what weight or reputation they brought to the fight. There are perhaps three wrestlers in all of India, all heavyweight Olympians, whom Sushil can't beat, by his own admission. The rest are too dazzled by his speed.

He is at his peak, though there had been a crushing blow a couple of years back. He had been in tremendous form leading up to the 2004 Athens Olympics, beating fifteen wrestlers on the way to qualifying for the Games. He had never felt fitter, stronger or faster. He had gone to the Athens Olympics, his first, convinced that he was about to do something very special. He had stormed through the first match 9-0. But in his second match he could not score a point. The Cuban who beat him went on to win the gold. There was no repêchage, so that was the end of the Olympics for him. In the second match. He could not believe the cruelty of it all. To add to that, the Ukrainian wrestler he had beaten at the 1998 Cadet Games so easily finished fourth, which was at least respectable.

A medal would have changed things, arrested kushti's terrible downward dive. People in cities didn't care about it any more, or thought of it as only fit for criminals and thugs. Villages were turning into towns, or, like Baprola, were being absorbed into big cities, and losing their interest in the game. In fact, the people from these places were sometimes ashamed of kushti; they wanted to distance themselves from this rural sport in their hunger for a more urban life. Worst of all, of all the countries with a rich tradition of wrestling, none fared as badly as India at the international stage. Rich countries like the US did well. Poor countries like Uzbekistan did well. Small countries like Cuba were winning. Huge ones like Russia dominated every competition. It didn't matter what race, colour, religion or economic condition, everyone got their share of medals—Japan, Belarus, Ukraine, Turkey, Iran, Kazakhstan—each of these countries won wrestling medals at the Athens Games. But not India.

A gloomy, despairing doubt had spread through the wrestling community. What if all this talk about India's great wrestling history and tradition—its obsession with the sport, all the champions of yesterday remembered through grand tales—what if this was all like that old story of the frog who thought himself king of a well he had never left? What if those arrogant sports administrators were right and Indian wrestlers were so unskilled that they did not deserve any infrastructure? India had only ever won one wrestling medal at the Olympics, and that was back in 1952.

But for now, as he stands there at the edge of the arena, he tells himself: forget these depressing thoughts. Get on the pit and do what you've come here to do. Look at the crowd. Remember how many times you've come here to see this very dangal with your father. Look at that—there's father sitting in the front row. Make eye contact. Smile. This is a great day, a glorious day. Feel that earth. Feel the power coursing through your body. This is where you belong.

Section II

Revival

6

The Body as a Wonderland

And if the body were not the soul, what is the soul?
—Walt Whitman

The intricacies of elite sports are hidden even from those of us who are its most ardent fans. The kinetic subtleties that athletes train for years to acquire, that process by which mechanical, explicit learning becomes a part of the basal ganglia, the realm of reflexes, so that an athlete can respond to a situation in a fraction of a second—these are hard to gauge from the outside. In common sports parlance, this ability to react is called 'touch'. It is a deceptively simple word for one of the most enigmatic of human skills.

In 1975, Janet Starkes, a graduate student at the University of Waterloo, Canada, invented what is now known as the 'occlusion test'.[7] The experiment was developed in response to questions thrown up by previous, simpler experiments to test the reflexes of elite athletes.

It was already known that the simple reaction time of top athletes—how fast they can hit a button in response to a light—was around 200 milliseconds.

Two hundred milliseconds is quick. It's the average amount of time it takes for the retina to register a stimulus and pass it on to the brain, and for the brain to respond with an action. Only a few involuntary reactions are quicker—it takes the eyes 150 milliseconds to blink when a light is shone on it.

Here was the puzzle, though: a 200-millisecond reaction time was not exclusive to athletes. In fact, most ordinary people could hit a button in response to light in the same time.

But elite sports was all about responding to things faster than that. The cricket ball, for example, arrives in a batsman's hitting zone in around 500 milliseconds. Take away 200 milliseconds as the time required for the brain to register that a ball has been launched, and that leaves the batter 300 milliseconds to decide what shot to play, get in position and execute the shot. An impossibly brief moment for that many actions.

If the batsman is not reacting faster than the average person, what is it that sets him apart? The difference, as Starkes—and others after her—found, lies in how an athlete reads and maps other visual clues. Through repeated practice and conditioning, elite athletes are able to tune in to critical visual information—like the angle of a bowler's elbow—and then rapidly, without having to really consciously think about it, predict a future event: where will the ball most likely be when it reaches the hitting zone?

Here was the answer to the reflex enigma: it was not reaction but informed anticipation, built through years of training, that held the key to success.

In a famous example from the 1980s, the South African batsman Peter Kirsten was made to face a static bowling machine releasing balls at 130 kilometres per hour (kph), a significantly lower speed than what Kirsten was used to playing in real match situations.

Kirsten failed against the machine, missing ball after ball. He was helpless without the complex series of visual signs that the batsman picks up from a real bowler's delivery stride and action.

In the original occlusion test, writes David Epstein in his book *The Sports Gene*, Starkes played out slide shows of photographs taken from volleyball games to pros and novices. Each photo flashed in front of the players for a fraction of a second and they were then asked if the photo that was shown to them had a ball in the frame or not.

'The difference between top volleyball players and novices was enormous,' Epstein writes. 'For the elite players, a fraction of a second's glance was all they needed to determine whether the ball was present.'

A member of the Canadian women's national volleyball team, Starkes found, could not only determine if a ball was present or not when shown a photo for just sixteen milliseconds, but gleaned enough information from the picture to be able to tell where it was taken.

At a press conference in Kinshasa in 1974 before his legendary fight against George Foreman—the 'rumble in the jungle'— Muhammad Ali, seated next to Don King, rapped about how fast he was: 'Fast,' he said, and then repeated the word like he was setting up a beat.

'Fast.'

'Fast.'

Then the rap: 'Last night I cut the light off in my bedroom, hit the switch, was in the bed before the room was dark.'

'Incredible,' King says, keeping the rhythm.

'Fast,' says Ali.

Ali was at his witty, poetic best, but the heart of what he was saying was true: *I'm so fast, you can't even see what I'm doing.*

In sports like boxing or wrestling (or, indeed, in football or cricket), where the objective is to keep your intentions hidden from the opponent, to feint in the subtlest of ways and then execute the real coup at lightning speed, the true nature of the move is necessarily hidden from the spectator.

Television coverage of sports has evolved steadily to address this space between what you see and what is really happening: cameras that are more and more advanced, super-slow-motion, ultra-slow-motion and heat-map recordings, graphs and statistics and animations on speed and trajectory and reaction times.

After being accorded the privilege of watching Sushil train week after week, I was being pulled deeper and deeper into this mysterious world of speed, anticipation and concealed motives.

One day, as Sushil and Pradeep were bringing their training day to an end with a sparring bout, I set up a video camera to record it. Then I watched the footage at one-sixteenth of its original speed.

This is what I saw.

First contact from Pradeep—start your stopwatch—he tries to grab the nape of Sushil's neck. Sushil reacts by bending low and reaching with his right hand across to the inside of Pradeep's left knee. It is only a feint; the hand that shot out like a whip is suddenly pulled back. As he is withdrawing his hand, Sushil propels himself backward. Pradeep, reacting to the feint, had moved one foot back to evade the hand. So now Pradeep is exposed to two opposing forces: his reaction to the feint has shifted his body's momentum backwards, and he has only one foot grounded; but the neck hold he has on a reversing Sushil is pulling him forward. Pradeep loses his balance, and, as he lurches forward, he makes a desperate attempt to get a grip on Sushil's ankle. This is a mistake. Sushil accelerates backwards, all the while circling out towards his left, and Pradeep lands in a heap, face down, on the mat, with no grip on Sushil.

But wait. Rewind. Rewatch. Before Pradeep has hit the mat, Sushil has braked his own movement, landed on one knee, and shot forward while grabbing Pradeep's right hand below the armpit and coiling his other arm around Pradeep's neck.

Stop the watch: six seconds have passed.

It's a breathtaking, breathless experience—like looking at the human body with new, fresh eyes. There is something primeval about it, something that makes the muscles of the watcher twitch involuntarily, a reaction that comes from the gut. Here are two people, built like trucks, moving with the speed and agility of cats. In real life, they look very fast and very powerful, but also jerky and fuzzy.

Slowed down, the movements reveal themselves as fluid, sinuous and so deliberate that not a finger moves without reason. The thunderous clash of two bodies transforms into the soothing, pure lines of t'ai chi.

Wrestling is a demanding sport, and it demands the kind of biomechanical mastery that can only come from years of training, beginning from early childhood. It calls for exquisite coordination between every moving part of the body. It needs quickness, brute strength, explosive power, preternatural balance, gymnastic agility and endurance. A single move can open itself to a hundred different possible permutations and combinations of counteraction. If your opponent has shifted his weight ever so slightly to the left, do you use that momentum or oppose it? Do you drop down for the legs? Do you follow a straight line as you drop, or go across? Has the weight shifted enough that your opponent is setting up for an attack or is he just looking for an opening? In that case, do you remain patient and hold your position, or do you move into a defensive posture, or do you execute a counter-attack?

Each of these questions can branch into a hundred more variables. You have 200 milliseconds, or less: it's a dialogue of split-second reflexes. Wrestling is almost all improvisation, caged within certain structural parameters like set-ups and standard opening moves, but within these it is a free-flowing call-and-response on hair trigger.

'There is no end of learning in wrestling,' Pradeep says later, cooling off in his dingy room under the stadium. 'No matter how much you know, it's never enough. You keep on learning new things, new techniques, evolve new daos.[8] That's what Sushil and I do every day. Sushil likes to dominate a fight. There is this one ability he has that is still a mystery to me: if you reach for him, he is light and nimble. But when he reaches for you to make contact, it's like he has suddenly put on 100 kilos more. He becomes really heavy. He knows how to use his bodyweight.'

'It's all about anticipation,' Sushil adds. 'When you are fighting, it's spontaneous, you are always improvising, and no two fights are ever the same. How well you anticipate and then react to your opponent's movements—that's the fight. That's wrestling. Wrestling is not dand-baithak, or climbing ropes, or running miles, or building muscles. It's about reading your opponent's body movement. Your visual awareness, your awareness of what you feel on your skin, the weight of a touch. When I'm on the mat, I'm so filled with this awareness that the slightest touch feels like electricity to my body, and my body reacts to that the same way it would have reacted if I touched a live wire. What you need to have to be a really good wrestler is phoorti. When I step on the mat and I can feel the phoorti, I know it's going to be good.'

Wrestlers are fond of using electricity as an analogy for speed and reaction time, just as Muhammad Ali did, but their physical self-awareness is based on the concept of phoorti.

Literally, it means 'agility'. But in the context of kushti, the semantic field is wider. It can be used to describe the 'electricity' in a wrestler's body, or the joy he derives from wrestling. It is nimbleness, but also the delight inherent in the nimbleness. This playfulness is integral to wrestling, the fun of fooling your opponent into thinking that you'll do one thing but then doing something else altogether. Phoorti is to revel in your body, and in the awareness of your own mastery of it.

Pahalwans draw a direct parallel between the health of the body and the health of the mind. They believe, without exception, that disciplining the body through exercise, and then allowing its expression through wrestling, inevitably leads to happy and uncluttered thinking.[9]

Walt Whitman could have been expressing the pehelwan's point of view when he wrote: 'But the expression of a well-made man appears not only in his face / It is in his limbs and joints also, it is curiously in the joints of his hips and wrists / It is in his walk, the carriage of his neck, the flex of his waist and knees, dress does not hide him...'

It is exactly this that I heard from numerous wrestlers and coaches, including Sushil and his father Diwan—the measure of a man is in how he stands and how he moves.

Other wrestlers used the word phoorti in other ways. An old wrestler in Varanasi spoke about his father, who was also a wrestler, saying that he had such phoorti that he wore langots made of silk. Satpal, Sushil's coach, said that the phoorti in him was such that if he woke up suddenly in the middle of the night, he would immediately start doing push-ups.

Phoorti is also the counterbalance for another concept fundamental to pahalwans: mehnat, hard work. The reality of kushti is that it follows a mind-numbing, gruelling training regime, consisting of hundreds of dands, baithaks, pull-ups, rope climbs, bridging and running that never varies, and has to be done at least 300 days in a year from the time you are twelve years old till the time you retire.

The most common trope used to describe mehnat is of the pahalwan who does hundreds of that excruciating combination of dand and baithak called 'burpee' in English (do a push-up, stand up, squat down, do a push-up, stand up, squat down, ad infinitum), with his feet rooted in a single spot, and his eyes fixed on a single point.

This is an exercise regime so hard that mind control becomes more important than any physical aspect, the wrestlers say. You can see this in action on any given morning on the stadium steps at Chhatrasal, or any akhada anywhere: the wrestler on his 350th burpee, eyes fixed on one spot, sweat flowing like water, body moving like an automaton someone forgot to switch off.

This is mehnat. It's scary and brutal. It's meditative and masochistic. It's the single-minded ability to do one thing without letting fatigue get to you.

Sushil tells everyone he meets 'mehnat karo' (work hard) with such regularity that it qualifies as a tic. His father has a simple explanation he repeats often when asked how and why Sushil achieved so much: '*Mehnat kiya*, focus *hatney nahin diya, aur kya? Koi bhi kar sakta hai.*' (He worked hard; he kept his focus, what else is there to say? Anyone can do it.)

But not everyone can do it. You need mehnat as much as you need its obverse, phoorti, otherwise the drudgery and pain will bring you down. You need both roots and wings. Phoorti then can be translated as ecstasy, literally, to exist out of time, to both embrace and escape the tyranny of regimented days.

'I do the same exercise, the same techniques on the mat almost every day. But there is not one day that I don't feel excited and happy about it,' Sushil told me. 'It's when I take a break that I get restless and bored and unhappy. If I'm not on the mat, the whole day seems wasted. This is how I felt when I first came to Chhatrasal, and I still feel the same way.'

The idea of ecstasy and playfulness might seem at odds with a combat sport. Joyce Carol Oates says of boxing: 'There is nothing fundamentally playful about it; nothing that seems to belong to daylight, to pleasure.'[10]

This is where wrestling stands apart from all other combat sports. Its fundamental singularity, its very soul if you please, is that it's a fighting form that shuns violence. It allows no hitting. There are no punches, no kicks, no knees and no elbows. You do not batter your opponent into submission, like you would in boxing or MMA, mixed martial arts. You don't break ribs, pound heads, harm the kidney, dislocate the nose, or cut open the eyes. The surface you fight on is soft, so a fall doesn't hurt. If you pick your opponent up, you are responsible for his 'safe return' back to the ground. Yet it is the manliest of sports, the very definition of masculinity, and has been used to judge the 'alpha male' from time immemorial, but we will come to that later.

Take away blood and gore and the intent to injure, and it is easy to see how the space for playfulness opens up, how you can revel in the joy of being able to call on all your muscles and bones and joints to action, to come up against another body, another force, and outwit and outplay it.

This euphoria ran through Sushil in the over sixty practice sessions I attended at Chhatrasal, and it never flagged. Everyone shared in it—from the oldest (thirty-eight) to the youngest (ten), and there was no attempt to separate Sushil, Yogi or any of the other Olympic medallists from even those boys who were at training for the first time.

Sushil is no pushover, but he routinely called children on to the mat and allowed himself to be taken down by them, feigning surprise and amazement that a child could throw him. It never failed to delight the little wrestlers.

Phoorti.

7

AN ANCIENT SPORT IS REVIVED

Sushil has a constant stream of visitors at the akhada. People come for all sorts of reasons, but most come with no discernible motive except to spend a few minutes with the pahalwan, the man who has become the saviour of kushti. Visitor or akhada-mate, they talk non-stop about wrestling—who's good, who's fading, who's not getting the proper diet but has talent, who's got a job with the police or the railways. Conversations inevitably drift to pahalwans of the past—'dangals are not what they used to be' everyone agrees. 'Those days are gone.'

'But you have brought us hope,' people inevitably say to Sushil. 'Because of you, people know kushti again.'

Sushil lies spreadeagled on the mattress, chewing a neem twig and checking his phone for messages. It's an off day, and time passes slowly.

A sad, dim-looking boy with a thin moustache, carrying a plastic packet with a stack of papers, comes to meet him. He is timid and weakly built, which immediately puts Sushil in a slightly abrasive mood, though he asks the boy to sit down and orders that almond milk be brought for him.

'So tell me, what can I do for you,' he asks warily.

The boy launches into a soft, flat monologue. 'My father knew your father and he told me, son, go to Baprola, and on the main road to Najafgarh, you will spot the pahalwan's house easily, so I took a train to Delhi, and then a bus, and then I came to your house…'

'No, no,' Sushil interrupts, 'I asked, what can I do for you? Why have you come to meet me?'

The boy continues the drone like he did not even hear Sushil.

'…so in Baprola I met your father, and I touched his feet, and I told him my father knew him and I have to come to meet pahalwanji, and your father said, no, pahalwanji does not live here, you have to go to Chhatrasal Stadium, take the bus from here, so I took the bus, I had to wait for a long time—'

'But why are you here?' Sushil asks again, more forcefully, but also with a hint of resignation in his voice.

'I want a job with the railways.'

Sushil, the man knows, works for the railways too.

'Ok. Have you given the entrance exam?'

'Sir, I am a pahalwan, I do zor[11] every day, I wake up at four, I never get time to study, and I am always tired…'

'But, but, you cannot get a job without passing the exam, no?'

'Pahalwanji, please do something, if someone can do something, my father said, pahalwanji can. The man who has raised kushti back up from nowhere, he can do anything. I have three bighas of land, and I will give it you—'

'Wait! Please.' Sushil sits up, snaps out of his stupor. 'Don't say things like that. I don't want your land, or your money, or anything from you! God has been good to me, and I have everything. If you need money, I will give you money. But I cannot help you—are you listening carefully?—I cannot help you if you don't give the exam and pass it, alright? So first, go home, study. Study hard like you do zor. Now go.'

Later, a young bedraggled new entrant to the Chhatrasal akhada is ushered into the room, and Sushil gives him a full set of wrestling gear. The young wrestler is told not to tell others whom he got it from, or else there will be a beeline of boys outside Sushil's door, and he does not want to refuse people.

'Shabash,' Sushil tells the boy affectionately. 'Mehnat karo.'

Back in 2008, when Sushil Kumar won a bronze at the Olympics, it had the same impact that an unexpected burst of rain has on a land made barren by drought. Millions of seeds buried under the baked earth were stirred from their lifelessness, and sent forth green shoots.

The obscurity of a rural pursuit was lifted. The most immediate effect Sushil's medal had was to bring a flood of new students to established akhadas like Chatrasal and Mehr Singh's. But it also seeded other, wilder dreams.

Billu Singh had missed watching that fight on TV.

It was a hot August morning in 2008, and the two standing fans that whirred furiously inside the small 'clubhouse' in a Muslim slum in Indore did nothing more than make noise. Billu had gathered there with some of his friends to watch the Indian wrestlers in action at the Olympics.

Twelve white plastic chairs and a TV stand were the only furniture in the room. The chairs were occupied, and a few others sat on the floor. The mood was not hopeful. They had gathered like this the day before and watched Yogeshwar Dutt lose in the quarter-final. There was no reason why Sushil Kumar, great wrestler that he was at dangals, could do any better.

Billu had hardly finished greeting everyone and settling down on one of the chairs when Sushil lost his opening bout. It was like the air had been sucked out of the stifling room. Within seconds, the clubhouse was empty, save a couple of old men. Billu got on his bike and went for a ride, feeling cynical and bitter. How could anyone from India win at the Olympics anyway? This corrupt, ruthless country, run by old men looking for nothing more than their own selfish gain at the cost of others. The akhadas are the same. Outdated hovels overseen by selfish dictators who are blind to what is happening in the rest of the world.

At some point, Billu found himself on the highway to Mhow, the road leading to the village where he was born, and stopped for tea. The shop owner knew Billu. 'What are you doing roaming around here, brother,' he asked.

'Why?' Billu was puzzled.

'That pahalwan, Sushil, he is winning, no?'

The owner turned up the volume on the radio, and yes, it was true! He had beaten two opponents and was already in the bronze medal match. Billu was transfixed (later, he would learn about repêchage). He felt such a surge of excitement, he thought he would go mad. He sat there right next to the radio, stiff and feverish with anxiety. Sushil Kumar against a Kazakh wrestler. The Kazakh goes down.

An Olympic wrestling medal for India! This is the moment Billu was waiting for.

'How do I look?' Billu Singh asks, with a look of deep concern. He turns to check his profile in the full-length mirror, then turns back to face it. He tugs down at his shirt, once deep red, now faded to a less glorious shade. He runs a finger carefully over his ear, fixing a lock of hair. He fusses with his jacket—it's the kind used by photographers, its entire surface stitched with pockets of various sizes.

'You look good,' I say.

'Do I look strong? Powerful,' he asks again, staring at the mirror as if his strength will grow the more he stared.

'Yes.'

'Good,' Billu says. 'I have a stomach problem; my doctor has said I can't exercise for some time. Still I did a few push-ups in the morning.'

Billu Singh Yadav is a tall, dark man with a lively sense of fashion. Everything he is wearing, including his skinny jeans, is a size too small for him. He likes to call himself Billu Singh Pahalwan, but immediately confesses that he is not a wrestler. He desperately wanted to be one, but that was not to be. He also wanted to work in Bollywood, starring in action films.

'I have the personality, I am good-looking, I sing like Kishore Kumar, and I would have done all my own stunts,' he says. 'But my skin is too dark.' He went to Mumbai, stayed there for a few months. It was not his thing. 'There were no honest people there,' he says. 'I couldn't stand the women. No morals.'

He came back to Indore, where he grew up, and where he lives now. Billu knows a lot of people in Indore, and organizes a lot of dangals. He also donates money to a dozen or more akhadas. He owns a cruiser bike, a Mitsubishi Pajero and an open jeep rigged up like a rally car. He wants to know which one we should take for our tour of akhadas in Indore.

This leafy city in Madhya Pradesh, once a royal principality, boasts a rich history of wrestling. Towards the end of the nineteenth century, the then maharaja of Indore, Shivaji Rao Holkar, set up many akhadas in the city, and kept a large retinue of court wrestlers. He also organized elaborate tournaments, and the best wrestlers of the time would stay for months to train in Indore and compete.

Billu Singh, pahalwan or not, knows every akhada in the city—the old ones left over from the royal past, perhaps the last functional remnants of that time, as well as newer ones. But first, there is the little matter of delivering a threat. 'Won't take five minutes,' he says.

We take the Pajero. Several other people are needed for the intimidation project, and a big car is necessary. He makes the calls, telling his men to gather at a cavernous tea shop inside an old building next to a busy flyover. It takes only ten minutes to drive to the shop, but a quartet of young men is already waiting for Billu. He swaggers in, eyes twinkling, smiling widely, and greets everyone in the shop.

His men tell him that he is looking very handsome. He smiles wider. The four are all carefully turned out. The most striking of them has skin the colour of polished mahogany, and is wearing a crisp white shirt, aviators, a well-tailored sleeveless Nehru jacket and fitted chinos ending in shiny and high black boots.

He shows Billu a cellphone video of a local politician exhorting a gathering of men to riot and arson, to attack a certain neighbourhood in rural Indore.

Elections are coming up in Madhya Pradesh.

According to Billu and his men, after the attack that took place as a result of this mobilization, the police arrested the victims. They used a video clip shot by a local TV channel that had captured some of the late, defensive violence from the community that was attacked. The TV channel had helped the attackers by suppressing the real facts of the riot. Billu and his men were convinced that the reporter who had shot the video had also filmed the actual attack.

'Let's go fuck his mother,' Billu exclaims with a big smile. Even before the car comes to a stop outside the channel's offices, with Billu at the wheel, the editor rushes out.

'You didn't have to come all the way here, why take so much trouble,' he fumbles. The bald patch on his head is damp with sweat, his shirt is soaked and his hair hangs limply. He fiddles with his hair as his eyes move uneasily over each man. The five pairs of eyes in the car are riveted on the editor.

Billu smiles widely. 'So you know why we are here.'

'We are going to play the video on prime time,' the editor says, his voice barely under control, fingers flying around his face. 'We will play it big. We have sent a reporter to the village also. Really, there was no need for you to come all the way here. It was an honest mistake, of course we will show the video, it will be done…I cannot even call you in for coffee because I was just leaving for a meeting—'

'We will be watching the news,' Billu says, and drives off.

The editor, who was leaning on the car, is jerked rudely. He just manages not to fall.

Billu and his men burst out laughing.

'Did you see the way he was looking at me,' asks the biggest guy—he is just over six feet tall and must weigh a hundred kilos. 'Like I would have killed him just by looking at him!' Big guy had latched on to that vibe, and kept up a brooding and bloodshot stare throughout. Now, caught up in the joy of being successfully scary, he begins singing: 'Hark the herald angels sing/glory to the newborn king/peace on earth and mercy mild/god and sinners reconciled.'

He spends the rest of the day repeating the line in a soft baritone.

'Let's start our own gang, eh,' Billu asks in his most charming voice, as we drive aimlessly around. 'We will rule the city. What do you say? All us good-looking people. We will be the most handsome gang in the world.' There is more laughter.

Billu wants to rule Indore, and wrestling is the foundation on which this rule will be based. He is a tireless organizer of dangals—in narrow lanes that snake through slums, in municipal parks strewn with garbage and in floodlit indoor stadiums with shiny new mats, he holds them everywhere. There's at least a dangal a month, sometimes as many as three or four during peak season.

'Everyone in the world, whether they know it or not, is a lover of kushti,' Billu says. 'Because it's what human beings have done since the very beginning of our time, you know? Men fighting one another. With nothing to interfere. No guns, motherfucker. No sticks or stones. Just the man and what he has in him. We are all brothers in this, all of us understand this. Man against man, on bare earth.'

Billu remembers the first dangal he organized in photographic detail. That was twenty years ago. He was fifteen.

It was a bright, sunny day in October. A sleepy breeze kicked up every few minutes, rustling through the narrow lanes of Goaltuli, near Indore's sprawling railway station. It had rained the night before, turning the road into a slush of mud and cow dung. Billu and a few other boys had been tasked with scraping the slush to the sides, creating a slightly cleaner strip about three feet wide in the middle. There were guests coming to the akhada at Goaltuli. Colourful little paper flags had been strung across rooftops leading up to the akhada, which gleamed in the sunlight under a fresh coat of paint. Flowers and mango leaves ringed the wrestling pit. Ashok Yadav and Vijay Mishra, two of Indore's foremost wrestlers, were visiting. They were accompanied by a small group of politicians and civil servants who were to donate a few lakh of rupees to this akhada: the money was for a new tin roof, a bathing area and, perhaps, if it could be arranged, a mat. Yet another glorious moment for the akhada, which had produced an Olympian, and had become famous when Amitabh Bachchan had said in a movie: '*Hum bhi Indore wale Vijay Bahadur ustad ke pathhe hain!*'[12]

Billu had no love for the place. He blamed the coach for systematically killing his dreams of becoming a wrestler, for never so much as glancing at Billu during training, never offering him a word. Billu wasn't picked for dangals, or even for practice bouts. The enterprising young man had been wracking his brain for a way to escape the clutches of the akhada without severing his ties with the sport. Perhaps there was something in the air that day, a day of festive, rain-washed joy, but he had felt an almost unbearable surge of excitement when the two wrestlers and their retinue had walked into the lane, watched by hundreds of people standing in their doorways or crowding the rooftops. Even the familiar prickle of self-loathing he felt when he saw big wrestlers in their glowing white kurtas—a reminder always of his own stick-like appearance—faded as soon as it appeared.

'These were two of the best wrestlers in India, and they had hardly ever fought each other, at least never in Indore, and I thought that I will organize a fight between the two,' Billu tells me over milky coffee in the same tea shop where I had first met his gang. 'If just the two of them appearing together to waste a little time on a Sunday could generate this kind of excitement, a fight between the two would be something people will talk about for a year!'

But how to do this? Billu had no experience, no contacts and never had more than twenty rupees in his pocket on any given day. The first thing, he thought, would be to know more about all the people who had visited the akhada that day. He put all his energy behind the quest. In a month, he knew everything that could be known about the two wrestlers and the three politicians who had made up the party—where they lived, their family trees, an exhaustive list of the fights that the two wrestlers had been involved in, and information about the politician's pet projects and electoral promises.

'Because I was always ignored in the akhada, I had made an obsession out of observing, of finding out information about other people,' he says.

He knew, for instance, that one of the politician's sons was training to be a wrestler. He knew the boy was sixteen, only a year older than him, and that he had lost in the semi-final of the recent state championships to a boy called Shankar, who lived near Billu's slum in Goaltuli. He knew that one of the wrestlers, Ashok Yadav, had old ties to Goaltuli, and was close to an uncle who lived there. At that time, Billu worked in a tiny roadside shop that stitched motorbike seats. He saw Ashok's uncle's bike parked outside his house and saw his opportunity—the seat was made of frayed black rexine, and little mushrooms of foam sprouted from the seams. Billu waited outside the house one morning, and when the uncle came out, he walked by casually and passed him before stopping and turning around.

'You are Ashok pahalwan's uncle,' Billu had asked, toothsome smile in place, eyes filled with awe. 'What a wonderful thing to meet you! Ashok pahalwan is like a god to me. The two of you look so similar! You must have been quite the wrestler too—do you still practise? I am Billu pahalwan; I work out at the akhada here. Maybe you could teach me some of those moves that Ashok pahalwan is famous for? Is that your bike? Oh how strange. I work in the seat shop on the corner of the main road. Why don't you bring me the bike and I will fix the seat for you. You won't have to pay anything. It is enough that you are Ashok pahalwan's uncle. It will be my privilege.'

The older man succumbed to that avalanche of charm. Billu borrowed the money needed to make a new seat cover from a tea shop, promising the tea seller free milk to cover the debt. He stole the milk from his own uncle's dairy. He made a shiny red seat cover for Ashok's relative for free, as promised, and began hanging out at the house, listening to stories of wrestling, never asking anything in return. One day, the uncle told Billu that Ashok was coming for dinner, and asked if he would like to join them, meet the pahalwan.

That night, having just met Billu, Ashok Yadav agreed to a fight. There were many compelling reasons to refuse: the organizer was an unknown, poor lanky kid; the fight would happen on a makeshift pit in a slum, and not in an established akhada; and there was no certainty that either the money or the infrastructure required for it could be put together by this upstart. Perhaps Yadav agreed because he thought it would never actually go through. He told Billu upfront that the minimum purse he accepted for fights was Rs 10,000, and this was not negotiable. If this could be arranged, with Rs 7,000 for the loser, he would convince Vijay Mishra himself.

Billu had an excellent plan for the money. He went to the politician with the wrestler son and made him a proposal: 'Finance the dangal, and posters with your name and your face will be put up everywhere in and around Goaltuli. For any campaign you run in the next few months, four–five boys from Goaltuli, including me, will be at your service for free whenever you want. And your son will be in an exhibition bout right before the main billing, introduced as one of the rising stars of wrestling in Indore. He will get to fight Shankar, the boy who beat him at the nationals. Except, this time, Shankar will be persuaded to lose the fight.'

Billu had his first sponsor.

There was no stopping him after this: he gave up his job at the bike shop and concentrated solely on organizing fights. Billu networked with the hunger of a man who has survived a famine, picking up information about each person he met. He trained himself in mnemonic tricks and observation skills, to be used when required to impress, cajole, threaten or influence people. He was omnipresent at dangals in the city. Within a short space of time, he went from a complete unknown to a small hurricane whirling through the wrestling community. The thin but indomitable Yadav boy who knew the lineage, history, medal count, wins and losses of every wrestler in the city—young or old, active or retired. He bribed local newspapers to carry reports and previews of his dangals with big headlines. 'We worked out a rate card: with picture, without picture, headline this size or that, page number this or that.'

Nonetheless, a decade later, Billu found himself still short of the mark he had set himself on the fame-and-money scale.

'Organizing dangals gets you no money, really. After you pay the wrestlers, the electricians, the tent guy, other workers, the police and the press, there is hardly enough to take home.'

So he branched out. The favours he did for politicians turned into a job in itself: transporting money and raising men for campaigning or organizing rallies. He took his logistical skills to a bigger platform. Then, almost inevitably, he stumbled on to something even more lucrative and perfectly suited for a man of his connections: real estate. Here, too, he found his own peculiar niche.

Slurping down thick, sweet coffee in a small hotel restaurant next to Goaltuli, he explains, 'A man owns farmland, and has three sons.' He holds up three fingers. 'None of these sons want to be farmers, so all of them live and work in the city. One day, the father drops dead without leaving a will. What happens to the farm? The three brothers immediately begin squabbling over it. As time passes, they fight more and more over this piece of land, till all they can do is threaten each other and file cases against each other while the land sits there and rots.'

Billu pauses for effect, taking his time to raise the cup to his lips. He takes a careful sip, smiles and says 'very good', and puts the cup down gently.

'I am the peacemaker,' he says, smiling. 'I show them reason. I make them forget about their ancient grudge and think of the money. I get the cases dropped, the land put up for sale, and all the paperwork done so that none of the brothers have to get involved with each other.'

Billu had struck a spectacularly rich vein with his diligent digging. Now he made money in a hurry. There were so many of these families, he said, that it felt like all of Indore was made of brothers fighting over land.

But what good was the money if it couldn't be used for wrestling? Billu was profoundly unhappy. No, not just unhappy. He was clinically depressed. The absence of wrestling was sucking the life out of him. By 2008, he already had two baby boys, and this just made things worse. He wanted them to become wrestlers so bad that it sent Billu into fits of misery that lasted for days. He began to dislike his job, and hate the families he had to deal with—their nasty, petty little quarrels made him feel ugly.

'I don't like violence, I don't like guns,' Billu says. 'But back then, I could feel the violence rising in me. I wanted to shoot people. If there was someone standing in my way, I felt an almost uncontrollable rage to finish him off.'

And then, there was a miracle in Billu's life. It came to him over the radio, on the highway that led to his village. He had sat in a tea shop by the road, transfixed at the news that India had won an Olympic medal in wrestling.

'It washed away all my anger,' Billu says. 'I had all these bad feelings for wrestling, but now there was hope. There was a way out. Things could happen, there were possibilities.'

His obsessive, restless nature had found the perfect outlet: building akhadas. There was a burst of new interest in wrestling in Indore. Boys were looking for akhadas to join. There were posters of Sushil Kumar everywhere. And Billu began turning the large roof of his house into a modern wrestling centre.

It is a peculiar sight, Billu's house. It rises like an antenna, three storeys high, in the middle of a makeshift slum where none of the other houses are more than a single storey. Very few are even brick structures—they are made of clay, reinforced with sheets of salvaged plastic, broken tin roofs, bicycle tyres and scrap metal. Open sewer lines criss-cross the area, leading to a central stream that circumnavigates the slum. Most people who live here are involved in recycling garbage, and the piles of newspapers and plastic rise higher than the houses. There are no roads, just huge craters and swampy cesspools, all the better for Billu's off-roader cars and bikes.

His house is a palace. It has a grand staircase spiralling up an atrium. Curtains the colour of mud drop twenty feet from the ceiling. There are mirrors everywhere, and an indiscriminate mix of decorative objects made of brass, steel, plastic or plaster of Paris. The furniture is either the colour of raw liver, or it's made of glazed glass. The most prominent wall in the living room is covered with a near-life-sized poster showing Sushil Kumar and Billu smiling for the camera. It was taken during the biggest dangal Billu has ever organized—there were wrestlers from eastern Europe, Sushil was the big draw, Indore's main stadium was booked, and a helicopter was hired to fly overhead and shower the venue with rose petals.

The true heart of Billu's house lies up the winding staircase, and through a small door that opens into a large covered terrace.

One part of it is taken up by an Olympic-sized mat, the other by a weight-training room equipped with a variety of machinery.

Posters of Sushil Kumar are on every wall. The large windows that line the terrace look out on a schematic view of the slum. It looks like the bombed-out ruins of a village.

'So what do you think? Isn't this like something you would see in America?' Billu is giddy with excitement. He looks at a mirror and smiles at himself and adjusts his shirt. 'This is where the next world champion will be made. Who will it be? Who will it be? Where is my tiger?'

Billu's younger son Vijay, all of eight, comes running from across the room. Billu picks him up in one sweep and repeats the question: 'Who will be the next world champion from India?'

'Me!' Vijay says and throws his arms up.

'That's my tiger!'

Billu has these running jokes for all his children. For his very sharp and sprightly five-year-old daughter Rani, he says: 'You know, you are very pretty overall, if it wasn't for your awfully big nose. Perhaps I will cut it off one day.'

One day, when Billu had used the line three or four times in an hour, Rani had startled him shut by saying: 'And you look like a black buffalo!'

For his quiet, serious, nine-year-old Rahul, Billu says: 'Who is my little lion? Who is it?'

Rahul does not answer. He smiles wanly and looks away.

The boy is suffering from trauma, Billu says. A couple of months back, at a school-level competition, Rahul had made the final, but lost his nerves once there. He kept going down too easily, and Billu, standing just outside the mat, could not take it any more. Billu had mercilessly bawled his son out.

'I forgot he was just nine,' Billu says. 'I screamed and shouted at him way too much and for too long.'

He had called Rahul a coward, a weakling, and a blot on wrestling and his family. He had taken hold of him roughly after the match, shoved him into the car and careened away. Billu had not spoken to the boy until the next morning when he had yanked Rahul out of his bed without warning, and carried him straight to the mat on the terrace and made him run rounds and do push-ups till he almost fainted with exhaustion. That day, Rahul came down with a severe fever that refused to leave for a week. He could not hold his food down either, and had to be taken to hospital. It had dawned then on Billu that perhaps he had gone too far. His psychiatrist told him to give Rahul a break from wrestling, and to bring him in for a few sessions.

'Yes, I go to a psychiatrist,' Billu says. 'Who goes to a psychiatrist in our country? My psychiatrist, she tells me I'm a role model because I go to her and I don't care what people think about me.'

Rahul has not wrestled since then, though during training sessions, he hangs out watching the other boys in the akhada.

Those other boys! They all suffer from malnutrition. They are small and thin, their limbs bony. They have slightly distended bellies and knock-kneed postures. Their wrestling leotards are torn in many places. They are running around on the mat and laughing and playing and tripping each other and falling. Billu surveys the scene and suddenly he becomes grim. He turns to a small round man with thick plastic glasses sitting slumped on one corner of the room and starts shouting at him.

'Why haven't you started training the kids?'

The man, the coach of Billu's akhada, shrugs expressively with his shoulders and mutters something indistinctly.

'What? What?' Billu continues screaming. 'Speak up! How will you coach them if you can't control them?'

Billu takes charge, gets the boys to line up and go through a lengthy series of calisthenics. Then he gets them to pair up and wrestle. Vijay, his younger son, is wrestling a particularly anorexic boy with awkwardly long limbs that he is using to his advantage. Vijay's face is pressed down on the mat, trapped under those tentacle-like arms. Billu gets progressively more agitated.

'Get your hips up,' he hollers at Vijay. 'Up, up. Get out of there, you fool. Drop the left shoulder. Left! Left! Put your heart in it!'

As Billu splutters and froths, others join in. Fathers of the trainees, some of the older boys who were lifting weights at the gym, they divide themselves into partisan camps. The gawky boy's father is here too—bent at the waist, so he has to support himself with a hand on his hip to stand straighter. He is emaciated, and wears glasses as thick as soda bottles, a frayed checked shirt so old it has lost all colour, and a torn dhoti.

He starts backing his boy, a crooked finger lifted at him, spouting advice in a slurry monotone. Vijay and the boy tussle silently but with great ferocity, their faces screwed up red and purple, teeth bared savagely, the hiss of their breath distinct even above all the shouting.

'Vijay will be a world champion,' Billu says later, quietly now, sitting in his room. For such a large house, Billu's room is small and unkempt. It has a double bed, a cupboard lining one wall with a huge flat-screen TV on it, and a muscular music system next to it. The bed sheet looks like it has not been changed in years. This is Billu's refuge. The place where he shuts the door, shuts out the world, and spends hours with himself and a karaoke machine hooked to the music system and TV.

'It's my best friend,' Billu says. 'I spend all my free time with the karaoke. It's my support system. Sometimes I sing all night because I can't sleep.'

Vijay is ordered to set it up, which he does, while Billu tells me that Rahul is a genius with electronics. 'He can fix anything. Vijay is not so good. Rahul will take things apart and put them back together perfectly. I tell all my friends, if you have any broken electronics, don't throw it away, give it to Rahul.'

Billu launches into a song. His daughter giggles, jumps on to the bed and hides under the sheet.

'You don't like my voice,' Billu asks Rani.

She says, 'No, no, you are an artist.'

Billu is very amused. 'No, I'm a fool!'

'No, I am a fool,' Rani returns.

'What have I told you about artists,' Billu asks her.

'That an artist and his art must never be separated,' she exclaims.

'That's my girl!'

Rahul, the traumatized electronics genius with large limpid eyes, brings us food—thin parathas, a very watery dal and some wilted onions chopped up. But Billu is not interested in the food; he is singing one song after another in a full-throated, tuneless howl.

'Kishore Kumar! What a singer, huh? People tell me I sound like him. Do I sound like him? How is my singing? I could have been a film star if I was not so dark-skinned. Would you like to hear a happy song, a sad song, a love song or an emotional song?'

Billu's mind is always on fire.

'Just like Sushil,' he says. 'I had such power in my hands, in my mind. You have to believe me because I don't lie or exaggerate. Nandkishore Yadav, who went to the world championship in Greco,[13] he is from here, and I used to fight him and he could never get even a point off me. But I had no godfather, no old fucker running an akhada who was my uncle. I did not know where to go, what to do, or how to go to qualifications and trials, and no one helped me.'

It seems like no one helped Nandkishore Yadav either, because he is now a cycle rickshaw driver at the Indore railway station, ferrying people for Rs 10 a ride from the station to the nearby slums.

'All those international medals, and now all his power is being sapped away by a rickshaw,' Billu says.

All his life, it seems, Billu has been trying to make a wrestler out of someone or the other in his family, with more or less disastrous results. When he was seventeen, and he had just given up hopes of ever becoming a great wrestler, Billu had turned his focus to his brother, then fifteen. He had funded his brother's shift from the village to Indore, and poured all his energy into this project. He had gone without food so that his brother could eat a wrestler's diet, he says. He had begged and stolen and schemed to get money. He had harassed senior wrestlers to teach his brother outside of class hours, and keep him informed about dangals and trials and state competitions. But his brother had broken his heart. He fell in love with a girl and ran away. Billu says he has heard nothing of him since, and has no wish to.

'He is the reason behind all my depression. I don't want to ever hear his name again. Or that girl's. Women are the root of all evil.'

Leaving aside his daughter, Billu's relations with women are not, on the whole, gentle. It is no wonder that Billu's wife never once makes an appearance in the many visits I make to their house. Sometimes she flits from one room to another, making a run for it as if avoiding a downpour, her face and head covered completely with a dupatta.

He disapproves wholeheartedly of this new evil that's growing in India—akhadas for women.

'It's horrible,' he says. 'How can women be wrestlers? All that is happening is that they are titillating men; the wrestling is a joke, and everyone just wants to see the girls sweat in tight clothes. The girls also want that. I have seen the way they look. Women's wrestling is the worst thing that can happen to the sport.'

Yet, a day later, he takes me to a slum where a former wrestler runs a small akhada, recently equipped with an Olympic mat that Billu has partly paid for. The akhada trains boys, but is mostly meant for girls. The wrestler's own daughter is a wrestler. She is about to leave for the national training camp. Billu is ecstatic at the news, and orders one of his men over the phone to bring a car to take her to the station.

'This is a big day, there's no need to take the bus. My cars are lying idle.'

At night, Billu is holed up in his room, singing songs. They are all songs of lost love. Billu's mood, correspondingly and theatrically, becomes more and more sombre, till he loses all his bluster and looks like a sleep-deprived, hollowed-out shell.

The songs give way to stories of his childhood. Billu's father was a landless farm labourer, and they lived in a hovel near the edge of the village's 'Dalit' zone, beyond which was the area the whole village went to defecate.

'I hate all this caste shit, this Chura, that Chamar...all those blind, horrible traditions meant to keep people down,' he says, softly. 'I was meant to stay down with my nose to the shit too.'

His father could never make enough money to feed anyone in the family properly, and as a result, Billu was born malnourished.

'When I was a baby, there was a plague of sukhi—malnutrition—in my village. A real plague, I tell you. None of the children were spared. They all looked like bones and skin. That's why I still have thin arms and legs.'

By the time Billu was born, his father was already an alcoholic, wasting away, getting drunk early in the morning and staying that way till he passed out. His mother laboured on farms, and also took care of the household. She took her son to Indore twice a week to get treatment for his malnourishment. They would travel in overflowing buses, and sit around for hours outside the hospital for treatment, before making their weary way back. It had almost killed her, and then one day, her brother, who used to run a mechanic's shop in the Goaltuli slum, told her to just leave Billu in his care.

'Then she would not have to travel all the way to Indore to take me to the hospital. And that way I could even go to school in the city.'

Billu's uncle took good care of him, but also put him to work at a tea shop in the area so that he could earn his keep. The tea shop still exists—a rickety slab of wood with a stove and other paraphernalia set on top of a few bricks, at the mouth of a narrow lane just wide enough for two people to stand side by side. The streets around it are full of makeshift shops with naked bulbs: car mechanics, cycle mechanics, cheap clothes, imitation jewellery, pots and pans, underwear, everything you need. Billu, breaking his coffee habit, speaks over a cup of tea.

'My father was always drunk, always hitting my mother, or me, or my brother. I got saved when I moved to Indore.'

When he was sent to deliver tea to the Goaltuli akhada, Billu would stand around watching the children wrestle, feeling a deep well of desire to join in. So one day he did. Soon, he gave up on school and started training, working part-time at the tea shop and part-time at his uncle's bike shop.

'But my guru did not want me there. He would never give me any bouts. He called me "sukha", so all the other boys called me that too. They would say, "What can you do, sukha, with your insect-limbs? Shut up and stay in the corner." And I would think, but these guys, I can beat them all, I have beaten them when I got the chance, so what's wrong? There was no fairness. It is like this in all the akhadas. What do these gurus know? They teach the same things they have been teaching for hundreds of years, as if wrestling has not moved on since the time of the kings and queens. Fine, it's our tradition, but that doesn't mean you never learn anything new, never change? Sushil Kumar—he is an anomaly, an accident. He clicked. There are hundreds of children in India who have his talent, but who will go to an akhada and go to waste. Not in my akhada. No. I learn from YouTube. I don't call anyone sukha. In my akhada, all children are the same, and I buy kilos of almonds for everyone so that they don't grow up with spindly legs. I go to the slums and pick out any boy who is interested in wrestling, no matter how poor he is. No one is poor in my akhada.'

The spindly boy who had fought Vijay at Billu's akhada is called Suresh. He lives a few steps away from Billu's house in a scrap hovel where the plastic sheet of a roof is barely six feet off the ground. Inside, the mud walls are blackened with smoke from the clay oven. A couple of charred old pots lie next to the oven. For a bed, Suresh's father has stacked tightly bound piles of newspapers end-to-end and covered it with a scavenged bed sheet. Five people live inside this tiny space: Suresh, his two wild-haired younger sisters, their father Laxman and mother Lila. Every one of them has tired eyes, their clothes glued to their skeletal frames with sweat. They move with stupefying slowness inside their house. Laxman apologizes for the size of the house, and peers at me from behind his thick glasses and rough stubble. He tells me how one day, barely a year back, Suresh had come home to say that he wanted to be a wrestler. Laxman had said, 'But then I have to buy you a langot, and where will the money come from? And who will buy you milk and almonds and ghee?'

'Papa, I have already got a langot,' Suresh had said, taking out a shiny new red one from his pocket.

'Go, I told him. Go then and be a wrestler,' Laxman says. 'Maybe this will take you away from this hell. I had tears in my eyes when I saw the langot.'

For the inauguration of his akhada, Billu had rounded up every young kid he could find in the neighbourhood, taken them to his house, given them samosas and sweets and a langot each. It was done. Suresh, instead of helping his parents sort garbage, was going to spend his free time learning feints and holds.

'How do you like Suresh's wrestling,' Laxman asks gravely, in his nasal, trembly voice. 'He can make it, can't he? He's a natural.'

'Yes,' I say, 'he looked good on the mat, very aggressive. How do you manage his diet?'

Suresh eats only one meal at home. Billu gives him breakfast and an early evening meal (almonds, bananas and bread) at the akhada, and at the NGO-run school Suresh attends (Billu arranged that too), he gets lunch.

'Yes, he will become strong, he is getting good food,' Laxman says. 'We give him extra bowls of dal every night. Sometimes we get eggs for him also. He will be strong like me.'

'Were you a wrestler as well?'

'Oh yes,' Laxman says. 'Even today my hands have such phoorti that if I get a grip on you, you will not be able to escape from it.'

He slowly rises from the bed and extends his long bony arm, his fingers trembling, and catches my wrist. He clamps it like a vice—it feels not human—I can feel it cut right to my bone, his blistered palm scraping through my flesh. For a second, I am scared.

Then his hands shake, and he lets go. 'Wrestling is in our blood. You would not believe if you saw a photo of me when I used to wrestle. I used to have a big black-and-white photo. I was very strong. Poverty killed everything.'

He shuffles back to the bed and sits down, exhausted. He has a cough that never goes away. Lila looks up at him, stops in the middle of making roti and fried potatoes, and says: 'I have never seen you wrestle.'

Laxman looks at her, but says nothing.

Laxman and his family are all involved in sorting trash. They spend the entire day slowly picking through plastic, paper and electronics from the huge sea of waste around them. Laxman then carries an absurd load of it, pedalling slowly with kilos of the stuff lashed to the back of a bicycle, to various recycling facilities. The family has been doing this for almost a decade now. Before that, Laxman says, they were farmers in a village called Mothala near Indore. He relates a confusing story of how he lost his land. First he says it was his two brothers who conspired against him, declared him mad, and took over his little patch of land after their father's death. The land was never enough to support a family, but

it was something—and Laxman and his wife made extra money as
hired farm labour as well. At another time, Laxman says his land
was taken by a politician's goon who runs a grocery store there
now, and that his brothers helped the goon. Lila offers no clarity
either—all she can say is that her marriage was arranged, and that
just a few days after their marriage, Laxman said that they had to
leave the village, and so they packed whatever little they had and
left. For the next one year, they lived on the platforms of Indore
station, or under the flyover near the station. They made their
money begging. No one in Lila's family knows where she is; she
says she was tortured at home till she got married and escaped.
She has never looked back.

'Now both my brothers are dead,' Laxman says. 'There is no
one in my family. One died of tetanus, the other of a disease I don't
know, but he had very high fever for many days.'

Lila still has nightmares of their time living on the platform.
There was never any certainty of food, and most nights, she
would stand outside a small restaurant outside the station hoping
someone will give her a few rotis. Or she would scour the platform
looking for half-eaten packets of biscuits. 'I thought I would go
mad,' Lila says. 'The hunger would enter my bones and it would
not leave.'

Yet, in these dark times of hunger, she got pregnant with
Suresh, and gave birth to him, deep in the night, under the flyover
outside the station. Another pavement-dwelling woman acted as
a midwife.

'Forget about that,' Laxman tells her. 'Why are you talking
about those things? Now look, we have enough food to make
Suresh into a wrestler, no? We buy milk for him, eggs for him.
He will be a strong wrestler. You come back in a year and meet
me again. You will see how Suresh has changed, how strong and
big he has become.'

The smoke from cooking dinner makes it unbearably hot
and stifling inside the house. The two young girls play outside,

digging the ground with flimsy sticks, burying a treasure of shiny plastic wrappers and shirt buttons. Suresh does his homework in the feeble light leaking out of the doorway. Laxman squats on his haunches, watching his daughters and smoking a bidi.

Billu's house looms darkly a few feet away, its lights hidden by curtains, like a solitary watchtower over a prison.

8

Peasant, Soldier, Wrestler

One July afternoon in 1809, soon after a torrential downpour, Thomas Duer Broughton witnessed the way kushti transforms a body, makes it big and strong.

Broughton was travelling with the maharaja of Scindia's army, as commander of the British resident of Scindia's escort. An intrepid military adventurer, Broughton had seen action in Seringapatam in 1799 and was involved in the battle that led to the death of Tipu Sultan, an event that would prove crucial to the rise of British power in India.

For a few years now, though, Broughton had led a largely peaceful life, training Scindia's soldiers in parades and manoeuvres. The rain had brought a temporary halt to such activities, and this had given the soldiers a chance to engage in some entertainment of their own.

'Our Sipahees have commenced the exercises which are customary at this season of the year,' Broughton writes.[14] 'The natives all over India are exceedingly fond of these diversions; which are regulated by certain ceremonials, observed with the most scrupulous etiquette. A sufficient space is marked out, generally in the smoothest ground, and, if possible, under the shade of trees, which is carefully dug up, and cleared of all the stones, hard lumps, &c. This is called the Ukhara, and is held sacred; no one entering it with his shoes on, nor any impure thing being suffered to be brought within its limits.'

He observes the rituals: the soldiers raise a heap of earth on one end of the akhada and pray to the mound before entering the arena. Then a senior wrestler is chosen as the 'Khileefu',[15] or instructor for the season.

'Every one strips to his dhotee,' Broughton writes, 'which is drawn as tight as possible about the loins, and rubs a particular kind of white earth on his body.' He goes on to describe the exercises, beginning with the dand. 'At first it is difficult to exceed ten or twelve, but by practice a man may bring himself to make so many as two or even three hundred.'

Broughton is impressed by the 'native's' skill in 'kooshtee' and notes that expertise is far more important than strength on the pit, 'yet a broken or dislocated arm is by no means an uncommon event'.

But he is moved most by the effect kushti has on the soldiers.

'All these modes of exercising tend to open the chest, set up the body, and strengthen the muscles,' he writes, 'and the effect produced by them upon a young lad at the end of the season is astonishing'. To make a career out of soldiering, to be able to survive the battlefield, a man first needed to build a foundation; that foundation was wrestling.

So to understand the deep roots of kushti and its great popularity in northern India, we must turn away from its sporting nature, its insistence on non-violence, and explore a peculiar and unique north Indian phenomenon called the 'military labour market'.[16]

From at least as far back as 1480, the many kings and emperors of Hindustan hired mercenary troops from a vast pool of rural agrarian communities stretching from the Punjab in the west to Bihar in the east, cutting a wide swathe across northern India.[17]

The Dutch scholar Dirk Kolff, who developed the idea of the military labour market, argues that this rural martial tradition permeated every aspect of Indian society, affording caste mobility (a skilled lower-caste fighter could find his and his family's status raised to a higher 'kshatriya' or martial caste as a recognition of his valour), and the chance to upgrade from a poor peasant to landed gentry through service.

On the other hand, the ruler who could forge the most alliances and exert the most influence on the military labour market held the key to expanding his kingdom, keeping it safe, and reigning successfully.

'...an enquiry into the nature of the military labour market is called for if we are to acquire a better understanding of the North Indian distributive system, the social history of much of its peasantry and the processes of state formation in ancient regime in South Asia,' Kolff writes.[18]

If kushti was the way to transform one's body, military service offered the possibility of a complete transformation of one's life. Kolff suggests that 'according to the ways of the North Indian military labour market, in the pre-Mughal period, "Afghan" as well as "Rajput" were soldiers' identities rather than ethnic or genealogical denotations'.

The British changed the nature of the military labour market completely, slowly and painfully forcing an end to the mercenary system of shifting alliances, in favour of a gigantic standing army (and disarming the peasantry in the process). But even during the final decades of colonial rule, the social mobility accorded by military service was still in play. Kolff quotes a British recruiting officer called Garrett, writing about a hiring drive in 1917 and 1918 in the Punjab: 'there were a large number of families of the Hindu Zamindar class of which those members who had enlisted in the army had, as a matter of course, become Sikhs...

'It was an almost daily occurrence for—say—Ram Chand to enter our office and leave it as Ram Singh—Sikh recruit.'

To ensure that the peasant could turn himself into a soldier when the time came, they needed to develop physical power, endurance and the ability to handle weapons. There were innumerable specializations on offer for weapon skills—musketry, stick-fighting, various kinds of bladed arms and archery. But, for the overall development of the body, the essential foundation for any kind of martial activity, there was only one way to go: kushti. You can't fight without strength and agility, and kushti offered the most well-established route to acquiring both.

The ordinary men—the rank and file—who trained in kushti rarely left accounts of their life. But Subedar Sita Ram did. In 1812, Sita Ram, who came from a farming family in Rae Bareilly, joined the East India Company's infantry regiment as a sepoy. He was following a family tradition of military service, and retired forty-eight years later as a subedar. By then, he was an old man who could barely hold a gun.

But back when he was just seventeen, after hearing stories of life in the service of 'Company Bahadur' from an uncle, Sita Ram decided that that's exactly what he wanted to do. He began neglecting farm work, spending his days learning to wrestle and playing with swordsticks.

Having so prepared himself, Sita Ram soon found himself in the army. His first meeting with his officers left him with little doubt that he had made the right move.

'There were eight English officers in my regiment, and the Captain of my company was a real sahib—just as I had imagined all sahibs to be,' Sita Ram wrote. 'His name was "Burrumpeel". He was six feet three inches tall, his chest as broad as the monkey god's, and he was tremendously strong.

'He often used to wrestle with the sepoys and won universal admiration when he was in the wrestling arena. He had learnt all the throws and no sepoy could defeat him. This officer was always known among ourselves as Pulwan Saheb.'[19]

Like the people of Oudh, the Marathas too were enthusiastic entrepreneurs on the military labour market, shedding their peasant background to become renowned warriors, generals and administrators, and finally, the rulers of their own independent kingdom. It is still widely believed among wrestlers that Shivaji, the greatest of the Maratha heroes, established akhadas throughout Maharashtra.

Shivaji's grandfather Jadhav Rao was a prominent general for the Nizam Shahi sultans of the Deccan. The Mughals too eagerly sought Maratha help, and in 1665 Shivaji assisted Aurangzeb's conquests at the head of 2,000 horsemen and 7,000 foot soldiers.[20]

But by 1674 Shivaji had carved out a part of the Deccan for himself, successfully fighting the Mughals away. Accounts of his coronation in 1674 often refer to champion wrestlers as being part of the procession, and some say they were given the honour of being seated on elephants, otherwise the exclusive reserve of the royals.[21]

Wrestling enjoyed both the widespread popularity of an indigenous martial art practised by a militarized peasantry, as well as a prestigious courtly and urban pursuit.[22]

By the early eighteenth century, with the Maratha kingdom well and truly established, the minister Ramchandra Amatiya was writing in a treatise on Maratha polity: 'Royal teachers, such as professional wrestlers and other experts (Jethi) who are well versed in the arts and knowledge of spear-throwing (bhejane) sword-playing (parajne) wrestling (kusti ghene) and athletic exercises (talimkarane) should be engaged. Under their instructions each of those arts should be taught.'[23]

Balaji Baji Rao, who was Peshwa of the Maratha kingdom from 1740 to 1761, was said to be a good wrestler, and kept a large retinue of wrestlers at his court.[24] The letters exchanged between the Marathas and their allies, as well as between members of the elite families, frequently referred to wrestling and physical training as well.[25] In early 1749, the younger brother of the Peshwa, Raghunathrao, then about fifteen, went out for a month of riding with the hunting party of Chhatrapati Shahu. During the excursion, he sent a letter to their brother Janardan to tell him about his interest in two Pune wrestlers, Muhammad Hussein and Dole. He had, he told his brother, asked Nanasaheb (Baji Rao) to arrange a fight between them, laying a bet that Muhammad Hussein would throw Dole.[26]

Broughton, who saw the transformation of the peasant to a soldier, the workings of an expedient akhada under the shade of a tree, followed the trail of the pahalwan to the Maratha court too, recording in detail the pride of place the athlete held there:

'A man who wishes for distinction as a wrestler prepares himself by a fixed regime; which consists chiefly in drinking a certain quantity of milk and clarified butter, and, if he ever eats meat, in devouring an increased allowance of it every day…

'When his body has by these means imbibed an additional portion of vigour, and he has acquired a certain degree of skill, he is dignified by the appellation of Puhlwan. The Muha Raj, who is a great patron of these people, retains a celebrated wrestler in his service, to whom he makes a daily allowance of a sheep and twenty pounds of milk. A Puhlwan came lately from Muttra, for the express purpose of trying his skill with this Mahratta champion, and was conquered—an event at which Seendhiya was so highly pleased, that he presented his favourite with a golden bracelet worth five hundred rupees. Great men in India take a pride in having the best wrestlers in their service, who are permitted to make use of their horses, elephants, &c., whenever they please.'[27]

9

WRESTLING WITH THE MUGHALS

In medieval India, there was hardly a royal court that did not venerate wrestling. Champion pahalwans were coveted and they travelled great distances to perform in front of kings and emperors.

In his memoirs, Emperor Jahangir recalls watching a pahalwan called Shir Ali making his debut at court:

'At the time when I gave leave to the ambassadors of Adil Khan of Bijapur, I had requested that if in that province there were a wrestler, or a celebrated swordsman, they should tell Adil Khan to send him to me. After some time, when the ambassadors returned, they brought a Mughal, by name Shir Ali, who was born at Bijapur, and was a wrestler by profession and had great experience in the art, together with certain sword-players. The performance of the latter was indifferent, but I put Shir Ali to wrestle with the wrestlers and athletes who were in attendance on me, and they could none of them compete with him. One thousand rupees, a dress of honour, and an elephant were conferred on him; he was exceedingly well made, well shaped, and powerful. I retained him in my own service, and entitled him "the athlete of the capital". A jagir and mansab were given to him and great favours bestowed on him.'[28]

Shir Ali came, Shir Ali conquered—his life transformed by his skills in wrestling.

With such prestige and fortune on offer, it is no wonder that the cities too were full of akhadas. In 1550, when Jahangir ordered a census of his capital city, Agra, he directed the kotwal to visit the city's maarekahs (akhadas). The kotwal reported that 'in none of these places did he find assembled less than two and three thousand persons, although it was neither the first of the new year, nor any of those days of public rejoicing on which it was usual for the people to appear abroad for amusement'.[29]

Did wrestling have significance apart from its usefulness in military preparations and a form of courtly entertainment? Why did Jahangir shower Shir Ali so lavishly with gifts and estates?

The Adil Khan that Jahangir refers to is Ibrahim Adil Shah II, who reigned as the sultan of Bijapur from 1580 to 1627. During his reign, a history of the Bijapur sultanate, the *Tazkirat al-Mulūk*, was completed.[30] The *Tazkirat* provides a romanticized origin story of the Bijapur sultanate; the story of the rise of Yusuf Adil Shah, the founder of the Adil Shahi dynasty and the first sultan of Bijapur, from slave to general in the Bahmani sultanate of the Deccan.

It begins with a dream. Yusuf, a young Iranian noble, is exiled to Turkey after a rebellion. One day, Yusuf has a dream in which he is told to seek his salvation in the Deccan. He goes to the slave market to seek a passage. When a merchant in the pay of the Bahmani emperor buys some Turkish and Ethiopian slaves, they convince the merchant to also include Yusuf in the deal—the slaves are smitten by Yusuf's powerful body and his sweet and refined disposition. The secret to Yusuf's physical beauty and his courteousness is revealed on the ship: he is a wrestler. On the voyage to India, he spends his time grappling with his fellow slaves.

At the Bahmani court in the city of Bidar, he is hired as a cook. It is a life of drudgery and tedium, and Yusuf runs away to Iran. He has another dream—a reproachful one that urges him to return to the Deccan and take up his humble job again.

Yusuf returns dutifully, but this time, he starts a wrestling gymnasium where he teaches his fellow cooks the art of wrestling.

Every morning, before the work in the kitchen begins, Yusuf takes the cooks through a rigorous series of workouts and wrestling skills.

One day, a wrestler arrives at Bidar from Delhi. He is a great champion of the Mughals, and brings with him the reputation of having beaten every wrestler in every town in Hindustan and Gujarat. He challenges the wrestlers of the Bahmani court, and beats them all. It brings great disgrace to the king.

It is then that Yusuf, the insignificant kitchen help, steps up. He pleads with the Bahmani king to give him permission to challenge the wrestler from Delhi.

'If I fall, it will become known that Yusuf the friend of the kitchen fell and if I throw him it will expel the vexation from the heart of the padshah and I will be set free from my adversities.'

Yusuf beats the wrestler, carrying him by his thighs and slamming him down on his back in front of the king. The Bahmani king's reputation, his pride, is restored.

Wrestling opens the path that leads to Yusuf's destiny, the fulfilment of his dream. From here on, he moves up rapidly, becoming a leading noble in the Bahmani sultanate, and eventually establishing his own lineage.

Wrestling could make or break the reputation of kings, and those who will be future kings. In its moves and countermoves, in its training for both mind and body, lay a whole moral and ethical universe. Yusuf's story is a masterly narrative structured around an ideal that was a lived reality for both kings and courtiers in India, whether they were from the sultanates of the Deccan or the Mughal Empire—the ideal of jawanmardi, literally, 'young manliness'.[31]

The set of ethics that inform jawanmardi include the idea of physical perfection as a reflection of inner beauty (the slaves see this in Yusuf); a commitment to repetitive, mundane work (Yusuf in the kitchen, and the disciplined physical regime needed to be a wrestler); participation and service to the community rather than a selfish quest for personal glory (Yusuf sets up a gymnasium and teaches wrestling to his fellow cooks); humility (Yusuf's plea to the king); and courage (Yusuf stepping up to take on the undefeated champion).

Wrestling champions also served as a symbol for the health and prowess of not just the king, but the kingdom itself—the *Tazkirat* was being written at a time of increasing Mughal aggression towards the southern sultanates, and the story of Yusuf's victory over the Delhi champion is charged with political importance.

The late fifteenth-century polymath and writer Husayn Vai'sh-i Kashifi wrote in his *Futuwwat Namah-i Sultani*: 'wrestling is a skill which is acceptable and pleasing to kings and sultans, and the strongest of those occupied in this work are those who possess purity and rectitude'.[32]

This symbolic relationship between wrestling skills, chivalric codes, and the fitness of the king was equally important to the Mughal nobility. If Yusuf, the future Sultan, rose to prominence through his victory over a wrestler from the Mughal court, the Mughal emperor Akbar is said to have thrown a much older noble boy at the tender age of two. Akbar employed the same move as Yusuf: picking his opponent up and flinging him down on the ground.[33] It's a feat so improbable that it can only be seen as symbolic. Akbar, who ascended the Mughal throne as a young boy, was a born wrestler—he was born with the qualities needed to be a great ruler.

This entwined world of wrestling, heroism, religion and kingship—the ideal of jawanmardi—had far older origins than medieval India. It held sway over a vast geographical area: from the Arab world in the west, through Persia and Central Asia and India, all the way to Mongolia and beyond.

A simple, clerical entry from the *Ain-i-Akbari* shines a light on the astonishing reach of wrestling. The entry lists the best wrestlers at Akbar's court, men who were paid hefty salaries and other privileges for their services to the sport.

'There are many Persian and Turani Pahluwans at court, as also stone-throwers, athletes of Hindustan, clever Mals from Gujrat, and many other kinds of fighting men. Their pay varies from 70 to 450 d.

'Every day two well-matched men fight with each other. Many presents are made to them on such occasions.

'The following belong to the best wrestlers of the age—Mirza Khan of Gilan; Muhammad Quli of Tabriz to whom His Majesty has given the name Sher Hamlah, or lion attacker; Cadiq of Bukhara; Ali of Tabriz; Murad of Turkistan; Muhammad Ali of Turan; Fulad of Tabriz; Mirza Kuhnahsuwar of Tabriz; Shah Quli of Kurdistan; Hilal of Abyssinia; Sadhu Dayal; Ali; Sri Ram; Kanhya; Mangol; Ganesh; Anba; Nanka; Balbhadra; Bajrnath.'[34]

Each name here is a door, a leap through time and space. Here are athletes from across Central Asia: from the kingdom of Turan, bordering Persia, inextricably linked to the myth that first exemplified the concept of jawanmardi; from the Persian city of Tabriz, one of the grandest cities along the Silk Route of that time; from Abyssinia, the great cultural link and trading link between Europe, Africa and Asia; and from the ancient city of Bukhara, also on the Silk Route. They live, train and wrestle with the Jyesthimallas of Gujarat, a Brahmin sub-caste whose very identity was founded on wrestling, Vaishnavites like Kanhya (another name for Krishna) and Balbhadra (another name for Balaram), Shaivites like Bajrnath, and warrior-ascetics like Sadhu Dayal.

Each of these athletes was brought together by a sport whose belief system was, and still is, an extraordinary example of a unified code that blurred the boundaries between the religions, myths and cultures of these realms.

We will briefly peek through each door and wonder at

wrestling's mystifying uniformity over the ages, and across lands, but first, to the source of jawanmardi.

The chivalric code of jawanmardi was indispensable to the Islamic rulers of medieval Asia since at least 1010 CE, when the *Shahnama*, the pre-eminent epic of the Islamic world, was completed. In the epic, 'wrestling is the test "'twixt man and man"',[35] and every hero in the *Shahnama* proves himself at least once through wrestling. Indeed, at the very core of the epic is the tragic wrestling match between Rostam and his son Sohrab.

The *Shahnama* takes us further back, because its ideals of jawanmardi are based on Arabic and Persian warrior traditions that existed before the advent of Islam, centred around the belief that 'wrestling rather than skill in weaponry was the test of superior strength'.[36] Essential to that tradition is a figure we are familiar with: the 'pahlavan', a 'champion whose duty consisted in protecting the kingdom by his selfless acts of valour'.[37] As Islam spread, Rustom became subsumed in the figure of Ali himself, and Muslim wrestlers still honour him as the 'true master of the wrestling pit and the founder of the path of pahlavāni and futūvat'.[38]

The pahlavan's continuing importance in Iran as well as its ancient provenance are both easily evident even now, in the traditional Iranian 'zurkhanas' or houses of exercise. The rituals of the zurkhana—'varshez-e-pahlavani' (the sport of heroes)—show distinct Zoroastrian and Mithraic influences, which means its origins may go as far back as 600 BCE.[39] The word 'pahlavan' itself is thought to be derived from the name of the Pahlava or Parthian tribe in Iran, and its Arcaside dynasty, dating back to 250 BCE.[40]

Like akhadas in India, zurkhanas still thrive in Iran, and they are the foundation on which Iran's exceptional record in wrestling at the modern Olympics is based.

In India, these traditions have left an indelible mark. Until the late 1990s, the winner of the most prestigious traditional kushti tournament was given the title Rustom-e-Hind—Sushil Kumar's coach Satpal Singh was one.

The word for a wrestler in India is pahalwan, of course, and it continues to embody the weighty ideals of the chivalrous man.

The origin of the word kushti is even older: it is derived from the Persian 'kushti-gir'—belt-grabber—which in turn is derived from 'koshti', the sacred girdle wrapped around the Zoroastrian initiate.[41]

10

WRESTLING AT THE HINDU COURT

In 1509, Yusuf Adil Shah was killed in battle by the forces of the other great Deccan kingdom, the Vijayanagara Empire, under the command of its king Krishnadevaraya.

They may have been competing kings, but Krishnadevaraya and Yusuf Adil Shah shared their belief in wrestling's profound importance, that 'the strength and vigour of the king was closely linked to the health of the kingdom.'[42]

In 1520, the Portuguese traveller Domingos Paes was given access to Krishnadevaraya's morning ritual. The king began his day by drinking 'three-quarters of a pint of gingelly oil'.[43] Then he put on a small loincloth before more oil was vigorously massaged into his skin. Then, 'taking a sword, he exercises himself with it until he has sweated out all of the oil, and then he wrestles with one of his own wrestlers'. All this happened before daybreak, and by sunrise, the king had been massaged and bathed, and was ready to hold court.

Paes's fellow traveller Fernao Nuniz commented on the importance of wrestling as a ritual activity during the festival of Mahanavami in Vijayanagara, and noted that the wrestlers, of whom a thousand are in the king's pay, 'do not perform any other service in the kingdom'. On the first day of the Mahanavami feast, the king sat in his 'victory palace', meeting every man of great importance in his kingdom: '...and all those that are inside make their salaam to him. As soon as they have done this the wrestlers seat themselves on the ground, for these are allowed to remain seated, but no other, howsoever great a lord he be, except the king so commands; and these also eat betel, though none else may eat it in his presence...'[44]

If Nuniz's account is to be believed, the court wrestlers were given extraordinary importance: they were the symbols of the empire's health and strength.

The Vijayanagara kings were following well-established norms. The Chalukya king Someshwara III, who ruled over the area that would become the Bahmani sultanate 200 years later (and parts of what would become the Vijayanagara Empire) completed an encyclopedic treatise called the *Manasollasa* in 1137 CE. Wrestling was one of the hundreds of subjects covered in the book.

The royal wrestlers, the *Manasollasa* tells us, were kept under strict observation, and trained rigorously every day.[45] They were provided a large allowance, and a special diet 'fit for the king himself', but were barred from mingling with women or having sex. On match days, they came to court on royal elephants, dressed in fine clothes and gold jewellery given to them by the king. Before the match, they rubbed themselves with sandal paste, and raised an earthen mandap to the god Krishna next to the wrestling pit. The king and the wrestlers worshipped together at the mandap before the match. Victorious wrestlers, the *Manasollasa* says, were given land, money, elephants, horses and jewellery.

Almost a hundred years after Nuniz passed through the Deccan, the Jesuit missionary Pierre du Jarric described a gymnasium at the Vijayanagara court: 'The house fitted for this has a yard in the centre, the pavement of which is covered with a layer of lime so smooth it looks like a mirror; there is a walk around it, spread over with red sand, on which they rest as on a soft bed. One who would wrestle strips himself. Then several strong and brawny youth called geitas,[46] who are ready beforehand, rub the nobleman; then they box, jump, fence and take other kinds of exercise with him, in order to strengthen him; and this they do until perspiration flows freely. Then the geitas cover the whole of the nobleman's body with sand, and massage him, and move his arms and legs in every direction as if they would disjoint his bones. Finally, the noble man is brushed, anointed and washed with warm water; and when dry, dresses himself. Noblemen take this kind of exercise almost every day before dinner, in order to be fit and healthy.'[47]

11

KRISHNA, THE DIVINE WRESTLER

We have already met the 'strong and brawny youth called geitas' who train and spar with the Vijayanagara nobility—they make an appearance in Abul Fazl's account of the wrestlers at Akbar's court as the 'clever mals of Gujrat'.[48]

They are the Jyesthimallas—literally, 'most excellent wrestlers'—and they are the only known example of a group who based their caste identity on their proficiency as wrestlers.[49]

Pre-dating the medieval period of Indian history, and right through it, the Jyesthimallas, originally from a town called Modera in Gujarat, moved across the subcontinent, establishing a highly successful 'network of patronage and employment', their skills in great demand in the courts as teachers, wrestlers and sparring partners for the nobility.[50]

If Ali, the son-in-law of Prophet Muhammad, is the 'true founder of pahlavani' in the Muslim tradition, for Hindu wrestlers, the founding father of the art of wrestling is Krishna.

The Jyesthis have left us an invaluable account of their beliefs and practices, a thirteenth-century treatise called *Mallapurana*—the 'history of wrestling'—a kind of 'guild manual' for the community.[51]

It tells the story of how the Jyesthis were singled out by Krishna as a people deserving of being taught the divine art of wrestling.

Krishna and his brother Balarama were passing through Modera on their way to Dwarka when they were struck by the village's exemplary religiosity. Krishna proposed that Balarama and he would reveal to the townspeople the secrets of wrestling. The Jyesthis were puzzled by this offer. As Brahmins, their duty lay in prayers and religious learning. The art of fighting belonged to the Kshatriyas.

Krishna replied that this was Kaliyug, a time when nothing was ideal, and to protect the dharma the Jyesthis were so fond of, they needed to learn 'the noble art'.

The *Mallapurana*, like the *Shahnama*, makes it clear that wrestling is greater than the mortals who practise it—it is of divine origin, and knowledge of the 'noble art' is not just desirable, but essential to a religious, spiritual life. It goes on to describe and categorize various aspects of training in wrestling that are startlingly modern in tone: different kinds of exercises and when to do them (including swimming, which is prescribed as a good cross-training tool, much like a modern wrestling manual would suggest); a detailed diet chart with emphasis on seasonal foods, fruits, nuts and vegetables; classification of wrestlers into different groups according to skill, age or weight; the dimensions of various types of wrestling pits, and the quality of the pit earth, which should be 'pleasing to see and as soft as that required for seed laying'.

The approach is holistic. Technique, exercise routines, diet, and even cleanliness and resting protocol are all prescribed with a view to the season, the kind of person and the mood of the person in mind. It also throws light on the cultural importance of wrestling, and describes it as a joyful, stimulating activity, a way to banish sorrow. It asks that the king himself must bring the earth to the akhada, and witness combats often, bringing friends, citizens, ministers and their family. At the end of a bout, the wrestlers should be given presents and sent around town on the back of elephants in a victorious parade.

Today, the *Mallapurana* is unknown in the wrestling community. I asked every wrestler I spoke to about it, and only a handful even knew of its existence, and fewer still had anything to say about it. But the text lives on in the actual practice of kushti, from the exercise and diet it prescribes to the way the akhada earth is constructed. Akhada gurus almost always refer to the earth prepared for wrestling as one that is fit for sowing seeds.

Wrestling is old. How old is wrestling? How far back in time can the idea of a divine fighting form reach?

The figure of Krishna as a wrestling hero is infinitely older than the *Mallapurana*. As early as 200 BC, Patanjali refers to the killing of Kamsa, and mentions that it happened a long time ago.[52]

The details of Krishna's battle with Kamsa comes to us from the *Harivamsa*:[53] everything revolves around a wrestling match.

Kamsa, the tyrant king of Mathura is told in a prophecy that the eighth son born to the princess Devaki, his sister, will be the cause of his death. Kamsa has Devaki and her husband Vasudeva locked up. In prison, she gives birth to six children, each of them murdered by Kamsa. Her seventh child, Balarama, is saved by divine intervention. The eighth child, Krishna, is slipped away secretly from the prison and given over to the head of a group of cattle herders, Nanda, and his wife Yashoda. It is under their care that both Krishna and Balarama grow up.

Here, the story of Krishna takes the form of the traditional strongman hero: he performs miraculous feats of strength as a baby.[54]

The tropes are immediately familiar to Indian wrestling: Krishna is part of the Yadu/Yadav clan, who are cattle herders. Kushti is still intimately linked to cattle herding. In a wrestler's family, owning cows and buffaloes is a matter of tremendous importance. The Yadav caste group still see themselves as the traditional keepers of wrestling knowledge: '*Kushti Yadavon ka khel hai*', wrestling is the sport of the Yadavs, is a common refrain in the community. In Uttar Pradesh and Maharashtra, Yadav wrestlers far outnumber wrestlers from any other caste.

The cattle connection is directly linked to the wrestler's diet. Krishna's prodigious appetite and love for butter and milk is a recurring motif in the colossal body of Vaishnavite literature and art, including the *Harivamsa*. And a pahalwan's diet is worth nothing if it does not include enormous quantities of milk and butter (or ghee), preferably drawn from the family's buffalo or cow by the pahalwan's mother, and brought to the akhada by the father.

In the Hindu tradition, milk is life-giving, the essence of condensed energy.[55] Butter or ghee is the distilled elixir of milk, a food without parallel in producing strength and virility in the body, a dietary means of controlling libido, as well as a cure for various diseases.[56]

Then there is the earth so revered by wrestlers as the akhada mitti, and which is ritually and liberally smeared on the opponent before they begin grappling. Krishna grows up always smeared in dust.

The *Harivamsa* says: 'Krishna and Sankarshana[57] had arms like serpent hoods, and as they moved about, their bodies covered by dust, they resembled a pair of proud young elephants. Sometimes smeared with ashes, sometimes sprinkled with cow dung, the two would roam about like the youthful sons of fire. Bodies and hair powdered with dirt, they crawled around on their knees while playing in the cowsheds.'

In their play, Krishna and Balarama innocently reveal their great power: 'Seeing them so determined to roam all over the camp, the cowherd Nanda could not restrain the two wild ones. Thereupon, the enraged Yashoda took the lotus-eyed Krishna to her wagon, rebuked him many times, and even bound him to a grinding mortar with a rope tied around his waist.'

Then, while Yashoda was busy, Krishna left the courtyard.

'Krishna, who was playing like a small child, amazed the herds-camp folk when he came forth from the courtyard, dragging the mortar behind. With the mortar in tow, Krishna proceeded away from the other children toward a pair of mighty Arjuna trees in the forest. The mortar to which Krishna was bound toppled and got stuck between the two Arjuna trees. And as he continued to drag, he pulled them both down, right from their roots. Then he just sat there, laughing, amid their forcefully shattered roots and branches.'

As Krishna grows up, he performs more and more elaborate feats of strength. The news of this miracle boy reaches Kamsa, who is told that this cowherd child is none other than the eighth son of Devaki.

It is here that we get the first explicit textual reference to Krishna as a wrestler. Kamsa is told of a way to lure Krishna to his capital, Mathura: 'O Deva, they are wrestlers, having organized a fight in the city, then, when they have come into the arena, having apprehended them, we will kill them.'[58]

Wrestlers gather from various parts of the country for the tournament, including two notorious champions, Mushtika from Andhra and Chanura from near Varanasi. Krishna and Balarama too reach Mathura. Walking through the streets of the capital, the brothers pass a servant girl carrying fragrant bathing lotions. She is hunchbacked, but Krishna calls her beautiful, and asks her for a lotion as dark as his skin.

'Lotus-eyed lady,' he says, 'we are wrestlers come as guests of the land to see the divine bow festival and the prosperity of the land.'[59]

When Krishna finally reaches the palace and enters the dazzling arena, he behaves just like a pahalwan in Mathura now would. He takes the earth and covers himself with it, claps his hands, and slaps his arms and thighs, the wrestling sign for a challenge—one that has changed not a bit over hundreds of years. He then pledges to fight according to the rules, so he may not 'cast a stain upon the fame of wrestlers'. He speaks of the importance of endurance, courage, firmness, skill and strength in wrestling.

Before the match begins, the rules of the game are outlined by Krishna's clan, the Yadavas. They speak of the 'ancient rules' of wrestling, where a judge must be present for a fight, and no weapons may be used and that the fight be arranged in such manner that the two wrestlers are equally matched in size, strength, age and skill. The onus of stopping a fight is placed on the wrestlers, who are told that they must not continue when their opponent is utterly exhausted or defeated. Even in the heat of battle, they are trusted to do the right thing.

Two things stand out in these pre-fight exhortations. One, that by the time the *Harivamsa* is being composed, the rules of wrestling are well established, and the game itself is clearly popular and highly regarded both at the court and in the countryside.

Two, that these rules are being told to bring to sharper relief just how evil Kamsa and Chanura—the wrestler chosen to fight Krishna—are: their plan is not to defeat Krishna but to kill him in whatever way possible, flouting the moral foundations of wrestling. Of course, Krishna, the master of subversion, will himself trample over the rules.

When the fight begins, the spectators cheer and howl. Divine music fills the air. The gods watch secretly from behind clouds. The two fight 'like elephants', and the fight goes almost immediately beyond all limits. In the end, Krishna kills Chanura, knees on his chest, with strikes to the head till Chanura's eyeballs pop out like 'golden bells'. A bloodbath follows, with Krishna and Balarama killing more of Kamsa's court wrestlers and finally Kamsa himself.

As wrestling matches often are in myths, this one too is transformative: it forms the basis of the transition of Krishna the cowherd boy god to Krishna the supreme being. He arrives in Mathura a rural nobody, and emerges as the prince and master of the city, and the leader of his clan.[60]

The Mahabharata, which can be dated back to 300 BCE,

features plenty of wrestling encounters in the heroic mode, but the one match that remains an integral part of the pahalwan's oral tradition involves Krishna as well. It's the fight between Bhim and the king Jarasandha, father-in-law of the slain Kamsa. To avenge the death of Kamsa, Jarasandha repeatedly raided Krishna's Yadav kingdom in Mathura. Such was his power as a king that even Krishna and Balarama had to flee each invasion. The hostility finally forced Krishna to take the Yadav clan and relocate to Dwarka, on the way to which he met the people of Modera and gave them the gift of his wrestling knowledge.

Many years later, when Krishna entered the lives of the Pandavas, he hatched a plan to eliminate Jarasandha. The king, who was considered an honourable man, was in the habit of fulfilling the wishes of Brahmins after a puja, and taking advantage of this, Krishna, Bhim and Arjun went to him in the guise of Brahmin priests. Their wish was that the king choose one of them for a wrestling match. Jarasandha chose Bhim, the strongest of the Pandavas, and one of the Mahabharata's central wrestling/strongman heroes. They fought a duel that went on for fourteen days. On the fourteenth day, with both wrestlers exhausted, Krishna signalled to Bhim the way to kill Jarasandha. There was a seam that ran through the middle of the king's body. Krishna indicated to Bhim that he must tear Jarasandha apart through the middle, and then throw the two halves in opposite directions so that they don't have a chance to join together again. Bhim, being extraordinarily strong, did just that.

The references to wrestling in both the Mahabharata and the *Harivamsa* differ in significant ways from the fundamental ethos of the sport. It is neither non-violent, nor fair. Everybody punches and kicks, making the fights more like the ancient Greek sport of pankration (one of the three combat sports that featured in the ancient Olympics and allowed punching, kicking and wrestling) or the modern sport of MMA. Most matches end in bloody deaths. The stress isn't on a chivalric or moral code, nor is wrestling explicitly prescribed as essential to the attainment of some physical or philosophical ideal. Yet, those ideals lurk in the background—Jarasandha, for instance, saw the Brahmin's wish for a wrestling match as a noble request. Sometimes, those ideals are made explicit, such as when the Yadavs expound the rules of wrestling, only to break them when necessary.

The word for wrestling used in the Mahabharata and the *Harivamsa* is mallayudhha. It is an ethnic term, 'malla' becoming the word for 'wrestler', derived from the name of an ancient and powerful tribe. The Mallas are mentioned in the Mahabharata, and there is evidence that they were around since the seventh century BCE, as one of the sixteen 'principal janapadas (territories)' in India at that time.[61] By the end of the fifth century BCE, during the time of the Buddha,[62] the Mallas were ruined by the conquests of Magadha, which emerged at that time as the most powerful kingdom in north India. Their name lived on as the word for a wrestler, perhaps as homage to their reputation as great fighters. In the *Harivamsa*, Krishna acquires the name Mallari (enemy of the mallas) after his wrestling victories at Kamsa's court.[63]

1 2

THE OLDEST SPORT

Wrestling in India is old.

'Wrestling is as old as India, it came out of India's soil,' wrestlers unfailingly said when asked about how old they thought the tradition of kushti was.

A combat sport that resembles wrestling has been around since at least the fourth century BCE in India, though textual and archeological evidence for wrestling as we know it—a man-to-man contest without punching, kicking or other strikes to the body, enclosed within a philosophy of non-violence, chivalry and fairness—begins to pile up only from the first century CE, acquiring real momentum in the medieval period of Indian history.

But wrestling is older, even if we can't always put our finger on a date. When the wrestlers say that 'wrestling is as old as India', they are pointing to an intangible, symbolic truth.

Towards the end of the fourth century BCE, a Seleucid ambassador called Megasthenes came to the court of Emperor Chandragupta Maurya. He wrote a book called *Indika*, which is now lost. But parts of *Indika* were quoted and referenced by later writers, including the Greek historians Diodorus and Strabo (first century BCE), and Arrian, who lived a century later. All three were struck by Megasthenes's description of an Indian tribe called Sourasenoi, who worshipped the Greek demigod Herakles, boasted of two great cities called Methora and Kleisobora and lived along a river called Jobares.

The Greeks were in the habit of describing other cultures and gods in Grecian terms. Megasthenes was describing Krishna worship in ancient India: the Sourasenoi are the Shurasenas, a branch of the Yadu dynasty to which Krishna belonged; Methora is simply Mathura; Kleisobora, Krishnapura, 'the city of Krishna'; and Jobares is the Yamuna.[64]

The reason Megasthenes identified Krishna with Herakles is simple: the two figures share remarkable parallels in the wrestler-hero arc of their stories. Herakles, like Krishna, grew up with cattle herders, and displayed amazing feats of strength as a baby. Like Krishna, Herakles fights many wrestling battles—with men, demons, demigods and great animals.

Herakles was the peerless model of the heroic athlete in ancient Greece, since at least the beginning of the old Olympic games, traditionally dated to 776 BCE—one significant Greek tradition credited him with re-founding the Olympic Games, and introducing the olive crown as a prize.[65]

The most celebrated athlete from the ancient Olympics was a wrestler too—Milo of Croton, who won six Olympic crowns and a total of twenty-six crowns in the Panhellenic games.[66] When Croton went to war with a neighbouring state called Sybaris, Milo led the army wearing his six Olympic wreaths and a lion skin. Milo was embodying Herakles—both the olive wreaths and the lion skin played prominent roles in the myths of the Greek god.[67]

If the myths made a direct link between Herakles and the sporting contests at Olympia, the Spartans worshipped Hipposthenes, a wrestler who also won six Olympic crowns in the seventh century BCE.[68]

The Spartans, famous for their skill as warriors, competed only in wrestling among the three combat sports in the Panhellenic games: boxing, wrestling and pankration. Why?

The answer to that brings us back to wrestling's ageless relationship with the ideals of non-violence, chivalry and manhood.

In the Greek sporting culture, wrestling held an all-important distinction when compared to boxing and pankration: it did not allow hitting, nor did it allow choke holds or holds that led to the breaking of bones or joints. It wanted to distinguish itself as a fighting method that was not brutal.[69] And, crucially for the Spartans, it was not a 'victory or death' contest.[70] Boxing and pankration ended either in a knockout or surrender, and sometimes, those rules led to the death of combatants. Wrestling was based on a far more technical rule, one that is familiar to us: the athlete who could make three 'clean' throws was declared the winner.[71] The Spartan warrior code had an ethos of not surrendering; they made an explicitly moral choice when they refused to participate in boxing and pankration. Wrestling was both morally acceptable and also the symbol of a heroic way of life for the Spartans.

The Ancient Greeks left us with such a rich and varied record of wrestling's tremendous popularity in the Hellenic times—through literature, art and historical documents spanning centuries—that as late as the beginning of the twentieth century, wrestling was thought to be a Greek invention.

The Greek veneration of wrestling was centred on the palaestra, and the focal point of the palaestra was the wrestling ground, skamma, which occupied an open space literally in the centre of the wrestling school. The word 'skamma' denoted a patch of land that had been cleaned, tilled and smoothed.[72] Before wrestling, the Greek athletes oiled their bodies and then rubbed each other with earth.

The palaestra was uncannily similar to the akhada.

Did some of the ideas of wrestling travel from Greece to India, the way kushti did from Persia? Did it travel with Alexander the Great as he made his way down from Greece, conquering Persia, and invading India in 326 BCE? Alexander, after all, grew up in a tradition that thought of wrestling as an essential part of schooling for men. Alexander was taught by Aristotle, who in turn attended Plato's Academy. Plato was a wrestler himself, and set several of his dialogues inside a palaestra.

Megasthenes's identification of Krishna with Herakles would not have needed much ingenuity.

How much wrestling knowledge passed back from India westwards along the same route that Alexander took?

We have no evidence of the exact transaction of wrestling ideas and knowledge along this great early highway, but there is no reason why we cannot make a similar leap of faith as Megasthenes. From Greece and southern Europe through northern Africa, Persia, Central Asia, to northern India, empires have fought and mingled, traded goods and gods, bartered in philosophy and wine, and shared their knowledge of architecture and art since time immemorial. From this limitless churning arose the akhada, the palaestra, the zoorkhana.

Wrestling is older still than the Hellenic times. It is older than the Vedic times. One of the oldest depictions of wrestling comes from the wall paintings of a group of tombs in Beni Hasan in Egypt, which date back to 2100 BCE. There are nearly 400 illustrations of wrestling pairs engaged in competition, wearing only loincloths, each pair rendered in different colours. The moves depicted are still in use in modern wrestling. No punching or kicking is shown. From an analysis of the figures, it seems the objective is to get the opponent on his back with his shoulders pinned.[73]

We can go back a thousand more years, and to a ritual knife from Egypt dated to 3450 BCE, and on display at the Louvre. Its blade is made of flint, its handle, ivory. There are carvings on the handle of a scene depicting a battle—various pairs of men engaged in armed combat. The pair on the upper right-hand corner of the handle, though, are unarmed. They grip each other in an unmistakable stance: they are wrestling.

Wrestling is not just as old as India, it is as old as civilization.

13

THE AKHADA EARTH

Perhaps the more important question to ask then is not who influenced whom in wrestling's vast universal history, but to ask: where can a living example of this heritage be found?

In Mathura, where the Krishna myth says he was born, and where he fought Kamsa, the Bhooteshwar akhada is full of the early morning sounds of training: the rhythmic thump of the wrestling pit being dug up, the strained breathing of wrestlers exercising and the lilting Radhe-Shyam Radhe-Shyam greetings as more wrestlers come in.

The akhada, one of many in Mathura, is made up of a series of small, whitewashed buildings with open windows on all sides and arched entrances. There are old, shady trees scattered across the space. A raised earthen platform in the middle of the space is the main wrestling pit. One of the squat buildings acts as a covered akhada, its floor is of soft, tilled earth.

The wrestlers here believe that this akhada was established by Krishna himself, after he defeated Kamsa. But they recognize that this is a spiritual belief—corporeally, they say, the akhada has been around since the middle of the nineteenth century.

'In the past, kings and great men used to sponsor the akhada,' an old wrestler called Bhagwan Das tells me. 'Even when the angrez ruled over us, there was a lot of interest, and people used to sponsor wrestlers here. We had great wrestlers, pahalwans who could fight with Gama. Now, no one pays for anything here. It's only us wrestlers who keep it going.'

There are three small temples inside the akhada, one for Krishna, one for Shiva, and one for the god who usurped the title of patron of wrestling from Krishna himself, Hanuman.

A few sadhus lounge around the temple area. Everyone else has crowded around the covered wrestling pit. Two pairs of wrestlers are about to start grappling. People watch from the doorway, or are seated on the various windows cut out on the four walls enclosing the pit. Some are wrestlers, some are just young men who have come to watch.

I ask Bhagwan Das if the akhada earth has special qualities. His eyes widen.

'It's as fine as talcum powder and as precious as gold,' he says. 'No, not gold—I would give you my gold, but I will not part with the mitti of the akhada. No one knows how old the original mitti is. We believe that Sri Krishna Bhagwan himself got the mitti here.'

'But you lose some of the mitti every day when the wrestlers leave the akhada covered in it.'

'Yes, every few months we have to add more mitti to the akhada. But that mitti must come from the banks of the river, from farms where they don't use pesticides or chemicals. It has to be pure. When we get new mitti, we mix many things in it.'

'Like what?'

'We add kilos of rose petals and pure turmeric. We collect ghee from all the wrestlers and their families—around twenty to thirty kilos of it, and add that too. We also add dried neem leaves. And then we do a puja, so that Sri Krishna Bhagwan and Sri Hanuman step on it, and the dust from their feet mingle with the mitti.'

The akhada earth is consecrated in this way not just in the birthplace of Krishna, but in akhadas everywhere in India. Even at Chhatrasal akhada, the elite Olympic training centre where

Sushil Kumar and Yogeshwar Dutt learnt their craft, there is an earthen pit in the basement parking lot under the stadium, along with rows of mats laid out next to the pit.

Some of the spiritual concerns are practical too: turmeric, rose petals and neem all have proven beneficial effects on the skin. The stress on only using organic earth is sound too; organophospate chemical fertilizers do terrible things when they come in contact with skin, and pesticides are best not inhaled on a daily basis while you are gasping for breath with your face shoved onto the akhada mitti.

In the evening, older people like Bhagwan Das come to the akhada just to lie in the wrestling pit. Many of the people who come are not wrestlers. They come because they believe that the mitti has healing properties for the skin and soothes the soul. They wash themselves afterwards from an old well at the akhada, the water of which is also said to be good for the mind and the body.

Bhagwan Das invites me to join him in this evening ritual. He asks a teenage wrestler to rub me down with some of the earth—'but not too hard,' he tells the boy, 'he is not a pahalwan'.

Then I lie down on the akhada mitti, surrounded by birdsong. It is cool and fragrant and smells of an obscure but pleasant childhood memory, a memory just out of reach. I lie there convinced it will come to me only if I can sink deeper into the reverie. But I fall asleep.

If Mathura is the kingdom of Krishna, to learn about Hanuman, who has almost erased Krishna's association with kushti, I end up in Varanasi.

It is dawn on the ghats, the river-front landings of Varanasi. The wide river shimmers, lapping softly against the anchored boats. Groups of people sing devotional songs and the serene melodies ebb and flow over the steep steps. There is the whiff of tea being brewed. The wind is cool, the sun pleasantly warm on the skin. Monkeys trace silent, shapely arcs through the air as they jump from temple spire to temple spire.

Sohan Lal, a Banarsi pahalwan, is done with his morning bath in the Ganga, and I watch him coming up the steps in his red langot, his wiry body shining in the sun. He wears a thin black thread around his thick neck. His chest has a light even coating of white hair, which turns black on his hard, flat stomach.

If it wasn't for Sohan Lal, it would have been difficult to find Tulsi akhada, hidden by the monumental white house of the mahant (head) of the famous Sankat Mochan temple. From the outside, it is just another walled compound in the warren of narrow lanes that stretch and twist along the river front.

Inside is a large open space where one expects crammed, narrow buildings. There are trees with generous canopies and luxurious hanging roots, soft earth underfoot, and a deep well in a corner. Next to it is a small changing room. Stuck to the back wall of the compound is a wrestling pit covered with a tin roof. On the wall, the words 'Sri Hanumanji' is written in a red scrawl, and below it there is a niche with a Shiva lingam the size of your palm.

It is a rare akhada that does not have some representation of Hanuman, even if it is just his name written on a wall.

But this is no ordinary akhada either—the local lore is that this is the akhada Tulsidas built.

Tulsidas, the prolific sixteenth-century writer, composed his Hindi retelling of the Ramayana—the *Ramcharitmanas*—in Banaras. Sohan Lal tells me that the house Tulsidas worked in while writing the book stood right next to the akhada and the ghat that bears his name, and that Tulsidas was a pahalwan too. He worked out in the morning, then bathed in the river and sat down to write, Sohal Lal says.

The *Ramcharitmanas* was the first major telling of the Ramayana in Hindi, and its loosening of the story of Ram from Sanskrit, the language of the elite, had an extraordinary effect.

Despite the absence of printing and large-scale illiteracy, Tulsidas's version of the Ramayana quickly became one of the most exalted books of its time. The poet-saint Nabha Das, a contemporary of Tulsidas, wrote in his *Bhaktamal* that Tulsi was Valmiki himself, reborn to bring the story of Ram back to the people.[74]

That's exactly what the book did. It brought the Ramayana to the people—not just as a text, but also through popular performance recitals, folk songs and as the basis of the theatrical Ramlila.[75] The *Ramcharitmanas* is the most widely known version of the story of Ram in India now. Mahatma Gandhi called it 'the greatest book in all devotional literature'.[76]

Though Hanuman is portrayed as Ram's most loyal follower in Valmiki's Ramayana, it is in the *Ramcharitmanas* that the monkey-god truly makes a colossal leap: Tulsidas says, 'My heart, Lord, holds this conviction: Greater than Rama is Rama's servant.'[77]

In his meticulous and festive exploration of Hanuman's socio-religious influence in contemporary India, *Hanuman's Tale*, Philip Lutgendorf says, '[I]n the experience and practice of many people, the most vibrant and endearing character in the story wasn't Rama, but rather Hanuman.' Lutgendorf then goes on to show, in loving detail, just how and why this is. 'Hanuman's devotees often point out, with a touch of both irony and satisfaction, that there are, in most regions of India, far more shrines to Hanuman than to his exalted master, and a modest number of temple surveys bear out this claim. These observations suggest that a commonplace scholarly assumption ought to be reexamined: namely, that Rama, as the seventh avatara of the cosmic preserver Vishnu, is a "major" god, and Hanuman, as his servant, messenger, champion, and general factotum, is a "minor" one.'[78]

Varanasi, the spiritual and scholarly centre of Hinduism, can be confidently included in the list of places where Hanuman out-shrines Ram. And Lutgendorf's proposal that Hanuman has more followers than perhaps any other Hindu deity is borne out unambiguously by the pahalwans.

How Hanuman replaced Krishna as the patron god of the wrestlers has not been documented, but Tulsidas may have had a hand in it: he helped shape Hanuman into the people's god, and wrestling already was, as it still is, the sport of the people. The various iterations of the *Ramcharitmanas* as performance art also often focus on Hanuman as a wrestling hero.

To this day, recitals of the *Ramcharitmanas* can involve detailed sports commentary, with mimed action, of Hanuman's many legendary wrestling bouts.[79]

Sohan Lal sits under the large peepul tree in one corner of the akhada, framed by a shower of twisted aerial roots. He is a clerk with an insurance company, but his life revolves around kushti. At sixty-seven, he looks at least ten years younger. Although, he no longer wrestles, his mornings must start at the shaded precincts of the akhada with a vigorous workout, followed by a rub-down with the cool akhada earth and a massage by one of the younger trainees, and finally a bath in the Ganga. Then he performs a simple puja for Hanuman and leaves for work. In the evening, he comes back to the akhada, just to sit around and watch others wrestle, though, increasingly, there are fewer and fewer boys who come. He sits around anyway, because it makes him 'happy and calm to be around Hanumanji's home'.

'Hanumanji belongs to all wrestlers, and all wrestlers belong to Hanumanji,' he says. 'We wear the langot in his honour. He is the greatest wrestler that lived.'

Did Tulsidas really build this akhada? Is there proof that the akhada was built in the sixteenth century?

'No one can tell for sure, but the likelihood is very high,' Sohan Lal says. 'Look, in this area, there are a lot of things connected to Goswamiji (Tulsidas). There's a little Hanuman shrine right outside which we believe was built by him. There is no doubt that he set up lots of small Hanuman temples all over Banaras. What they say about this akhada is that Goswamiji always started his day here. He was a great believer in strength. He believed that you have to be strong in your body to be strong in your mind and live a moral life. He found the strength to write the Ramayana because he wrestled here, and because Hanumanji granted him that power.'

Perhaps Tulsidas did wrestle here at this akhada and bathe in the Ganga before sitting down to his daily writing, moulding the divine monkey in the image of a Banarsi wrestler. Perhaps he never stepped foot in this akhada—maybe there was no akhada here at that time at all. There is no certainty beyond the romance of the stories that pahalwans tell, and Sohan Lal makes that explicit with his next nugget:

'You know how we wrestlers are always climbing ropes for exercise? Well, Goswamiji was married to a very beautiful woman and she had gone to her parents' house once and he couldn't bear her absence. So he swam across a flooded river in the middle of the monsoon, reached the in-laws' house and then climbed two storeys up to the balcony of his wife's room using a vine that was hanging on the wall. It was only after he had reached the balcony that he realized that he was climbing up a snake.'

Sohan Lal says this with all seriousness, and then breaks into a smile.

'It is difficult to find snakes in Kaliyug, so we use ropes.'

It can be said with certainty though that the current akhada was refurbished and popularized in the early twentieth century by Swami Nath, the then mahant of the Sankat Mochan temple, who was a wrestler. It is also known as the Swami Nath akhada, and it is more a spa than a competitive training centre. There are very few who come here to learn or practise wrestling—a sixteen-year-old student whose older brother is a national-level wrestler and a couple of his friends, two young rickshaw pullers, a labourer who works at a sheet-metal factory, a shopkeeper and a cloth merchant made up the morning attendance. There were also three old men—all at least a decade older than Sohan Lal—toothless, wrinkled and slightly stooped, who spent half an hour doing squats and push-ups as Sohan Lal and I spoke. Then they rubbed the akhada earth on themselves, shook it off as it dried, and went to bathe in the Ganga.

Watching them, I felt a strong sense of yearning: may I too, if I live to be eighty, spend my days like this.

When he is done with his morning ritual, Sohan Lal takes me to his office on his bike. After the peace of the akhada, the crossing at Godhulia, just off the ghats, comes at me like a screaming bomb. I feel disoriented and deaf. The crowded, crater-ridden roads of Varanasi are not for the unprepared. Cars, bikes, people, cows, handcarts, hawkers and garbage jostle for every inch of space. The air is thick and hot with car fumes. Blaring horns cut through it and through the brain. We move an inch at a time, legs always brushing past the nearest vehicle or person. Even at that speed, it is a shuddering ride.

'Banaras roads,' Sohan Lal bellows over the noise. 'They are meant for VIPs! You travel on them, and get a full-body massage for free.'

It is a relief to enter the dusty little office, and watch the nightmare traffic crawl past outside.

Sohan Lal's table is piled high with documents and folders. He takes a deep breath, then sits down and starts sorting through them. He sits very straight, and soon, when he gets into a rhythm with his sorting, he begins a monologue on Hanuman for my benefit.

'Hanuman is everyone's god. He is the god concerned with human difficulties, the things that people like you or me face.'

'Like the pollution and traffic here?'

Sohan Lal laughs. 'Yes, but perhaps there are limits to what even he can do.' Then he's more serious. 'No, look, it's not about Hanuman's limitations. It's about us. Hanuman will show the way. It is up to us to follow. He won't carry us on his back.'

'What is Hanuman's greatest attribute? What makes him so close to wrestlers? Is it because he is incredibly strong?'

'No, that's not it. Where does his strength come from? That's the real question. His strength comes from brahmacharya, his celibacy.'

'Other pahalwans have told me that that's why they wear the langot.'

'Yes, of course, Hanuman keeps his langot tightly bound, to show his celibacy, that's why we do the same. But there is something more that makes Hanuman the greatest wrestler who has ever lived. See, he had immense shakti, right? Unlimited power. But he never uses the power for himself. Never. The only time he uses it is in the service of Ram, in the service of the greater good. He is ready to give his life for it. If Ram says, in the middle of the night, I want this mango from this district of Poorvanchal, and they are sitting in Kashmir, Hanuman will leave immediately to get that mango.

'Hanuman thinks of himself as nothing, a vacuum, if he is not serving Ram. Now, *this* is called bhakti. Even if you know everything, and have been taught all the secrets by Shiva, Vishnu and Vayu, you remain a humble servant. That's bhakti, and what we aim for with our mehnat is not just shakti, but also this bhakti. Keep working, no matter what. Ask Hanuman to get a plant from a mountain, he gets the mountain. That's mehnat.'

'That's just stupid.'

'Well, he is a monkey. Sometimes he forgets he is a god. But it's bhakti and mehnat all the same, and that's the point. Whether you are strong or weak, wise or stupid, the ideals of bhakti and mehnat apply equally to you.

'Most people will say that strength and humility are two opposite things—that's why, if you're into kushti, you're not most people. Pahalwans have to embrace both things.'

Hanuman's embodiment of the ancient Hindu constructions of shakti and bhakti is perfectly in sync with the tradition of the wrestling hero that we encountered earlier, the tradition of the *Shahnama* and the *Futuwwat*, of Rustom and Yusuf Adil Shah. Even the name Hanuman points to this duality. There are two common interpretations of it: One whose jaw (hanu) is broken or prominent (mant), referring to the story of a baby Hanuman trying to devour the sun and injuring himself in the process—a tale of innocent hubris and supernatural strength. The second interpretation says the opposite: one whose pride (mana) has been destroyed (han).[80]

14

PAHALWAN HANUMAN

For pahalwans, Hanuman is neither a myth, nor just an abstract god-figure whose divinity is incomprehensible. He is real, grounded. He is always present in the akhada, they say. Along the winding cobbled lanes in the older part of the city, you come across a shrine every few metres. The Hanuman idols in them, covered with layers and layers of red lacquer (with which he is worshipped), have acquired a strikingly amorphous, prehistoric look. Each of them, according to the locals, has his own particular persona. One, next to a defunct akhada above Darbhanga ghat is said to be greedy for milk and sweets. Another, next to a busy hotel, restores virility in men and fertility in women. The chief of them all, the idol at Sankat Mochan (which is said to have been Tulsidas's) is self-explanatory—the remover of difficulties.

Sohan Lal takes me to akhada Bada Ganesh. It is, as usual, hidden away from the choked iron-and-steel-parts market where it is located. The whole akhada is on a raised buff, sheltered by foliage, overlooking the stark red-and-yellow Bada Ganesh temple. One part of the akhada is a cattle shed. The owners are dairy farmers, and also run a sweet shop and a metalworks shop. The Hanuman shrine is at one corner of the akhada.

Kallu pahalwan, a big, shambling man with a foot-long belly, is the patriarch here. He is easily amused, and laughs with abandon. Sohan Lal and he take me to the shrine.

'He is a very loving Hanuman,' Kallu says.

Sohan Lal nods.

'What does that mean?'

'Everyone who spends time at this akhada becomes happy,' Kallu says, with his disarming laugh. 'That's why we say he is loving. Isn't he beautiful?'

To my unbesotted eye, he looks a lot like the rest. Covered in bright red lacquer, shapeless, except for the big eyes.

Kallu's father Lallu, a man even bigger and more formidable (going by the photograph that hangs inside the weight-room), was a revered guru. He had travelled and taught in many places in eastern India—Calcutta, Kharagpur, Puri, Patna—before settling down here in the 1950s. Gungey Baba, a deaf-and-dumb sadhu and wrestler who lived in the Bada Ganesh temple, inspired and partly funded Lallu's endeavour.

It was a success. Lallu's fame spread, and the akhada overflowed with young pahalwans. Kallu was one of them. He was around ten, he says, and had just finished bathing one morning when his father came and picked him up and dropped him on to the mitti.

'In Banaras, who doesn't know Lallu pahalwan,' Sohan Lal says fondly.

Kallu agrees. 'He had no vices, and loved life, and loved food. Milk, cream, ghee, he lived on the pure stuff. He was always happy, and I have never seen him sick. Every day at four in the morning he was at the akhada. Never saw him miss a day, except the last four days of his life. He was eighty-five—ill for three days and died on the fourth. What a beautiful way to go. All thanks to our loving Hanuman.'

The wrestler's affectionate embrace of Hanuman has one unfortunate parallel: extremist and supremacist Hindus also call on him as their martial deity. The destruction of the Babri Masjid happened amidst cries of 'Jai Bajrangbali'. The most notorious Hindu right-wing organization, the so-called 'youth wing' of the

Vishwa Hindu Parishad (VHP)—'Bajrang Dal', or the army of Hanuman—is also named after the god. Its role in the communal riots that followed the destruction of the Babri Masjid is well documented.

The Rashtriya Swayamsevak Sangh (RSS), the umbrella Hindu nationalist outfit, was even modelled on the principles of the akhada, and in fact drew its first members from one.[81] Dr K.B. Hedgewar, the founder of the RSS, was a Hanuman devotee, and always carried a small statue of Maruti, as Hanuman is better known in Maharashtra, with him. Early RSS members took their membership oath before a framed icon of Maruti. Like the pahalwans, RSS members follow a regimen of workouts, equate physical strength with moral grit, and believe in the ideal of celibacy.

But this is where the similarity ends.

The RSS shakha—their version of the akhada—is in many ways the antithesis of the wrestling school. Its ideology is focused on communal discourse, a Hindu-centric nationalism, the importance of community over the individual and politics. Everything else is subjugated to this ideological framework. The akhada philosophy is about the primacy of the individual; its main thrust is towards developing somatic skills and an understanding of one's own self, and it is a decidedly apolitical space.[82]

Akhadas make a conscious effort to distance themselves from right-wing politics and communal discourse, and it is rare to find a wrestler who advocates violence of any kind. But wrestlers, like anyone else, are shaped by their family and their community, by time and circumstance and individual motivations. They may become goons for hire for politicians or crime bosses. They may hold deep communal grudges. They may join a communal riot if it breaks out in their neighbourhood. During elections, they have a reputation of being hired by politicians to strong-arm people into voting for them; so much so that well-known gurus make public statements asking pahalwans to refrain from doing such things.

But choosing violence, crime or communal hatred inevitably results in a backlash from the akhada. If a pahalwan decides to join a criminal gang, the akhada doors are closed to him. If a pahalwan is a well-known rioter, most akhadas will refuse him.

Early on, Sohan Lal had to choose between these two opposing forces.

The RSS had a shakha in a small park near the house where he grew up. When he was ten, he started attending the shakha, pulled in by his peers and the chance to play kho-kho with other boys. For a year, he was a regular. Then a gang of boys at school, the most notorious ones, began picking on Sohan Lal and his friends. They would casually snatch their books and toss them in the sewer. They would demand that pocket money be handed over to them. They would make Sohan Lal stand at attention and throw ink on him. After such things had gone on for some time, Sohan Lal and his two friends went crying to a teacher.

'The teacher looked us up and down, and asked, "What's your full name?" Because we only write Sohan Lal, Kanhaiya Lal…So I said, Sohan Lal Yadav.'

'"Yadav," our teacher said. "You are a Yadav and you are scared of a few boys? *Yadavon ka kaam kya hain? Marna, pitna, harkana.* (What do Yadavs do best? Beating people up, threatening them.) What are you doing here, crying? Don't you go to an akhada?"'

'I said, "No, I go to a shakha." He said, "Leave that immediately, and go and join an akhada if you want to really be a man."'

And so Sohan Lal did. Within a year, he says, he got so strong and so confident that he felt like a different person.

'Then I started picking on those gundas one by one,' he says. 'I waited for one guy in the gali near his house and took him down. I kept him pinned to the ground and I told him, "I am a Yadav, and the next time you come for me, I will not stand around, and I will pick you out first. Then your friends can do whatever they want, but you will go down." Then I picked on the next, told him the same thing.'

The leader of the gang was next, and once he had been brought down, the rest of the boys fell in line. Over the years, the boys in the gang (most of whom are schoolteachers now) and Sohan Lal became friends.

'And that was it,' he says. 'I have never gone to a shakha again, but the akhada has stayed with me.'

At dusk, Kallu pahalwan and Sohan Lal decide to walk to the ghats.

It's what they do every evening. They keep away from the more crowded ones, the places where tourists and devotees throng for the evening aarti. The ghat of their choice, under the shadow of a hulking old palace, looks abandoned. A naked bulb hangs from the wall of the palace where the curving steps meet an octagonal stone platform raised above the water. It casts a feeble yellow light on the final few steps. A few feet away, on the next ghat, a band of children run around playing a game of tag, casting long, fleeting shadows over the palace ramparts. Boatfuls of tourists go by, the boatmen shouting out inane bits of information: 'This is Darbhanga Palace, it was made by the maharaja of Darbhanga; This is Ahilya Ghat, built by Maharani Ahilya'—and so on.

But mostly, there is silence. I sit with the two friends on the platform and watch the water turn black.

'So why exactly are you here,' Kallu pahalwan asks.

'I am writing a book on kushti.'

'A book? Then you've come to the right place. This is a place of learning.' He smiles widely.

'*Banaras ki kushti, aur Banaras ki masti!* (Wrestling in Varanasi and ecstasy in Varanasi!) You must experience both, and write about both!' He smiles, then: 'There is one very important thing about wrestling that you must understand. It is the most important thing. If it can be grasped, everything else is unnecessary.

'Kushti is not about fighting at all. It is about spreading love. That's the main reason why akhadas exist. To spread love. Some people call it bhaichara (brotherliness). When we put mitti on ourselves, we are saying many things. We are saying that we come from mitti, it sustains us, and then we go back to mitti. What that means is that we are all the same. Hindus, Musalmans, high caste, low caste, Brahmin, Chamar, brown skin, white skin, black skin, ugly, beautiful—you know what happens to them when they enter the akhada and wrestle?'

'What?'

'They all become the same. They have a body of one colour. They are all covered in mitti. They become members of the same caste—the caste of pahalwans.'

Kallu and Sohan are only telling me what I have heard repeated endlessly by other wrestlers and gurus: kushti is against the divisions of caste.

'See, this is the only sport where two naked bodies meet. Your sweat, blood, saliva—all of it mingles. If you haven't broken the barriers of caste and religion, how can you allow this to happen? That's why kushti has no caste, and it has no religion.'

'Who is India's most famous pahalwan?' Sohan Lal asks.

Without thinking, I say, 'Gama.'

'And he is a Musalman,' Sohan Lal says.

'Yes. And every pahalwan in India knows of him, and keeps him in his heart, just like with Hanuman,' Kallu says. 'I remember—and this was a long time back—when I was twenty or twenty-one, and I had travelled for two days to go to this akhada in Punjab for a competition. I was not feeling too well. But I went to the akhada, and inside there was this huge portrait of Gama—the moment I saw that, I felt the illness leave me.'

Kallu pahalwan's akhada stands in solidarity with his ideals. The current coach, who was one of Lallu pahalwan's first students here, is a Brahmin. There are two Dalit boys, both in school. One's family runs a tailoring shop, the other's works in a railway engine manufacturing factory. There is a Muslim man, who goes to work in his family's garments shop after his morning practice. The twenty other practitioners at the akhada are from various Hindu castes.

'They all have to eat together, bathe together and massage each other,' Kallu says.

'It would be nice if these ideals spread outside the akhada, became part of our culture,' Kallu says, following it up with his throaty laugh. 'And it already has. Caste is an old idea, and its time is almost over. Why, in twenty, maybe thirty years, it may be forgotten entirely.'

Perhaps not. It has survived for thousands of years, fought and adapted through hundreds of anti-caste movements and revolutions. What cataclysm can destroy it in the next twenty?

The pahalwans try.

The anthropologist Joseph Alter clearly agrees. In his detailed investigation into wrestling and caste in *The Wrestler's Body*, he says that it undermines the very basis of caste, challenging its most fundamental concepts of ritual purity.

'This is not because wrestling provides a forum for social protest against stratification,' he writes, 'but rather because it is a context in which the meaning of particular key symbols that relate to the embeddedness of caste are significantly reinterpreted through the medium of the human body.'[83]

Wrestling is not an anti-caste movement, and its ideals stay inside the akhada. Pahalwans who forget caste distinctions at the akhada remember them when they go back home. There are not that many wrestlers from the 'lowest' caste groups, the Dalits and Balmikis, at akhadas. This, many gurus say, is because people from these groups are poor, and sending a boy to an akhada is a serious investment with no guarantee of any returns.

'Pahalwans,' Kallu says, 'are not restricted by caste, but by their ability to provide for their diet. Those who have land and buffaloes, they can do it. Like us. We have never wanted for milk, ghee, paneer, or wheat or vegetables, so it was easy for us to become wrestlers, and it's easy for us to put our sons in it.'

Akhada gurus though take real pride in their lower-caste students, if they get any. When I asked many of the gurus in Delhi who their favourite wrestler was when they were wrestling themselves, an overwhelming majority named Vijay Chura.

Most wrestlers drop their surname so that their caste does not become a badge of identification, adopting casteless monikers like 'Kumar', 'Singh' or simply 'Pahalwan'. Vijay, a national champion from Delhi from the 1980s, did just the opposite. He flaunted his caste.

He was also Captain Chand Roop's favourite student, a role model, and still is. Even now when a student complains that he can't work any more, the captain tells him: 'Vijay Chura could do twice as much and still not stop till I told him to stop.'

15

WRESTLING IS DYING

The wrestle of wrestlers, two apprentice-boys, quite grown,
lusty, good-natured, native-born,
out on the vacant lot
at sundown after work,
The coats and caps thrown down,
the embrace of love and resistance…

—*I Sing the Body Electric,* Walt Whitman

Sohan Lal and Kallu pahalwan say wrestling is dying.
The more people move away from their roots, the less popular
wrestling gets, they say. Like many wrestlers in India, Sohan Lal
and Kallu think that modern India has no identity of its own, and
does not care for one.

'There was a time,' Sohan Lal says, 'not so long ago, when
langots flew from the windows of every home in Banaras. Proud
little red banners. You would walk through the lanes and look up
and see them and think, life is good.'

Those days are gone now, and talking about them depresses
him. He sits slumped on a plastic chair in the small front room
of his house. The room is bare, except for two chairs and four
framed pictures on a wall. One, larger than life-size, is a portrait
of his father. The others are all wrestling-related—Sohan Lal and

the rest of the Banaras Hindu University wrestling team in the 1980s, his brother with Satpal Singh, Sohan Lal with his closest friend and wrestling teammate.

'So many akhadas have closed down in Banaras, I have lost count,' he says. 'Why, right here in Beniabagh, there used to be four akhadas—one on each corner of the park here. Now there is one. The others…basically people either shit there or shoot heroin.'

The wrestlers in Varanasi say, there used to be an akhada in every mohalla. But a walk along the ghats is easy proof that the city has forsaken its wrestling past. Every single ghat—even the ones where bodies are cremated—used to have an akhada. Now the full stretch of the river front has only two that are still running. Three have turned into weightlifting gyms, their wrestling pits neglected. The rest have been abandoned—luxurious banyan and fig trees have taken over, their trunks breaking through tin roofs, their roots clasping the stone weights that have been left behind.

'Children now, they think that mitti is dirty,' Sohan Lal says. 'They are restless and impatient. They want to be wrestlers in one year, make money, and get a government job. This is kushti's birthplace, and yet, who cares? Boys now, they want nice clothes, they don't want to take off their shoes, they want to put some music in their ears and lift some weights. The akhada guru will say, you must be celibate to be a wrestler, and these kids run away immediately.'

Sohan Lal was ten when his father brought him to the akhada he now teaches in. 'My father would say, "*Mitti nahin lagaoge toh khana nahin milega.*"' (If you don't rub that mitti on you, you won't get fed.)

It's kushti's stress on celibacy that is the real reason for its decline, Sohan Lal says.

Akhadas have a strict decree enforcing celibacy. This too is tied to Hanuman, whose 'adamantine langot'[84] is iconic with pahalwans. A good wrestler is identified by his tight langot. Like the amount of milk or ghee the wrestler can consume, how firmly he binds his genitals is a common theme that runs through the wrestlers' world. They will often say that such-and-such 'pahalwan wore his langot very tight' to convey just how good that wrestler was.

Even Sushil Kumar wears a langot under his singlet when he competes at international tournaments, though he does not talk about celibacy. He says he wears the langot as a sign of respect for Hanuman, and also because it keeps the groins protected. He is a rare example of an active wrestler who is also married.

Most wrestlers and gurus avoided questions on the role abstinence plays in kushti. Many just said that it's an ancient belief, and thus its wisdom cannot be questioned. Others had more practical reasons: sex distracts men—and wrestlers, who need to stay focused, cannot afford that.

Sohan Lal, though, does not shy from the topic.

'The sperm,' he says forcefully. 'The sperm is where all the power of a man is stored. The reason for celibacy is simple. You hold on to the sperm, and thus you hold on to all your power.'

It is evident, though, as Sohan Lal goes on, that it is not so simple to hold on to the sperm. For one, it is not just a question of not having sex, or not masturbating. Just denying sexual release is worse than actually indulging in it.

'Because then, since sperm is in continuous production, it will mess with your mind, it will wreck you, your balls will burst,' he says.

So what then? What is it that one must do?

'You have to rise above sexual desire. The sperm must be channelized to go into the Ajna Chakra: the source of phoorti, of power, of the electricity running through your muscles.'

I am reminded of a line from *On Boxing*, where Muhammad Ali's manager Bundini Brown had this to say about the secret to Ali's success: 'You got to get the hard-on, and then you got to keep it. You want to be careful not to lose the hard-on, and cautious not to come.'[85]

Brown is using a metaphor all too common in the male-dominated world of sports, these retellings of the myth of Samson and Delilah, where men lose power through sexual contact with a woman.

Football teams are often banned from having sex or bringing their wives or girlfriends along during big tournaments. This denial gives them an edge, the reasoning goes, that sexual fulfilment will take away.

The wrestler's engagement with sexuality, linked to dietary beliefs, has complicated origins in Hindu philosophy,[86] and is wrapped in a paradox. This is apparent in the figure of Hanuman, whose connection to celibacy and the langot began to take shape at around Tulsidas's time.[87]

In Hindu ascetic thought, unbroken celibacy is linked to great virility, and the common expression 'lal langotwala'—the one with a red loincloth—refers to both Hanuman and the common rhesus monkey with its red hindquarters. Male monkeys are popularly associated with an unhindered libido, not abstinence, and this only serves to highlight Hanuman's supernatural status: the fiery girding of his loins is both a sign of charged virility as well as of celibacy.[88]

Wrestlers live out this paradox—the super-virile man, yet a virgin; his naked body unadorned except for the fiery red cloth wound tightly around his loins, and yet it speaks not of sex, but its denial.

What sport is as vividly erotic as wrestling? It is the entangling of two bare bodies, honed to perfection. It is the meeting of two hunky men who must prove their physical domination over the other by getting seriously intimate. The tensions of wrestling's homoerotic power have rippled through the ages.

It found its highest expression in ancient Greece, in sculptures and in painted pottery—the male nude in its most vividly idealized form. The Greek palaestra was an idealized school for the training of a man, but it was also a 'prime arena of pederastic courtship'.[89]

There is only circumstantial evidence of wrestling's erotic flowering in India. The passion with which sexual control has been enforced is in itself a clue: the need to construct this elaborate philosophy of strength through abstinence may have developed in reaction to wrestling's inherent eroticism. Classical Greece too reacted against sexuality in wrestling. By the end of the fifth century BCE, a law was enacted to protect pupils from relationships in palaestras.

The hidden erotic paradox of wrestling, and the very claustrophobic atmosphere of an akhada where nothing is private, must be terrifying for young boys. The age at which most boys join akhadas is the age of puberty.

Just how do young boys handle their sexual awakening when they are inside the strict boundaries of the akhada? Surely, the exhausting and supremely rigorous physical regimen of the akhada helps. Extreme fatigue is an excellent demotivator of sexual urges.

Only one former wrestler gives me a peep into this aspect of growing up in an akhada: the Olympian Ashok Aggarwal, who coaches at both the Mehr Singh and Captain Chand Roop akhadas.

Celibacy is easily enforced in an akhada, Ashok says, simply because there is always someone watching. 'Even if you spend a little extra time in the toilet, there will be a heavy knock on the door,' Ashok says. 'If you left the akhada for fifteen minutes, some senior or some coach will catch you and say, "Where did you go, and to do what?"'

'But sexual desire is the strongest impulse in the world,' Ashok told me one hot afternoon after a training session at Captain Chand Roop akhada. 'For most people, this kind of sexual control is impossible. The bounded akhada life can become impossible. Boys go through twenty days of continuous nocturnal emissions, two or three times a night, and they are terrified by it. All this talk of celibacy…I will swear on Bajrangbali and tell you that it's a lie. Hanuman is celibate—but he is a god. We are only humans. Look at Mahatma Gandhi. He was steeped in sex, and we talk about his celibacy!

'Look, if you had no desires, you are hardly human. Athletes desire success, desire power and strength. Without it, there will be no passion, and no goals. Similarly, you can desire sex, desire a woman, and there's nothing wrong in that. The problem is when you have no control and you give up everything else, forget everything else because you are in love or lust. That is your own fault. It's not the fault of the woman, or the fault of sex, or desire itself.'

Getting married when he was still an active wrestler, Ashok says, is the best thing he did. It made him a different person; more relaxed, more light in his body, happier and hungrier on the mat.

'If I had sex the night before a bout,' he says, 'I would want to eat up my opponent, my body had a different kind of power and agility running through it.'

Even Sohan Lal agrees that celibacy, in the context of a wrestler, is a strange and complicated beast. 'Yes, desire is important, you must have desire. But desire comes from the head, it comes from the heart, and it comes from the balls, and it gets all mixed up. How do you separate them? That's the mystery, that's what a wrestler must strive towards. If you simply let go of yourself, submit yourself to sex, it's so easy.'

Yet, he says, he has stopped talking to his students about sex and brahmacharya. 'It's better to leave these things out, focus on the sport,' he says. 'At least I will have some students left to teach.'

When we finish talking, Sohan Lal asks me to join him for a walk to the ghats. We stroll through the now-familiar mazy lanes, winding our way through crowded tenements and smoky, clamorous temple fronts and shops. Sohan Lal, wearing shorts, a cheap, imitation Brazilian football jersey and a muffler the size of a blanket, stridently leads the way. We skip past mounds of trash, reclining cows and trails of cow dung. Sohan Lal keeps his eyes peeled, peering up often, perhaps to check for langots flying from the windows. There are none.

Sometimes the weight of tradition can sink the very thing it is trying to uphold. If wrestling in India is alive and well because of the vibrancy of kushti, it has also held India back from more robust success in international wrestling.

Kushti's complex and rigorous links to many schools of thoughts—Hindu philosophies, chivalric codes, questions of morality and love, the embrace of mitti, the dietary codes—are often rigidly opposed to modern methods of training, nutrition science and modern techniques.

In Kolhapur, an agrarian–industrial belt in Maharashtra, kushti enjoys a popularity unrivalled by any other sport. Here, wrestling schools are not called akhadas, but talims, from the Arabic word for instruction. There is nothing quite as dreamlike and hypnotic as a Kolhapur talim.

They are often single-storeyed L-shaped buildings with high, sloping roofs, like the Sri Shahu Vijayi Gangavesh Talim, which was established some time in the first decade of the twentieth century by Shahu Maharaj, the maharaja of Kolhapur from 1894 to 1922.

Shahu Maharaj was a direct descendent of Shivaji, and a fiery social reformer who campaigned tirelessly against the Brahmin hegemony of Maharashtra's administrative and educational institutions and for the upliftment of the lower castes. He established boarding houses for low-caste students and made primary education compulsory and free for all. He passed an Act legitimizing inter-caste marriages, and imagined the unification of backward classes against the Brahmins.[90]

Powerfully built and barrel-chested, Shahu Maharaj was also a wrestler. He viewed the patronage of wrestling as one of

Pahalwans in Hyderabad in 1870, photographer unknown

Krishna and Balarama fight Kamsa's wrestlers. From a dispersed Bhagavata Purana from Malwa, Madhya Pradesh, dated 1650. In the possession of the Metropolitan Museum of Art, New York

A fifth-century terracotta sculpture from Uttar Pradesh depicting a wrestling match

Hanuman vanquishes the demon Nikumbha in a wrestling match. From a Ramayana produced during the reign of Akbar in the possession of the Freer Gallery of Art, Washington DC

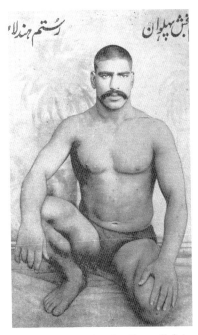

A poster featuring Gama (left) for a wrestling tournament in Bombay, 1940, promoted by prince Ranji
Source Wikimedia Commons

Gama's younger brother Imam Baksh, photographer unknown
Source Wikimedia Commons

Early morning at an akhada in a bylane in Banaras © Amit Bose

Mahavir Phogat in his akhada at Balali village, Haryana, training his daughters Priyanka (in red) and Sangeeta (in white) © Pradeep Gaur/Mint

Priyanka with her mother Daya after the training session © Pradeep Gaur/Mint

A dangal in Haryana © Rudraneil Sengupta

Crowds at a dangal © Pradeep Gaur/Mint

A wrestler dejected after losing a dangal in Uttar Pradesh © Rudraneil Sengupta

A wrestler gets some advice before his next bout at a dangal © Pradeep Gaur/Mint

A wrestler cools off after a dangal in Haryana © Rudraneil Sengupta

Prince Go-Ho Gobar Meets Champ in Main Event at Auditorium Tomorrow Night

An article announces a Gobar Goho fight,
LA Times, 23 August 1925
Source Wikimedia Commons

Sushil Kumar before the 2012 Olympics
© Priyanka Parashar/Mint

the many ways to uplift the lower castes, and promote a society without caste divisions. To this end, Shahu Maharaj sponsored the establishment of many talims in Kolhapur. He also built the Shahu Khasbag wrestling stadium in 1912, a kilometre away from the Shahu Vijayi Gangavesh Talim, and it remains the only dedicated wrestling stadium in India.

On the day he was crowned the maharaja of Kolhapur in 1894, Shahu Maharaj marked the occasion with a wrestling tournament.

The Shahu Vijayi Gangavesh Talim is in a crowded place in a green, hilly area, with the wrestling stadium, two large markets, one of Maharashtra's most popular temples and a dargah all in a one-kilometre radius. The talim itself is in the shadow of a fabulous peepul tree that dwarfs everything around it. In keeping with the reformative zeal of Shahu Maharaj, the talims of Kolhapur are the most mixed-caste wrestling gymnasiums I have come across. The strict vegetarianism of the north Indian Hindu akhadas don't apply here.

Though dairy farmers still outnumber others, there is every kind of profession and social class represented at the talim. There are the sons of daily-wage labourers, schoolteachers, tailors, butchers, government clerks, poultry farmers, vegetable sellers, shopkeepers, restaurant owners and real-estate dealers.

Inside the building, thick shafts of light from rows of windows illuminate the wrestling pit. The earth of Kolhapur is the colour of rust; it glows an ethereal red. The pit is encircled by a raised stone structure the colour of coral. The walls are daubed an earthy crimson. A row of boys in red langots, made indistinguishable by the dust that covers them, sit on one end of the stone platform, watching. Pairs of massive wrestlers tussle in the shadows or tumble in and out of the golden blocks of light.

Dadu Chaugule is a Kolhapur legend. A former Rustom-e-Hind and the champion of innumerable dangals, Chaugule, now fifty-four, stands just a shade below 6 feet and weighs close to 100 kilos. His neck is as thick as a block of wood.

Chaugule, who also wrestled in international competitions for a brief period in the 1970s, and won a Commonwealth Games silver in 1974, is conflicted about just how the tradition of kushti can merge with the requirements of international wrestling.

'The mat is a bad thing, you see,' Chaugule says, 'but perhaps it is necessary. I grew up wrestling on mitti, and I believe that when you take the mitti away from kushti, you lose everything.

'The Khasbag maidan is like a temple for us pahalwans,' Chaugule says. 'We worship the soil of the maidan. We worship the soil of the talim. Our strength, our peace of mind, come from it. How can we wrestle on mats?'

The talims of Kolhapur have few mats, and even the ones they have are just thin foam-and-jute crash pads with a cloth cover sewed on—nothing at all like Olympic mats.

While Maharashtra has a robust and well-entrenched tradition of wrestling, it produces very few international wrestlers. Between 1996 and 2012, only two Maharashtrian wrestlers have represented India at the Olympics.

'Mat wrestling can kill our tradition,' says Chaugule. 'But it is also true that if we don't do well in international tournaments like the Olympics, kushti itself might die. Look at Mumbai, or Pune. When I was growing up, there were talims everywhere in those cities, everyone wanted to be a wrestler. Now you will only find a handful struggling along.'

Older wrestlers and wrestling patrons often think of the mat as a Western aberration that will destroy an indigenous way of life.

'Wrestling on mitti is heaven, wrestling on a mat is hell,' says Ratan Patodi, an ageing wrestling patron and scholar in Indore and the publisher of India's oldest-running wrestling periodical, *Bharatiya Kushti*.

Ashok Aggarwal feels that those who oppose wrestling on mats are missing the deeper truth—mat or mitti, the techniques and rules of kushti and international freestyle wrestling are more or less the same.

'This is a great, great opportunity for us,' he says. 'People say India is not a sporting country, that we have no culture of sports outside of cricket, but this is not true at all. We have a great culture of wrestling, and what we do on the mitti is no different from what you have to do on the mat. Then why are we so opposed to it?'

Sushil Kumar feels the same way.

'There is no reason why akhadas can't have both,' he says. 'Twenty years back, you would have found no mats in Delhi or Haryana. But look now. There are mats everywhere. But does that mean pahalwans from Delhi or Haryana are any less skilled at mitti ki kushti? They are champions on both. My wrestling is focused entirely on the mat, yet every week I practise in mitti at least once. Because I love it, because it gives me peace, it gives me strength.'

The economics of mitti dangals too prevent the spread of mats. In places like Maharashtra and Punjab, where there is an annual calendar full of tournaments fought on mitti, a wrestler's career and fortune is built on fighting the traditional way.

'It is a blessing and a curse,' Ashok says. 'Many, many wrestlers—hundreds of wrestlers—can have a proper career fighting on mitti. But only maybe the top twenty or twenty-five international wrestlers in India make any money.'

16

SATPAL GETS A MAT

Behind the revival of wrestling wrought by Sushil Kumar stands his coach, Satpal Singh. A contemporary of Dadu Chaugule, Satpal Singh has worked miracles with his wrestlers.

At the 2008 Olympics, the seven-member men's wrestling team from India featured five wrestlers from Satpal's akhada at Chhatrasal; it was the same in 2012. He taught both the wrestlers who won medals at these Games—Sushil and Yogeshwar—since they were children. Of the five Indian medalists at the wrestling world championships since 2000, three are Satpal's students. At the national championships, it is common occurrence that both finalists in almost all weight classes and age groups come from Chhatrasal.

The extraordinary role this akhada has played in India's recent international wrestling record is founded on three simple things: shifting the training focus to Olympic mats; access to a number of high-quality mats; and giving a free hand to athletes like Sushil and Yogeshwar to set modern training protocols.

If the techniques of kushti and international wrestling are the same, why is the difference between fighting on mats and in pits so important?

It is because earthen surfaces offer far more friction and traction, allowing wrestlers to be stable on their feet, and slowing down the speed of the fight. On the slippery surface of the mat, keeping yourself grounded is an altogether different matter, and fights are furiously pacey.

It's the difference between driving a rally car on dirt tracks and racing on asphalt.

Satpal fought at the 1972 Olympics, and got to train on a thin jute mat—for the first time in his life—for just a month before the Olympics. It left him wholly unprepared for the surface actually used at the Games.

'My only thought was, how do I keep myself from losing my balance,' Satpal says of that experience. 'I went there thinking I would beat everybody. Instead, I could not sleep at night thinking about just what a fool I was making of myself slipping around on the mat. I decided back then that if I ever get a chance to teach wrestling, my students will not face this humiliation.'

By the time Satpal went for the 1972 Munich Games, wrestling in India was already in the grip of a protracted death. The chief reason for this was the loss of the sport's most enthusiastic patrons, the rajas of various princely states, who were rapidly losing their money and power post-independence. By the 1970s, the last of the princely states had been dissolved, and the onus of sponsoring the sport was left to the government.

India's engagement with international wrestling had started with some promise. Bombay wrestler Rashid Mian Anwar won India's first individual medal at an international event at the 1934 British Empire Games (the precursor of the Commonwealth Games). In 1952, K.D. Jadhav won India's first individual Olympic medal, a bronze. At the 1962 Asian Games, India won twelve wrestling medals, its best ever, a record that was only broken in 2010.

None of those wrestlers had ever practised on mats, and had no structured training in the international style. They practised kushti on earthen akhadas, fought in local dangals, and took their slippery chances on unfamiliar mats at international competitions.

Till the middle of the 1960s, it was still possible to do this and win medals at international events, because Olympic wrestling rules and systems were still very much a work in progress.

At the 1960 Olympics, for example, American Shelby Autrie Wilson, twenty-three years old, won gold without ever having fought at an international event before.[91] By the 1950s, the US had introduced foam-core mats with a smooth, bonded vinyl surface that had revolutionized wrestling in America. The mats at the 1960 Olympics, however, were very different. Wilson's teammate Ed DeWitt described it as 'felt' in an interview: 'Never saw anything like it…I'm not sure what it was filled with…could have been horsehair,' he said.[92]

By the middle of the 1960s, these differences were blurring, and international rules and regulations were becoming more consistent. Countries with a rich history of traditional wrestling—the USA, Japan, Iran, Turkey, the states of the Soviet Union—quickly adopted Olympic protocols for the sport, including the surface on which to wrestle.

The first mat at a private akhada came to India as late as 1979, when a basic jute one was installed at the Guru Hanuman akhada in Delhi, where Satpal trained. The next one came in 1992, at Chhatrasal akhada. At that time, there were less than ten mats in all government-run training centres—thin jute ones with little resemblance to Olympic mats.

Satpal is not only at the centre of India's wrestling resurrection, he has lived through the transformation himself.

His father was a farmer and a 6′2″-tall fairground wrestler from Bawana, which was once a village on the outskirts of Delhi, and is now very much a part of the city. Satpal was the only one of his three boys (he also had two daughters) of comparative height and built. He put the boy into the village akhada, and travelled with him for local dangals. When he was fifteen, Satpal's father decided to take him to Delhi, to an akhada run by a wrestling guru he had once learnt from and deeply respected. It was an old

akhada, established in 1947 with money from the Birla famil
of the foremost business dynasties in India. The Birlas had been
impressed by Guru Hanuman, who until then had led a largely
itinerant life, training pahalwans in Calcutta, Banaras, Lucknow
and various other cities famed for their wrestling schools. The
Birlas gave Guru Hanuman a small piece of land next to their
mills in the north of Delhi.

When Satpal arrived at the akhada, it was in dismal state.
There were barely ten pahalwans who came for training, and none
of them lived on the premises. Not that there were living quarters.
The akhada had nothing except for a tin-shedded wrestling pit, a
6-foot by 6-foot Hanuman temple, and a large, shady sheesham
tree.

Satpal had never been to Delhi before, and the big alien city
and the spartan, run-down akhada reduced him to tears. When
he went home to Bawana for the weekend, he refused to go back.
Satpal's father was having none of it. 'Either you become a wrestler,
or you work full-time looking after the cattle,' he told the young
boy. That settled it. Satpal went back. He made the wrestling pit
his home, sleeping on the cool earth in the summer, or under
the sheesham tree. Winter was another matter. He would have to
crawl into the mandir to escape the cold at night, curled into a
foetal position, hemmed by walls that could barely contain him.

His family sent him fresh milk, ghee, fruits and vegetables
every day. A driver on a bus route from Bawana to Delhi, a friend
of the father, would make the delivery. Young Satpal would wait
at the bus stop at the appointed time to receive it, and sometimes
the driver would tell him, '*Pahalwanji, aaj toh hum thoda doodh se
chai pee liye, toh aadha doodh hai.*' (Today I made some tea with
some of the milk, so you only get half.)

There was only one thing that helped Satpal keep the
loneliness at bay—he was falling in love with wrestling. Sundays
were the best. On that day, there would be the big dangal for
schoolchildren at the park next to Jama Masjid. Satpal would get

to test himself against people his own age. He would get some money if he won. One Sunday, he won nine fights in a row. He bought himself a pair of canvas shoes with the money.

'At that time there were hardly any TVs, so these things were huge,' Satpal says. 'The park would be packed with people to see the fights. For a young boy, that kind of atmosphere is just an out-of-body experience. I used to tell myself that no matter what happens, I will never lose a fight at Jama Masjid.'

Guru Hanuman tapped into this thought. He improved on it, polished it and strengthened it, until Satpal became the country's strongest, most invincible wrestler.

'Guru Hanuman filled me with awe,' Satpal recalls. 'He did not know much about mat wrestling, but he had the spirit of the wrestling god moving through him. He spoke little, but saw everything. He would go to dangals, make a note of every mistake we made, and then come back and drill us till those flaws were ironed out. He could make you tough like no one else.'

In his first year with Guru Hanuman, Satpal won the U-19 National Championship—he was still only fifteen. Next year, he competed in the senior nationals and won. Satpal was responding to the wrestler's training and diet with alarming potency. He fought the first junior national in the 46 kg class, but was fighting the senior nationals the next year in 62 kg, and the next at 80 kg.

Attracted by Satpal's success at the nationals, other boys began trickling in to the akhada. The construction of squat little living quarters became a necessity.

Four years after he came to Guru Hanuman's akhada, Satpal was selected to compete at the 1972 Munich Olympics. Here was a completely new experience—the wrestlers in the team were expected to wear shoes, but no one could tell them what kind of shoes. They got cheap canvas shoes from the government, and old wrestling leotards that were already frayed and discoloured—'We had to sew them in places ourselves,' Satpal says.

They were going to fight on mats, and Satpal had never seen

one till he went for the month-long national camp before the Games. But there Satpal was in the presence of some of the legends of Indian wrestling—people like Jagroop Rathi and Chandgi Ram, also known as the 'Master', and he basked in the knowledge they shared freely.

When they finally landed in Munich, Satpal was dazzled.

'I had no idea that such places even existed,' Satpal exclaims, the memory clearly fresh in his mind. 'The hotels, the transport systems, the buildings and roads, the gyms and the shiny mats… there was an abundance of everything, and everything was beautiful and clean and sparkling. I felt awed and amazed, but at the same time it was a massive psychological setback. I thought, "How am I going to get on the mat wearing my old discoloured leotard? How am I going to explain the canvas shoes? What kind of a country do I come from? Are we really this poor?"'

Even though Satpal won four of his bouts at Munich, he still finished sixth. A medal was never within reach.

When he came back to India, he found out that his eldest sister had died of an illness. In fact, she had died soon after the trials, six months earlier, while he was still in India, but Satpal's father had made sure that the news did not reach him—he felt that it was necessary to cut his son off from the family altogether.

'He thought it would only distract me,' Satpal says. 'He used to get angry if I went home for holidays. He stopped coming to see me at competitions. He stopped coming to the akhada.'

Satpal became what Guru Hanuman wanted him to be. From 1973 to 1980, he won every major national competition and dangal—Rustom-e-Hind, Bharat Kesri, Rustom-e-Bharat, Hind Kesri. He was invincible.

'By this time, Guru Hanuman was everything to me. Coach, father, mother, everything. If I won, no one was happier than him,' he says. 'I remember in 1976, I won the Rustom-e-Hind in Rohtak. It was a very big deal then. My final was with Jagdish Mittal, who was at that time the most famous wrestler in Delhi and Punjab.

A huge guy. Just a year before that, Guruji had asked me not to fight with Jagdish at a competition because he thought I would get injured. There was more history as well—Jagdish's father and my father had trained under Guruji together many years back. There was lots of excitement about this, lots of tension. Journalists had come, All India Radio was broadcasting the fight.

'I pinned him in three minutes. Guruji went mad with happiness. The All India Radio reporter had told Guruji that he should wait at a certain spot after the fight, and he would get me there as well so both of us could be interviewed together. Guruji forgot all about it. He forgot about his things at the guest house where he was staying. He was so happy that he just started walking from the venue back towards the train station. I can imagine him smiling to himself as he did this. That day, no one could find Guruji! It was only the next day, when I came back to the akhada, that I found out that he had come back to Delhi.'

In 1975, Satpal became Bharat Kesri, and a month later, he was also in the final of Rustom-e-Bharat. The venue was the historic Shahu Khasbag Maidan in Kolhapur. His opponent: Dadu Chaugule.

'It was the biggest dangal I can remember,' says Satpal. 'Every famous heavyweight pahalwan in India was there—Master Chandgi Ram, Kartar Singh, Sukhchain Singh, Birajdar, Vijay Chura. Thousands of people had gathered to watch the fight, the stadium was full and there was a thick crowd of people outside it as well. It was madness.'

The final lasted over fifteen minutes. 'But in the end, I pinned him. People went wild!'

Satpal, in his langot, covered in earth, was hoisted on an elephant and taken around town. He can still recall the peculiar odour of the elephant.

'I was bloodthirsty,' Satpal says. 'Bloodthirsty. There was a saying that if you could withstand three minutes in a wrestling match with Satpal, you would be offered a job in the armed forces or the police.'

Satpal had some success on the mat as well, winning medals at three consecutive Asian Games and Commonwealth Games from 1974. He is still the only Indian to have done so. But an Olympic medal eluded him.

'There was no reason why I could not have won an Olympic medal,' he says. 'The man I beat at the 1982 Asian Games final had won the World Championship that year. If we had the right support and the right coaching, many of us could have won at the Olympics. We have never had any officials who really cared or knew how to nurture athletes and do what is good for them, so we never had a system to back us. The sports administrators were only looking to make money for themselves, consolidate their own political powers. The sport was not their priority. It still isn't. The only thing sports federations do is push files.'

In 1983, using his influence as a top athlete, Satpal wrangled a position in the Delhi government's sports administration. He was sent to look after Chhatrasal Stadium. He got a wrestling pit made next to the main stadium and started an akhada.

Soon after, Sushil Kumar and Yogeshwar Dutt joined the akhada.

When Sushil won the World Cadet Games in 1998, Satpal began his campaign for an Olympic mat. The next year, he got one from the Delhi government. Two years later, he got another one. Now there are enough mats for a hundred wrestlers to train simultaneously.

There is a clear reason why Delhi and Haryana are so over-represented in India's international wrestling teams. There are Olympic mats in every major akhada in these two states, and a fair number of mats in smaller akhadas too. Politicians in Haryana must—almost compulsorily—sponsor an akhada and furnish it with an Olympic mat if they want any influence over their electorate.

'In sporting terms, this is just the beginning,' Sushil says. 'The effects of this access to mats will start showing results now.

Of course, there are still many things we need to modernize, including our knowledge of training techniques. For example, we still think that the only measure of how well you are training is how *long* you spend working out. How many dands did you do today? Our idea of mehnat is unscientific and narrow, and coaches don't know any better than what tradition has taught them. There has to be a lot more learning, a lot more exchange of knowledge.'

17

THE MASTER

At the time Satpal was sowing the seeds of transformation in Indian wrestling, there was another influential wrestler who campaigned hard for the introduction of mats in the akhadas of Haryana and Delhi.

But he did something else, something that dug far deeper into the roots of kushti and ripped them out, sending out shock waves that still resonate in the world of Indian wrestling.

Master Chandgi Ram did the unthinkable. He let a woman enter the akhada and made her a pahalwan.

It was a strike at the most conservative, unchanging core of kushti: wrestling was not just a manly sport, it was the sport that defined manhood. Women never had a place in it. They neither wrestled, nor were they expected to watch wrestling. They were not welcome at akhadas or dangals.

The Chandgi Ram Vyayamshala (literally, gymnasium) is surrounded by history. It lies hidden between the reedy banks of the Yamuna and a highway thick with speeding cars. This is the edge of Delhi's Civil Lines, the name given to non-military British residential areas in Indian cities during the Raj. Now at the northern edge of Delhi, the locality used to be the very centre of the city. Opposite the hidden vyayamshala once stood Ludlow Castle, the chief residence of the British administrative head of

Delhi. The original building is gone, replaced by another built in the same style of architecture—the Ludlow school.

During the siege of 1857, the final wave of attack that broke the Indian resistance came right through where the vyayamshala now stands, using the cover of the extensive gardens and forests that lined the Yamuna then. John Nicholson, the indomitable Scotsman who led the attack and was so fiery that he inspired a cult among his enemies—the Nikkal Seyn—is buried barely a kilometre from the vyayamshala.

Surrounded by such potent history, yet cut off from it by the highway, the vyayamshala and its inhabitants lead a quiet, sleepy existence.

When you enter through the low gate, the first structure that meets the eye is the akhada itself: a cavernous hall in poor condition, just to the left of the entrance, sunk two steps below ground level. Two old mats take up the whole flooring of the hall, and old portraits of Chandgi Ram recede in the shadows.

A small courtyard with a couple of trees separates the wrestling hall from a flat single-storey building on the right. On the left, hidden from view behind the hall, is another residential building of similar style. The back of the vyayamshala is bordered by a sparkling Hanuman temple, an outhouse which contains a shiny gym and a small office, and another small detached building which functions as a guest room. Behind this, through a small door in the back wall, is the river, an earthen wrestling pit and a patch of farmland. Even in the middle of the day, the only sound here is of cicadas.

Chandgi Ram's daughter, Sonika Kaliraman, has just woken up. She is on holiday. She lives in Los Angeles, and the jet lag is yet to leave her system. She is tall, and stoops slightly from her broad shoulders. Dressed in an oversized T-shirt and pyjamas, she fixes her long hair lazily into a tousled ponytail. She is beautiful, in a big hulking way, with large almond-coloured eyes, long eyelashes and a perfectly straight nose. It's the first time in a long while that her nose is straight and not broken, she says, and I can see evidence of that from the photographs that hang on the walls.

Sonika is India's first woman wrestler.[93] She retired recently, got married, moved to the US and became a mother.

'It's been a long time since I have been on a mat,' she says. 'It seems so far away. I live such a peaceful, calm life now—wrestling seems like it happened a lifetime ago!'

A lifetime packed into ten short years of turmoil and rebellion.

Sonika was born in a hospital near the akhada in 1983, the second child of Chandgi Ram's second wife, and grew up at the vyayamshala.

Here, she discovered an early love for nature, and spent her days helping her father with his gardening, catching frogs by the bank, watching spiders spin webs, and bringing in stray dogs and cats to adopt. Chandgi Ram had a large family, and was entirely without regard for social conventions. He had three wives, even though polygamy was, and is, illegal in India. When he married for the third time, a police case was filed against him and he lost his post as a sports administrator. He wrangled out of stricter legal action by claiming that he was 'looking after' the wives and children of his brothers after their deaths as was the custom in their area, and that the third wife was actually his only wife.

Chandgi Ram had a daughter and a son from his first wife, and put the son, Jagdish Kaliraman, straight into wrestling.

'When I could crawl, I was crawling in the akhada,' Jagdish, now a police officer, says.

He had three daughters with his middle wife, and all three are built to be athletes—Deepika, a year older to Sonika, also called Lucky; and Monika, or 'Chhoti', a year younger than Sonika.

Chandgi Ram and his youngest wife had a son and a daughter too.

The family lived together—a big, boisterous and freewheeling life—bound together by the three wives, and a father who seemed never to leave the wrestling arena.

'Ever since I can remember,' Sonika says, 'it was pahalwani, pahalwani, pahalwani—papa on the mat, lots of noise, lots of thudding and slamming and screaming and shouting...'

The girls were not allowed near the akhada though. 'Too many sweaty, muscular men in langots...not a fit sight for young girls,' Sonika says.

In the early 1980s, Chandgi Ram's vyayamshala was rivalled only by Guru Hanuman's school in popularity. A decade earlier, Chandgi Ram was second to none as a competitive wrestler. A tall, long-limbed man packing in 100 kilos of pure muscle, Chandgi Ram was a handsome man, with a wide, lopsided smile that was positively Bogart-ish. He was sought after and offered quintessentially masculine roles in Hindi films—of Tarzan in a movie called *Tarzan 303* (thus continuing the long global legacy of Olympians playing Tarzan), and of the mythical eponymous hero in *Veer Ghatotkach*.

Jagdish offers an elegant critique of *Tarzan 303*, which he remembers going to see in a hall with the rest of the family, as well as students from the akhada, when it released.

'Now what's Tarzan like,' Jagdish asks rhetorically. 'He doesn't talk, because he was raised by wild animals, and he has a great physique because he lives in the jungle and swings from tree to tree. It was perfect for father who had no experience in acting, and was shy in front of the camera. He didn't have to speak, he had to do amazing physical stunts. And he looked really good!'

This foray into films was a short-lived experiment, something to do after Chandgi Ram retired from a long and distinguished career in wrestling in which he won, much like Satpal, every big championship in India.

In 1968, when he beat Indore's Meheruddin pahalwan in Delhi to win his first Rustom-e-Hind, he was widely reputed to be the first Hindu wrestler to have won the title (though no official records of this exist). Meheruddin had, in fact, beaten Chandgi Ram in the same competition a year earlier. Soon after Chandgi

Ram's triumph, he was called to Indore for a felicitation parade, and a communal riot broke out at the parade. The effects of that are still felt in Indore: Hindu–Muslim wrestling matches remain banned in the city.

Chandgi Ram also won the 1970 Asian Games heavyweight title and went to the 1972 Olympics. By then he was thirty-five, and approaching the end of his career. Soon after, he retired from wrestling, dabbled in movies, decided it was not for him, and opened his akhada.

Like in his wrestling days, Chandgi Ram soon acquired the reputation of being an excellent coach—so far, so predictable.

In 1997, twenty-two years after he started his school, Chandgi Ram's life took an abruptly stormy turn, precipitated by an announcement that bypassed most of the wrestling community in India. Women's wrestling was to be added to the Olympic programme—starting from the 2004 Games in Athens.

'I remember that I was playing with a tap in the courtyard, spraying water on the plants,' says Sonika. 'And papa came back home looking all excited and the first thing he said was "They've put women's wrestling in the Olympics! Who wants to be a wrestler?" And he was looking straight at me.'

Sonika was flummoxed. She had been a laughing stock in school for her antics on the sporting ground. She was tall and well built for her age, giving the appearance of being sporty, but in fact she was particularly uncoordinated. Others were always tickled by this contradiction.

'I was the joker of the pack,' she says. 'I was a…what do you call those funny animals? Sloths! I was a sloth—slow, shuffling, baby fat—so when papa said this, I was like, yes! I want to be a wrestler!'

Deepika, a year older than Sonika, was less enthusiastic when Changdi Ram made her the same offer. So, one day, Chandgi Ram bundled the two sisters into an autorickshaw and took them to a government-run sports training centre, where a small team of women wrestlers from Russia had come for an exhibition.

'It was the weirdest thing—girls wrestling,' Deepika says. 'It was funny, scary, liberating, elating, all at the same time. We laughed at the "costumes"—we had never seen girls dressed in shiny body-hugging clothes. Look at those muscles! Those thighs!

'As we were taking it all in, one of the girls picked up another over her hip and slammed her down on the mat—*phatak*!' Deepika slaps her thigh with the hollow of her palm. 'And that sound… it was like a dazzling light switched on in my head. I had an incredible urge to slam someone on to a mat.'

The two sisters, so far barred from being near the akhada, were now practising moves on it, along with their brother Jagdish and the other men.

'How life changed,' Sonika says. 'We forgot everything but wrestling. Papa seemed to be bursting with a new kind of energy. I forgot my animals, my friends. There was time for nothing but wrestling. I forgot what Diwali meant. For the next ten years, there was not a single festival that we were home for. We were out fighting, going from village to village, from dangal to dangal.

'I remember that there was a black cow in my house I was very attached to and she was pregnant, and I had to leave for a dangal. I remember my mom telling me about the birth of the baby, and I was so sad that I couldn't be there and I cried over the phone. So it was like that. Many things would happen at home, life would go on, and all that news I would get over the phone from my mother.'

The band of wrestlers travelled with their home on their backs—clothes, utensils, stoves, fuel, all bundled into army holdalls. They practised in trains and train stations and farmlands.

No dangals were open for women then, so Chandgi Ram took Sonika and Deepika of his own accord, staging exhibition matches between the two in far-flung villages, as Jagdish battled in the main competition.

The Master had begun his campaign.

'At six in the morning, Papa would sit in front of the phone and start calling coaches and wrestlers all over India,' Deepika says. 'He would say, "Look, the boys of my akhada will only come to your dangal if you allow a girl's bout as well—just a couple of exhibition matches." He had a lot of patience and a lot of drive. He would call, write letters and meet people all day with just this agenda: start getting women into wrestling.'

Dangal organizers were not happy about this. Some refused straight away, others hesitated because of Chandgi Ram's stature as a wrestler and coach, yet others had long associations with him and could not refuse out of courtesy. Nowhere were they made to feel welcome.

'We were always fending for ourselves, which is why we carried all the necessities with us,' Deepika says. 'Once in 1999, we were in a village in Uttar Pradesh, and were received in a small house on a farm by the organizers. We thought, this is not bad—a room with electricity, a toilet, a kitchen and fans—it's got everything! But then they told us, okay, wash up here, and then you can go to your room downstairs. We thought, downstairs? There is no room downstairs…only a garage with a tractor!'

What the organizers meant was the gap under the staircase. They had put a bed there, and a naked bulb hung over it for light.

'Papa saw all that calmly, and then he told us, you girls must be stiff after the journey, why don't you go for a long run,' Deepika says.

When they came back two hours later, Chandgi Ram had taken over a small, empty granary in the middle of the farm, got it cleaned, got a generator and hooked it up to an electric line, and put lights and fans in the room. Because the path from the main house to the granary was unlit, he had also stuck two poles there and hung light bulbs on them.

'There were charpoys inside the room, with mosquito nets, and the kitchen had been set up,' Deepika says. 'We spent three nights in that room, and though millions of tiny insects would come into the room and take over everything at night, it was the best time of our lives. We used to go and fight, and then come back into the insect-filled room and talk deep into the night hidden under our mosquito nets.'

The backlash was severe.

'No self-respecting woman should go to watch a dangal,' Sushil's mother says. She too has never seen her son fight in one. 'This was the thought. It is still what people think.'

Often, at these village exhibition matches, Sonika and Deepika would be at the receiving end of obscene commentary.

'People would throng to see them because they thought they will get some freak value from it, some sort of fantasy, watching two women in tight clothes tear each other's hair out,' Jagdish says. 'They were disappointed that they fought like real wrestlers, with technique and power and grace.'

At first, many in the wrestling community thought that Chandgi Ram's experiment with his daughters, like his experiment with films, would be short-lived. When they realized that it was not to be so, the counter-campaign heated up.

'One time in 2000, we had gone to a dangal in a village in Palwal,' Sonika says. 'It was a clearing in the middle of a sugar cane farm. The moment Sonika and I got on to the pit, stones started flying at us, and people were shouting obscenities and surging towards the pit, some brandishing sticks.'

'Papa rushed at us,' Deepika says, slapping her thigh hard with the palm of her hand. 'We ran. Papa bundled us into the car, and we drove off with people chasing.'

For the next few months, Chandgi Ram became obsessed with Palwal. He financed dangals in the surrounding area himself, and took his daughters to fight there.

'By the end of it, the very mention of Palwal made me sick,' Sonika says. 'I must have fought thirty or forty dangals in that place in two to three months.'

Guru Hanuman, who claimed to have been celibate till his death at the age of ninety-nine, was one of the main dissenters, and used his considerable influence on the wrestling circuit to stop women from wrestling.

Despite its modern set-up and Olympic success, Satpal's akhada is still all-male, even though all the other sports training units at the stadium are unisex. Guru Hanuman's decaying akhada, which has lost much of its earlier glory, is resolutely all-male too.

The campaign against women in wrestling reached Chandgi Ram's akhada. Some of the vyayamshala's own coaches and students rebelled. One day in 2000, they attacked the akhada.

'It was the worst thing I have ever seen,' Deepika says. 'Stones being thrown from everywhere, papa running, blood flowing down his head, mummy running, the electricity lines cut off. I was told to take all the kids and lock myself up in the inside room. People hammered on the doors. I could hear papa screaming "Deepika pahalwan, don't open the door!" I could see one of papa's coaches lying on the floor with his legs broken.

'Then the police came. Later, we were packed off to the village. All except papa, who remained here with five or six coaches and students who were on his side. Papa was heartbroken after this. They wanted to destroy the akhada, and take over the space. But papa was a lion.'

Perhaps Chandgi Ram knew always what it was to forge his own path through humiliation and defeat. He came from a small village called Sisai, far in the interiors of rural Haryana. He left his village in anger when he was eighteen, tired of being mistreated for being weak and thin. He never really spoke to anyone—family or friends—in any detail about this, except to say that his father too was mistreated in the same way; that they were always a sickly family, and people took advantage of that. So, soon after he finished schooling, Chandgi Ram left home. He worked as a teacher for a brief while in Rohtak (thus the epithet 'Master'), but was haunted by his own weakness. He began working out with a vengeance. He started travelling to Delhi on the weekends to seek out an old and very reputed wrestling coach called Chiranji Lal. Soon, he had quit everything to live in Chiranji Lal's akhada, determined, despite the late start, to become a wrestler.

Not everyone was unmoved by the determination with which Chandgi Ram stood his ground. The few people who remained loyal to him took the fight forward. Jagroop Rathi, one of the coaches at the vyayamshala, brought his daughter Neha to the akhada—she became an international medallist. A wrestling coach from Meerut, Jabbar Singh Sone, stayed at Chandgi Ram's akhada for a few months of training and went away transformed, beginning his own long battle to get women into the sport by starting a women's wrestling programme in a university in Meerut. Sone's student Alka Tomar became the first Indian woman to win a wrestling medal at the World Championships in 2006. Her sister, Anshu Tomar, became an international wrestler. Yet, in 2013, a village panchayat near Meerut banned its girls from wrestling, and Jabbar lost four students.

Deepika had to give up wrestling early in her career after a back injury, but now runs her own training school, for both boys and girls, in Delhi. Jagdish won the national championship and competed at the Olympics. Sonika too won a national championship, though she never qualified for the Olympics, and retired from wrestling in 2010.

18

Six Sisters

The distinction of being India's first woman wrestler to qualify for the Olympics belongs to Geeta Phogat, who competed at the 2012 London Games, two years after Chandgi Ram's death.

Geeta belongs to what is perhaps wrestling's most remarkable family. Her father, Mahavir Singh Phogat, came to Delhi from the village of Balali in Haryana to train under Chandgi Ram when he was just sixteen.

He has four daughters—each of them an international wrestler—and two adopted daughters after his brother was killed in a land dispute. They too are international wrestlers. And he managed all this not from a city, but from his own village.

Balali is deep country. It is still untouched by Haryana's hurried pace of urbanization, and sits hidden in the middle of wheat fields and guava and citrus groves. In the afternoon, you can walk around Balali's slim tracery of cobbled streets and meet not a single person.

Inside Mahavir's house—an elongated rectangle of flat white—there is a stirring of post-siesta activity. There is a gathering of village elders, all in white kurtas, who have lit the communal hookah and broken out the cards. Mahavir himself is on his charpoy, eyes still resolutely closed. His wife Daya has swung into action. The family's immense black buffaloes have been led out of the shed, their troughs filled with feed. Daya is laying out the buckets she will use for milking.

Mahavir opens his eyes abruptly, pulls out his phone and scolds someone at the other end: 'Where's your daughter? We start in five minutes. Tell her to run.'

He stands up and shuffles towards the house. It's not a house. It's a large wrestling hall: a double-sized mat on one side, top-of-the-line weight machines in another, thick ropes dangling from the high ceiling, and a series of small windows overlooking lush farmland.

Mahavir's six girls are the first on the mat—Geeta, Babita, Ritu, Sangeeta, Vinesh and Priyanka—all dressed in dry-fit tees and training tights. Two more girls come running in. Then three boys. 'Warm up,' Mahavir barks, pointing to the mat.

That there are girls wrestling at all, in these rural settings, is in itself a miracle, let alone the quality of international success they have managed.[94]

Geeta is a gentle, soft-spoken woman with an aquiline nose and an easy smile. She is the only one of the six sisters with long hair, which she ties in a high ponytail during her bouts. The rest have identical short crops that barely cross the nape. As the eldest sister, Geeta has forged a remarkable path for the rest to follow—Commonwealth Games (CWG) gold in 2010 was followed by a bronze at the 2012 World Championship, a first for Indian women; then she qualified for the Olympics. The sisters are not far behind. Babita won silver at the 2010 CWG, and gold at the 2014 version, where Vinesh also won gold. Ritu has every major international medal at the junior level (including multiple World Championships), and is about to make her leap to the senior team.

Sangeeta and Priyanka have medals from junior Asian Championships.

What if all six of them land up in the same competition one day, and all of them finish with medals?

'Let that be the Olympics!' Babita is thrilled with the idea. It has occurred to her before.

'Well, perhaps not all six. Let's say three,' Geeta says. 'Now that's not fantasy—that can happen in Rio.'[95]

'Yes, and then papa will finally say—' Now Babita makes her voice heavy and manly: 'Fine, not bad. Now you can rest a little.'

The sisters laugh.

Despite Chandgi Ram's efforts, no village in India has a wrestling school where women are allowed, except here, in Balali. Even in the cities, the number of private akhadas that allow women can be counted on your fingers—Jabbar's centre in Meerut; Indore, where former Olympian Kripa Shankar Patel campaigns for akhadas to open their doors to women, and runs his own centre; Rohtak, where the University of Rohtak runs a popular training centre; former Olympian Prem Nath's akhada in Delhi; Deepika's school.[96]

Chandgi Ram's campaign has spread, more than a decade later, and consolidated in these little pockets of resistance.

'The general atmosphere is still strongly against women in wrestling,' says Kripa Shankar, who was a former coach with the national women's team.

His family, who have been in wrestling for generations, were Chandgi Ram's chief patron when he opened his vyayamshala.

'We have a very small talent pool to pick from,' Kripa Shankar says. 'Maharashtra, which produces hundreds of male wrestlers, has nothing for women. Madhya Pradesh has very little, Jabbar Singh is alone in Uttar Pradesh. Only Haryana is really trying. Women's wrestling is still new to the world, and we could have stepped ahead, taken the lead and dominated it for years. But no, we are stuck being backwards, judgemental and idiotic.'

Not Mahavir, not in Balali.

'Masterji opened my eyes,' Mahavir says. 'He used to tell me, "What you are doing for your girls, you will see one day that it will bring you great happiness. So keep doing it, don't be scared, face your difficulties like you face opponents, and be deaf to the criticism."'

Geeta remembers that morning when her father woke her and Babita up at five one morning, and said, 'I want to see how well you two run.'

She was ten then, Babita eight, and they were both a bit puzzled.

'It was fun though,' Geeta says. 'We ran laughing through the fields when everyone else was asleep, it felt like a secret game.'

A week of that, and Mahavir in the meantime had finished making a level square of soft earth next to his house, and had raised a tin roof over it. The akhada was ready.

'People said, Mahavir has lost his mind,' he says. 'They said, he is destroying the village, he has no shame, and he is making an exhibit out of his own girls.'

But there was only so much the villagers could do to oppose this unprecedented development—Mahavir was the sarpanch, and the family had both influence and land.

'So we were spared the worst of it,' Daya says. 'They could not come up to me and say these things to my face. But I was told many times, "Your daughters will become like boys, their faces will get messed up, they won't be able to bear children, their ears will get mangled, and who will marry them?" I felt the stress of that. But I felt angry that there was so much opposition to the girls doing anything different, so I wanted to see the fight through the end.'

Geeta and Babita were exposed to some of this harassment; people in the village stopped talking to them. They would not even make eye contact with the sisters.

'After a few months, there were a couple of boys also at the akhada, and papa started training us together. We would fight the boys, and wrestling's such an intimate sport,' Babita says. 'That was a step too far for most people in the village. There was constant trouble during that time.'

Despite the social boycott, the Phogat girls loved the life of the wrestler—the pain, the euphoria, the fighting, sleeping exhausted after a hard day's training, the liberating experience of wearing shorts and T-shirts, all the fuss over their diet.

'It was a great adventure,' Babita says, 'And what made it special was that we knew no other girls in our village or in any nearby village who were doing this!'

In 2010, when Geeta won India's first Commonwealth gold in women's wrestling, Balali went berserk. The celebrations lasted ten days. The word spread to nearby villages. So many girls started coming for training that Mahavir had to build a hostel for them. Thirty-six girls live there now. The girls in Haryana, Rajasthan and Punjab are big and strong, says Mahavir, and they will take women's wrestling very far.

'Just don't hide them at home,' he says. 'When I was growing up, girls did not go to school here. Now every single one in the village is working for a college degree. So, things are changing.'

Mahavir dreams of Olympic gold. He drills this into his girls.

'Give it another ten years,' Mahavir says. 'And people will forget that they ever resisted women in wrestling. Look, already, this year at the Commonwealth Games (2014), India won sixty-five medals; forty-nine of those were won by women.'

It is spreading, ever so slowly. Dangals in Haryana still don't have official competitions for women, but nearly all of them hold exhibition matches, sometimes allowing the girls to fight boys as well.

I remember a slow Sunday morning at Mehr Singh's akhada. Everyone had slept late. There was an easy lightness to the day, and the mood was gently joyous, almost festive. The wrestling halls with their mats were empty, but some of the pahalwans were getting a light workout by digging, tilling and flattening out the earthen wrestling pit.

A senior wrestler had brought his two young daughters to the akhada. One was eight, the other a year younger, and the two of them tumbled on the tilled earthen pit, with their father yelling out instructions with a big smile on his face. Wrestlers crowded around the pit, divided into neat little camps—each side had picked a girl to support and instruct. The young girls were already technically adept, and it was both amusing and thrilling to see the two tiny figures so seriously engaged in combat, while their father shouted out things like 'get your elbow on top of her neck and push down hard' or 'jam your knee into her stomach, c'mon, you can do it, bring your left leg in, no left, and jam the knee into her stomach. Good, now push-up with the knee. Yes!'

The girls showed no signs of tiring, their pretty pink and white dresses covered in dirt.

Chandgi Ram would have thrilled at the sight.

SECTION III

THE ANNALS OF WRESTLING

19

THE GOLDEN AGE

If Sushil Kumar revived kushti in India, it was because the sport had been forgotten. It was once the people's sport, the sport of kings, the sport of champions, a military sport, a loving sport that broke the artificial barriers between man and man. Then it was hit by a series of body blows.

First, the military labour market was demolished by the British by the 1850s because they wanted a more centralized control of the armed forces, a monopoly over violence for the state. The onus of developing martial skills shifted from the individual or the community to the state.

The British were keen on sports, but they wanted to introduce their own varieties of it. They brought boxing, football, hockey, gymnastics and cricket.

To effectively control India as a unified nation state, the colonial administrators had to pull the rug from under the feet of the Mughals, and the various rajas, maharajas and sultans of India. Kushti began to lose its chief patrons.

Independent India, struggling with extreme poverty, deep social inequality and widespread illiteracy, had little time for sports. The government-controlled sports bodies were poor, corrupt and ineffective. When a sport did emerge as India's own, widely loved and widely followed by people from all walks of life and independent of government funding, it was not wrestling, but cricket.

But just before it went into hiding, wrestling enjoyed one brief moment in the sun. A great golden age. The age of Gama.

The Great Gama is central to the oral history of Indian wrestling, and a sketch of his life, with the structure and brevity of a fairy tale, is known across India.

The details of Gama's life that can be found in these oral tellings is pithily consistent: his father died when he was young, but he impressed the maharaja of Patiala in a physical contest for which the biggest names in wrestling from across India had gathered. They were asked to do baithaks and Gama, around ten years old then, outlasted everyone. A little child, bobbing up and down tirelessly even as the champions of the land fell away one by one in exhaustion. The maharaja himself had to intervene to stop Gama, who had gone into a baithak-induced trance, the story goes. At this point, the maharaja of Datia, who was also present at the competition, decided to adopt Gama for his royal akhada. Gama developed as a wrestler under the careful and affluent patronage of the court. By the time he was in his twenties, he began to acquire a reputation of being unbeatable. Soon he was winning every major competition in the country. Yet he remained elusive and solitary; a humble man so dedicated to his art that he had time for nothing else. And then, in 1910, no one can tell for sure why, but either the maharaja of Patiala, or the maharaja of Datia, or the great Congress leader Motilal Nehru sponsored him to go to London as a challenger for the world championship of wrestling. The organizers of this competition did not think it was appropriate for a dark-skinned man to fight against the racially superior whites, so they did not allow Gama to wrestle.

Gama's backers, incensed by this slight, threw an open challenge: any wrestler who can beat Gama on an appointed day will get a fortune. Many wrestlers came, and Gama beat them all—ten, eleven, twelve, thirteen…twenty of them—one after another, no rest in between. He did not need it, none of the wrestlers could stand against him for more than two minutes. The people of London and the press then raised some serious noise: let Gama enter the world championship. So he did.

He fought the world champion, and had him on the defensive within minutes. So much so that the world champion, realizing he was entirely out of his depth, lay prone on the mat, a cowardly move, employed with the sole purpose of not allowing Gama to lay him flat on his back. Two hours passed. The world champion remained in this shameless position. Gama attacked relentlessly. Finally, the fight was called off, declared a draw according to the rules of the day, and a second meeting between the two were arranged a week later. By then the world champion had had enough. Refusing to be humiliated on the mat, he ran away. Gama was declared the new world champion.

Undefeated Gama! Not just poor little Rustom-e-Hind, the champion of a vanquished race in a starved, crude country, but Rustom-e-Zamana—champion of the whole wide world.

In India, the news swept people up in a triumphant storm. It became a matter of the deepest pride: an enslaved nation standing up against their overlords and beating them.

Thousands turned up to receive the Great Gama at the port in Bombay. The maharaja of Patiala gave him a ceremonious welcome usually reserved for royalty. He was flooded with gifts—land, jewels, money, clothes, livestock—and he rode an elephant around town, sitting next to the maharaja, while hundreds of people showered them with flowers. Gama was a hero, Gama was the pride of the great nationalist leaders, from Nehru to Gandhi to Muhammad Ali Jinnah.

He continued wrestling in India, but was never beaten. When India was partitioned, he moved to Pakistan, where he became a guru, a khalifa.

He died unconquered.

20

THE EFFEMINATE INDIAN

Where can Gama and his legacy be found beyond wrestlers' tales?

In Datia, the princely state the pahalwan grew up in, there is nothing to remember him by. His akhada is long gone, turned to dust, just like the royal buildings of Datia are turning to dust. In Patiala, where he was based during his glory days after that fateful trip to London, nothing is left except for a hasli—a doughnut-shaped stone worn around the neck while doing squats—that supposedly belonged to him. The hasli lies in a dark corner in a dark 'museum', a forgotten room with a completely arbitrary collection of sporting memorabilia, at the National Institute of Sports, which is housed in the maharaja of Patiala's palace.

Miraculously, an akhada still operates where Gama's wrestling school used to be. The new school is run by one of Punjab's most reputed wrestlers, Sukhchain Singh Cheema. Sukhchain's father, Kesar, was given the reins of the akhada by the maharaja himself a few years after Gama left for Pakistan. Cheema lives in a sprawling compound right across the street from the main entrance to the National Institute of Sports in what used to be Gama's land.

When I asked Cheema for any material remains of Gama—letters, clothes, wrestling equipment or medals, anything at all—he said there were none.

'When a man decides to leave his country, his land, he takes everything he can,' Cheema said.

I wished I could trace Gama's legacy to Pakistan, but that was not to be. Instead, I picked up the paper trail.

The core of Gama's gilded myth is that fateful trip to England. To understand just why Gama became, and continues to be, wrestling divinity in India, we have to begin a little before his time.

We have to begin with the rise of the East India Company (EIC). By the early years of the nineteenth century, the EIC had grown, with terrifying pace and purpose, from a trading business to the rulers of large swathes of India. Not only did it hold trade monopoly over India, it also had the right to tax Indian citizens, had control over 2,43,000 square kilometres of land, had a standing army of over 2,00,000 men, and issued its own currency.

The British government had been uncomfortable with the EIC running a continent since at least the middle of the 1700s. The nawab of Bengal had surrendered his dominions to the Company after losing the Battle of Plassey in 1757. When a famine wiped out a third of the population of Bengal and struck a blow to its business in 1770, the EIC had to beg the British government to bail them out, opening the way to increasing government control. The Company was finally dissolved in 1873, and the British government directly ruled India.

The early forays of the EIC, despite the many battles it fought, was also marked by a level of equality between the British and the citizens of the country they were trying to take over. Large numbers of Company men 'went native', adopting the customs, clothes and habits of the Indian states they lived in. Eventually, though, with the aggressive military, trade and political expansion of the EIC, a very different relationship between the colonizers and the colonized evolved.

As far into the history of the EIC as 1825, the British in India were still fascinated by the country and its people.

Captain Godfrey Charles Mundy, aide-de-camp to the

commander-in-chief of the British forces in India in 1825, described a dangal in glowing terms:

'The Commander-in-chief having expressed a wish to witness the athletic and gladiatorial performances of the seapoys of the 39th infantry, sixteen of the most skilled in these sciences were drawn from the ranks, and in the cool of the evening repaired to Mr Stockwell's garden.'[97]

A soft spot of earth was selected for the fight, and the English were provided chairs under the shade of trees.

'The games were opened by the sword-players, who, as well as the wrestlers, were entirely naked, with the exception of a cloth bound tightly around their waist and reaching a few inches down the thighs. Such perfect models of the animal man I never beheld!'

Mundy liked the swordsmen's display, but found the wrestlers 'infinitely more interesting'.

'On meeting, they placed their heads firmly together, like butting rams, seized each other's wrist with one hand, whilst the other was twined round the back of the adversary's neck. In Indian wrestling a fair fall consists in being thrown flat on the back, a consummation which, owing to the extreme agility and suppleness of the wrestlers, is seldom accomplished. A front or side fall is not accounted disgraceful; on the contrary, it is common for the spent combatant to throw himself flat upon his face to gain breath; in which position, with outspread arms and legs, he defies the utmost attempts of his adversary to turn him, like a turtle, upon his back.'

Mundy was most taken by a young boy of twenty-two, who defeated six opponents in a row, four of whom were heavier than him. Mundy does not provide us with a name for this champion, but we do know that he had a 'remarkably handsome and classical countenance, with a figure of perfect symmetry'.

'And as he sprang into the circus looking sternly and confidently round for his first antagonist, I would not have wished for a better representation of a youthful Roman athlete.'

Mundy then described the wrestlers' body: 'I was much struck by the similarity of make in the several seapoys who contended—the chief peculiarities in their form being the immense expansion of the chest, breadth of shoulder, flatness and hollowness of back, and extreme smallness of waist.'

He concluded: 'These skillful seapoys seemed to me to understand the mechanical application of their strength better than any British wrestlers that I have seen. The legs were brought much more into play; and at the commencement of the bouts, when the combatants were fresh, the falls were dreadfully heavy. The young Roman, after a series of intricate combinations which I could not trace, twice threw an opponent heavier than himself quite over his head...'

Mundy may have written admiringly of the sepoys, but the official British view of the people they were colonizing was moving in quite a different direction. When Robert Orme, the historiographer to the EIC said back in the 1770s that Indians were 'the most effeminate inhabitant of the globe',[98] he was voicing an opinion that was still in its infancy among the British in India. But less than a century later, that thought had become firmly entrenched among the colonizers. The assimilation had given way to grim apartheid.

The EIC chaplain Reverend Midgeley John Jennings, a fervent missionary who had come to India in 1832 and had moved to Delhi in 1852, gave voice to the popular British view of the Mughals in his description of Delhi: 'Within its walls, the pride of life, the lust of the eye and all the lusts of the flesh have reigned and revelled to the full, and all the glories of the Kingdoms of this portion of the earth have passed from one wicked possessor to another.'[99]

Apart from the Mughals, Bengal too was characterized as a degenerate race without manly qualities; perhaps because it was the first area to fall to a British military campaign, and certainly because Calcutta became the administrative capital of the British. Other parts of India had their martial races—especially the north and west of the country, the cradle of the military labour market—but Bengal had no redemption.

In 1897, in a lavish book of hand-coloured photographs called *Typical Pictures of Indian Natives*, Frank Morris Coleman, the co-owner of the English daily *The Times of India*, wrote this description to accompany the photo of a Bengali man: 'The Bengali, or as he is more often termed, the Bengali Baboo, belongs to a class who are as little distinguished for courage as any race in the world. It is not uncommon indeed for them to expiate upon their own extreme cowardice, as if alluding to a special gift. They are consequently thought of by all the up-country tribesmen of the North-West, many of whom are soldiers born, and consequently do not take kindly to a people who are wanting both in physical strength and moral courage.'

The historian John Rosselli notes that the Bengali 'elite'—by which he means the 'upper, and in part self-made, sections of Hindu society', a group whose growth and evolution was triggered by their close association with British government services and the rapid expansion of Calcutta into a metropolis—made this degenerate stereotype their own.[100] If the British were convinced of the racial inferiority of the Bengalis, the Bengali Hindu elite, many of them products of a British education system, were no less convinced of it themselves.

The Bengali novelist Bankimchandra Chattopadhyay, in an essay published in 1874 called 'Bangalir Bahubal' (The Physical Valour of Bengalis), said simply: 'Bengalis never had any physical valour.'[101] We are not courageous, Bankimchandra wrote, because 'the physical is the father of the moral man', and Bengalis had no physical culture.

Many Bengali writers and thinkers offered many explanations for this lack of valour. Some were genetic, some environmental; some blamed the aping of British lifestyles, some the bookish bent of Bengalis, others the diet. 'But the most important explanation of Bengali "effeteness"', Rosselli writes, 'was historical and cultural. We may call it a myth of physical downfall.'

The nineteenth-century social reformer and early nationalist Rajnarayan Basu elucidated this idea in a lecture delivered in 1874 titled 'Ekal o Sekal' ('The present and the past'). Basu's lecture, published as a book the next year, extensively listed the reasons for the downfall of the Bengalis as a race, and the ways to overcome it. Heading that list was the body (followed by education, work, society, character, statehood and religion, in that order.) Like Bankimchandra, Basu too regarded the loss of physical valour as the foundation of this downfall.

'Firstly, bodily fitness and courage,' Basu wrote. 'With regards to this, a distinct erosion can be seen when compared to early times. If you ask anyone they will tell you, "My father or grandfather possessed great strength." When you compare people now to people then, there is really no strength left to speak of...'[102]

Basu circles in on an idea that became pervasive as an explanation for Bengali weakness: the dying of akhadas, a result of the rejection of traditional modes of living by the Bengali elite to align themselves with British ideas and lifestyles.

'Earlier, each village had a kushtir adda (wrestling gymnasium) and everyone from young men to the old practised kushti. Even in winter, at four in the morning when it is pitch-dark, the old and the young, gentlemen all, would go to these wrestling gymnasiums and start training. The sound of these men slapping their arms and legs in readiness would serve as a wake-up call for the entire neighbourhood.'[103]

As Rosselli points out, locating this idea of weakness in a myth of physical downfall, and invoking a recent age when gymnasiums were an integral part of daily life were a call to action: we had it before, we just have to find it again.

This idea of regaining a lost physical valour became an obsession among the Bengali Hindu elite. It was a powerful idea, and it dovetailed perfectly with the first stirrings of nationalism, and with other social, cultural and religious reform movements. It led to a proliferation of physical clubs and circus strongman acts, inspired the first hot-air balloon flight by an Indian, led to ever-increasing participation of Bengalis in British-introduced sports such as boxing, football and cricket, as well as a resurgence in indigenous physical culture like wrestling and lathi-khela (stick-play), and finally, almost half a century later, exploded into armed insurrection against the British.[104]

In its early years in Calcutta, this call to action found its most popular expression in the 'Hindu Mela', a festival organized by Basu, members of the great Tagore family and the untiring activist Nabagopal Mitra, whose obsession with all things 'national'—in his stormy career he had founded a National School, a National Gymnasium, a *National Paper*, a National Circus and a National Theatre—earned him the delightful sobriquet 'National Mitra'.

The first Hindu Mela was organised on 12 April 1867, in the 'garden house' of the late Raja Narsingh Chunder Roy in the suburbs of Calcutta. At the festival, the secretary of the Hindu Mela, Ganendranath Tagore, presented a six-point action plan for subsequent editions. Point six was: 'Those who are experts in Mallavidya (wrestling) and are famous for it, they will be called to attend each Mela and honoured for their achievements, and through this we will also promote exercise training among our own people.'[105]

For each of the six points (Hindu religion, social development, indigenous arts, crafts and skills, music and physical culture), a list of prominent people who would lead the movement was drawn up. For physical culture, the most important name on that list was of a man called Ambikacharan Goho. Ambu Babu, as he was popularly known, became the shining light of the Bengali physical movement.

Wrestling was a problematic sport for the Bengali elite: it was indigenous, which was good, but it was also disreputable, a sport practised by people of the lower classes, by the peasants and the poor.

In affluent Bengali homes, wrestlers worked as guards—a

lowly occupation. The young men of these families were allowed to learn exercises and wrestling from them, but they were not expected to become wrestlers themselves.

Rabindranath Tagore wrote: 'I used to get out of bed when it was still dark, get ready for kushti, while cold shivers ran down my body. There was a famous pahalwan in town, Kana pahalwan, he used to train us.'[106]

The makeshift akhada was right next to the courtyard of the Tagore house, on fallow land which used to be a grain storage before. The ground was dug up, and mixed with mustard oil.

'There, learning the holds of wrestling was, to us, child's play,' Rabindranath wrote. 'After rolling around in the mud for a while, I would put on some clothes and leave.'

This is as far as wrestling went in rich Bengali families. Anything more than a passing interest would have been disastrous for any young man. As for actually competing, or fighting for a purse, it would have led to immediate and full severance from the family. Wrestling was subaltern.

'Many of them who complained of Bengali effeteness clearly had in mind English-educated, mainly high-caste Hindus,' writes Rosselli.

This is precisely what made Ambu Babu so unique, and so important to the Hindu Mela and the general physical movement: He was a 'gentleman wrestler', no less. A high-caste Hindu.

Ambu Babu traced his ancestry to the sixteenth-century Jashohar[107] king Pratapaditya Guha Ray. Brajaram Guha, a scion of the family, moved to Calcutta in the late eighteenth century and joined the British in business.[108] He was a facilitator—a mutsuddi—supplying and managing manpower, transportation, the sourcing of materials and goods, acquiring land and overseeing construction projects; basically everything that was needed for British businesses to establish themselves and run in Calcutta. Brajaram was phenomenally successful in this, and in his short life (he died at thirty-seven), he had amassed great fortune and bought large spreads of land. The British pronounced Guha as 'Goho', and Brajaram adopted this slightly altered surname. Brajaram was the father of Ambu Babu's grandfather.

The story goes that in 1857, the year of the Sepoy Mutiny, Brajaram's son Shibcharan had taken his grandson Ambu to Srirampur, a town close to Calcutta, on a work trip. The British had started running train services in Bengal in 1854, and while returning from the trip, Shibcharan and Ambu reached Srirampur station only to see the train to Calcutta already pulling away. Shibcharan had given up, but Ambu had other ideas. Before he could protest, Ambu picked up his grandfather in one arm and raced down the platform, jumping up on the slowly moving train. By then, Ambu had already shown a keen interest in wrestling, and was generally thought to be spending too much time in the company of the family's 'north Indian' wrestlers and guards. Impressed by his strength and courage, Shibcharan promised his grandson that he would fully endorse and support Ambu's interest in wrestling. Soon after returning to Calcutta, Shibcharan commissioned a sculptor in the northern town of Mathura to make a large idol of Hanuman. He then had the idol transported to Calcutta and installed at the family's large mansion at 65, Masjidbari Street. A famous wrestling guru from Mathura was hired as Ambu's personal instructor. A cattle shed was set up next to the house with forty cows and thirty goats to provide the necessary diet.

Soon, the akhada began to attract more students, and more gurus were brought in. By the time Ambu turned eighteen, he was already a well-known pahalwan, though he was still not allowed to compete because of his family's social standing. In wrestling circles, Ambu became known as 'Raja Babu' because of his propensity to spend on the sport. In 1888, we have news of a grand dangal organized by Ambu Babu at the Masjidbari akhada. Among the wrestlers competing was a nineteen-year-old Karim Baksh—the Great Gama's brother. The dangal was won by the pre-eminent wrestler of the time, Gulam pahalwan.

Though he did not compete, Ambu did one unprecedented thing—he became a guru at his own akhada. This made him an icon among his peers, and high-society families could more easily send their children to his school. The list of students at Masjidbari has an extraordinary number of the who's who of Bengal society of the time, and many who would later become great leaders: Vivekananda is perhaps the most glittering example, but there was also Major Phanindra Krishna Gupta, a muscular doctor who served in the Army Medical Corps during the Second World War and was involved heavily with the physical culture movement in the first decades of the twentieth century.

From the very first Hindu Mela, Ambu Babu was a regular fixture, giving lectures about the benefits of kushti, and taking part in demonstrations along with others from his akhada.

In 1868, after the second edition of the Mela, 'National' Mitra could proudly proclaim: 'In the Mela, indigenous wrestlers displayed their skills. The skills and techniques demonstrated were created entirely by Indians, and in this regard we have no debts to anyone.'[109]

Ambu Babu had many children—and though some of them died young, or at birth, eight of them survived. Of them, Khetracharan and Ramcharan became wrestlers. Ramcharan did not have much success, but Khetracharan rivalled his father in his popularity as a wrestler and a guru. Around 1900, after a dispute with his father, Khetracharan left their Masjidbari house and akhada and established one of his own.

By this time, wrestling had become a matter of pride: an indigenous somatic pursuit that stood against the British stereotype of the weakness of Indians.

21

THE MAKING OF GOBAR GOHO

Wrestling and royalty were entwined for centuries, the body of the wrestler representing the symbolic might of a king.[110]

As princely states began to lose real power in the colonial era, the relationship between the wrestler and his king became perversely important. The maharajas of Patiala, Jammu, Datia, Indore, Baroda, Kolhapur and Jodhpur obsessively patronized wrestlers, organizing grand competitions between them and poaching the best athletes from each other.

Nationalistic leaders also picked up on this. Motilal Nehru, the patriarch of the Nehru–Gandhi family and two-time president of the Indian National Congress, took the pre-eminent wrestler of the time, Gulam, to the Great Exposition in Paris in 1899.[111]

Here, a match was made with the Turkish wrestler Kurtdereli Mehmet Pehlivan, or Cour-Derelli as he was known in France.

There is a detailed report of the match in Edmond Desbonnet's 1910 book *Les Rois de la Lutte*, 'The Kings of Wrestling'. Desbonnet saw the match, held at the hippodrome at Boulevard de Clichy, from a box at floor level.

'No detail of the bout escaped us,' he wrote.[112] 'From the beginning of the bout Gulam demonstrated a crushing superiority over the Turk Cour-Derelli. As soon as the whistle signalled that the two contestants could come to grips, the Hindu, agile and swift, sprang on his adversary and threw him with a marvellous "flying mare (tour de bras)". Both of his shoulders touched the mat but, as this match brought into play big financial interests, after interminable discussions, the throw was not admitted and the bout recommenced.

'Several times the Hindu used his terrible arm roll and each time Cour-Derelli rolled on his two shoulders, but got up at once. Finally, realising that his opponent was too strong, the Turk decided to crouch down on the mat, and not budge from that position for an hour and a half… Finally, the only recourse was to the points system, and, to avoid harming those interests of which we spoke above, the bets were called off. It was declared that Cour-Derelli had not been thrown, Gulam was proclaimed the winner, but all bets were reimbursed.'

Desbonnet arrived at the conclusion that 'no current wrestler could stand five minutes against Gulam in fair wrestling, that is to say, without grovelling on the mat, a system of defence which should be banned as anti-sporting'.

Ten years later, the 'world champion' wrestler who fought Gama was to adopt this exact same system of defence, but more on that later.

From Paris, Gulam travelled to Calcutta, where he was received with some fanfare. He met both Ambu Babu and Khetracharan, and the latter proposed the holding of a grand wrestling demonstration with him. Gulam agreed, and Khetracharan fixed a date and a venue and printed posters for the show. A few weeks before the exhibition, Gulam was hit by that scourge of the Gangetic plains, cholera. He died within a few days, and was buried in Calcutta.[113]

Khetrababu's invitation to Gulam was no doubt meant to inspire his students. Like Ambu Babu, Khetracharan had his own roster of extraordinary wrestlers-in-training: among them were Jatindranath Mukhopadhyay, later to become 'Bagha Jatin', one of the most dynamic leaders of the armed guerrilla warfare against the British, and Gobar Goho, Ramcharan's son.

Gobar Goho was born Jatindracharan Goho on 13 March 1892, and was a lazy and overweight child. Ambu Babu gave him the loving moniker 'Gobar'—cow dung.

'He sits around like a heap of cow dung,' Ambu Babu would say.

Gobar grew up in an atmosphere that was as partial to wrestling as it was to music—the Gohos were all patrons of music, and both Ambu Babu and Khetracharan were known to hold regular soirees in their house, with some of the best musicians of the day in performance.

Until the age of eight, Gobar had shown no interest in wrestling. Then, in 1901, Ambu Babu died. This shook up Khetracharan: there was a crisis brewing—will the Goho family's engagement with wrestling end with him? None of Ambu Babu's other sons had continued with the sport, and Khetracharan's own sons were still babies. His attention turned to Gobar. The overweight boy was being picked on at school. His mother too was worried about his health. Khetracharan met with no resistance when he decided that Gobar must be trained in wrestling.

Gobar proved to be a natural. By the time he was fifteen, three or four years after he started wrestling, Gobar had become a proper pahalwan. Khetracharan hired a well-known guru from Amritsar, Rehman,[114] as Gobar's personal trainer. Then, in 1909, Khetracharan died. The then seventeen-year-old Gobar was beginning to feel stifled by the social restrictions that stopped him from being a competitive wrestler. He wanted, more than anything else, to be a pahalwan—not just a gentleman hobbyist.

It was not just wrestling that was seen as a disreputable and low-class activity, but any kind of sport. Perhaps the reason for this is partly economic—making money in sports has been, and continues to be, a very unsure proposition.

Gobar had other problems to contend with as well. In the early years of the twentieth century, when he was trying to make his mark as a wrestler, the physical culture movement in Bengal had undergone a massive shift in trajectory. Wrestling schools were being seen not just as places to build an indigenous martial ideal, but as training bases for armed militants against British rule. This made it attractive to some, but repugnant to many.

As far back as 1876, Bipin Chandra Pal had founded a 'secret society', not just to train the body, but also to teach people the handling of weapons and to propagate the idea of self-government. The Hindu Mela, and the kind of physical reform it advocated, had already lost steam by the early 1870s. The political climate in Bengal had changed by the 1890s to one of outright opposition to British rule and apartheid. The Swadeshi agitation was taking shape. The mood was militant. In 1905, with the partition of Bengal, the dam burst, and anti-British demonstrations and armed attacks spread through the country.

The new focal point of the physical movement in Bengal were the Anushilan Samitis. Taking off from Bankimchandra's idea of Anushilan—the full development of all faculties, physical and mental—and modelled around Bipin Chandra Pal's secret society, these were an underground network of armed revolutionaries operating under the guise of wrestling akhadas and gymnasiums.[115]

Many of the early adherents of the physical movement, men who had trained in wrestling under Ambu Babu or Khetracharan, became the leaders of this rebellion.

The mood of the time was summed up perfectly by the fiery Sarala Debi, a niece of Rabindranath who tirelessly spread the idea of militant nationalist physical culture, and established an akhada in her own mansion in Calcutta. Sarala Debi had been exposed to nationalist ideals from her early years. In her autobiography, *Jibaner Jharapata*, she writes of a conversation she had as a teenager with a family friend, a Cambridge-educated assistant magistrate called Loken Palit:

'One day, he told me, "I was so convinced that there is no difference between me and my English and Scot classmates—yet, when I heard them singing, '*Rule Britannia! Britannia rules the waves! Britons never shall be slaves,*' that day I felt it to my deepest core—how far removed I am from them, how different.'"[116]

As the physical culture movement gained momentum and anti-British sentiments ran high, Sarala Debi wrote bolder calls to arms: 'Learn to welcome death, don't go to it helplessly. Cross the oceans, go to the desert, climb the highest peak...man's greatest gift is a strong and healthy body. For this, Bengalis must give themselves up to building their bodies.'

'A punch for a punch', she wrote. 'On trains or steamers, on the streets, wherever you are, if a white soldier or civilian insults you, or your wife, niece, or daughter, don't be crestfallen, don't go to a court of law to complain; settle it then and there with your fist, and then write to me about the incident.'[117]

Sarala Debi held festivals to foment her ideas of physical valour and violent dissent. When asked to speak at a literary meet in Calcutta by a friend, she demanded that he go and 'comb through the city to unearth Bengali boys who know wrestling, swordplay, boxing, stick-fighting. Let them put on demonstrations.'[118]

Her friend agreed. Swordsmen, boxers and stick-fighters were sought out. For wrestling, they brought 'the boys from the Guha family of Masjidbari'.[119]

Appropriated for other symbolic needs, wrestling itself was lost. In this fevered atmosphere, what chance did Gobar have to express himself fully as a competitive wrestler? He knew the answer only too well.

In 1909, soon after Khetracharan's death, a young Gobar, accompanied by his brother-in-law Sarat Kumar Mitra, an affluent businessman with a love for wrestling, travelled to Lahore to witness the most legendary rivalry in wrestling at that time: a bout between Gama pahalwan and Rahim Sultaniwala.

22

ENTER GAMA

Rahim Baksh Sultaniwala was a giant. Born in Gujranwala, Rahim trained under Gulam, the wrestler Motilal Nehru took to Paris. At 6′9″ and over 130 kilos, Rahim's sheer physical presence made him a fearsome opponent. To take further advantage of his overwhelming size, Rahim also came to his fights covered in vermilion—like a red demon coming out of the underworld.[120]

By 1909, when Gobar and his brother-in-law went to Lahore to see Rahim fight Gama, the two had already met twice. The first bout was in 1902, when Gama was still a young tyro looking to make his mark, and Rahim was the chief court wrestler at the princely state of Junagadh. They met in a wrestling festival in the state, and though Rahim towered more than a foot above Gama, the match went on for nearly an hour without a fall. Four years later, Shivaji Rao Holkar, the great wrestling patron and raja of Indore, invited Rahim and Gama to come and fight in his court. Yet again, after almost two hours of wrestling, the bout ended in a draw. The legend of Gama had started to coalesce.

Gama was born Ghulam Muhammad in 1878 or 1880 in a family of wrestlers of Kashmiri heritage. Gama's father, Aziz Baksh, a court wrestler in Datia, began taking his son to the akhada when he was just five. When Gama was eight, his father

193

died and the responsibility for training him passed to his maternal grandfather, Nun pahalwan. When he too passed away a couple of years later, Gama's uncle Ida pahalwan took over the tutelage. Ida pahalwan is said to have reminded Gama daily that it was his duty to become a great wrestler, because that is all his father would have wanted from him. In any case, that Gama's devotion to wrestling was of a rare variety was made apparent when he was just ten years old, in a competition organized by the raja of Jodhpur, where wrestlers from around India came to test who could do the most baithaks. Over 400 wrestlers competed, and after several hours of non-stop squats, only fifteen were left. Gama was one of them. The rest were all well-known wrestlers. The raja of Jodhpur had seen enough—he stopped the competition and declared Gama the winner. Gama had later said in an interview that he could not remember how many squats he had done, but it was probably several thousand, and that he was bedridden for a week after the competition.[121] By fifteen, Gama had been formally appointed court wrestler in Datia.[122]

Between 1904 and 1909, Gama's fame started to spread as he won a series of courtly tournaments across India. He won at the court of Rewa, at Orchha, in Gwalior and Bhopal, Tikamgarh and Indore, Baroda and Amritsar, and at Datia, where he pinned another famous upcoming wrestler, Ghulam Mohiuddin, in only eight minutes. There was only one man Gama had not beaten: the giant Rahim.

The match Gobar and Sarat Mitra witnessed in Lahore—Gama and Rahim's third encounter—lasted for around two hours, with neither man able to pin the other.

The fight inspired Gobar. What if these incredible wrestlers were taken to London? To the heart of the Empire? To prove once and for all that Indians were neither cowardly nor lacking in physical prowess. That, indeed, they were masters of a sport, of an art that tested the strength, courage and will of a man to its extreme.

Sarat Mitra agreed to pay for the trip. He acquired the services of London wrestling impresario and circus promoter R.B. Benjamin.

In April 1910, the troupe of wrestlers arrived in England. Gama, his brother Imam Baksh, Ahmed Baksh and Gamu—all from the same akhada—accompanied by a cook, some helpers, Sarat Mitra and Gobar Goho. R.B. Benjamin had arranged living and training quarters for them at the Oak Hotel in Surbiton, at Kingston-upon-Thames.[123]

But the young Gobar had travelled without letting his family know, and when the Gohos did come to know about it, a terse telegram was sent to him: 'Come home, mother seriously ill.'[124]

Soon after he arrived in London, Gobar was back on a ship headed to India. There, with the hope of domesticating him, he was married to Radharani, the ten-year-old daughter of an influential landowning family.

The rest of the wrestlers, meanwhile, began preparing for their European adventure.

In its 14 May 1910 issue, the London magazine *Health & Strength* announced 'The Invasion of the Indian Wrestlers'. The wrestlers were to fight in the 'catch-as-catch-can' style—the precursor of freestyle wrestling, very similar to kushti—as opposed to the Greco-Roman style, which was more popular in Europe and involved standing wrestling with no leg holds, a style unknown to the Indians.[125]

The magazine carried this challenge:

The sensation of the Wrestling World
Exclusive Engagement of India's Catch-as-catch-can Champions.
Genuine Challengers of the Universe.
All Comers. Any Nationality. No One Barred.

Gama was billed as the 'undefeated wrestler of India, winner of over 200 legitimate matches'. Imam was the 'Champion of Lahore', Ahmed the 'Champion of Amritsar' and Gamu the 'Champion of Jullundhur'.[126]

The challenge was that any wrestler who withstood five minutes against these Indian champions without being thrown would be awarded five pounds. From Gama, there was a further challenge—he would take on any three men who agree to fight him, without weight restrictions, one after the other, for one throw.

For good measure, the magazine made it clear that the wrestlers 'are all British subjects'.

There was only one problem. There were no genuine challengers to be found. Wrestling had already started to lose its value as a real sport, and was fast becoming music-hall entertainment, at least in the big cities: showy, scripted matches between giant muscular men full of 'flying holds' and dramatic reversals.

Just a year before Gama and company reached England, George Hackenschmidt, a Russian wrestler who at the turn of the century had been a genuine European champion, wrote in *Health & Strength*: 'Wrestling is my business…I am certainly very fond of the sporting element which enters into it, (I) should be absurdly careless if I allowed my tastes in that direction to interfere too seriously with my career.'[127]

Nonetheless, Hackenschmidt was, at the time Gama was looking for challengers, one of the most successful professional wrestlers[128] in London, so the Indian issued a direct challenge to the Russian. Hackenschmidt denied him a fight.

Gama and his troupe stuck to a strict training routine: 'They would rise at 5:30, wrestle for two hours, then drink a quart of milk with Indian spices,' an article in *Health & Strength* reported.[129] 'Breakfast at around 11:00 would consist of eggs, dahl, and rice, prepared by their own cook, who had travelled from India with them. A rest followed and then at 3:30 there would be two hours of exercise. About 7 o'clock, the main meal of chicken or mutton would be eaten. Finally, before retiring for the night at 9:30, another quart of milk with spices: the wrestlers had brought twenty varieties of spice with them.'

Gama and his men waited. April turned to May, May to June, June to July. A whole summer spent in the London house, practising, hoping and wondering why their European adventure had died before it even got a chance to take off.

Magazines carried reports of Gama's 'Hopeless Quest'. *Health & Strength* made the reasons explicit: Gama had many offers of 'lucrative employment', the magazine said in an article, if only he would be willing to 'go down'—fight a pre-scripted bout, throw a match. 'He simply doesn't understand what that means,' the article said.

Benjamin raised the prize money, directing his challenges at other pro wrestling stars of the time: to the polish wrestler Stanislaus Zbyszko, known as the Greco-Roman champion of the world, promoted by Hackenschmidt's former manager (and manager to Harry Houdini as well), Gama will 'throw him three times in one hour for 100 or 200 pounds a side'.

To the American Frank Gotch, known as the catch-as-catch-can 'champion of the world', a sum of 250 pounds was offered.

To the world: any man for 100 to 500 pounds.

To the Japanese champions who had come for the grand Japan–British Exhibition in London: 'Gama is prepared to throw every one of the thirty Japanese wrestlers…in one hour.'

No luck.

Gama and his men went out some evenings, to some music hall or the other to put on an exhibition, where they showed how Indian wrestling exercises were done and then a few wrestling moves.

Finally, at the end of July, an American wrestler called Doc Roller accepted Gama's challenge. He was a real doctor, Dr Benjamin Franklin Roller, but with his powerful, 6'1" muscular physique, he was well inclined towards rough, physical sports. Roller had played American football, and had made the switch to pro wrestling only in his thirties—just around four years before this match. He had made a reputation for himself working[130] matches with Frank Gotch.

Training began with renewed vigour at the Surbiton house. A correspondent from the London daily *The Sporting Life* was invited to come and witness a session.

'To watch Gama at work is to realise that one is looking at a master of his craft,' the correspondent wrote. 'He is there on the mat to get his man down on his shoulders, and it is obvious that the paramount thought in the Indian's mind is that the quicker his opponent is defeated the greater is the credit due to himself.'[131]

That journalist, used to seeing the show bouts of pro wrestling, had met a real wrestler: 'He is not wrestling with one eye on his adversary and one on the spectators. There is no wasting of time playing for head holds or holds of any other kind. He doesn't play for holds at all, he goes in and takes them, and should it happen that his opponent is clever enough to avoid the first attack he also has to be ready to meet the next, which comes upon him with lightning rapidity.'

In every way, the correspondent realizes, Gama is a wrestler of the highest order—he has speed, technique, power and execution: 'He is a worker and he sees to it that his opponent needs to be a worker too unless he is to go down on his shoulders within the first five seconds. There is no letting up, no breathing time, no holding off to gather wind and strength when Gama is wrestling. Move follows move with such tremendous rapidity that it is not entirely easy to distinguish the particular chip which brings about a fall. From grip to grip he changes with the quickness of lightning, arms and legs both at work, the one ready at an instant's notice to supplement the movement of the other. Thus it is that one loses sight of the man's enormous strength.

'But his opponent knows it's there. There is no violent

striving for half-nelsons; there are no deliberate movements by which an opponent may be held so that a particular hold may be obtained. An uninitiated person might almost consider that he was witnessing merely a rough-and-tumble, get-hold-anywhere encounter, but it is not so. There is a purpose behind every movement. Both offensively and defensively he knows the value of leg work and in addition he knows a good deal about leg work which the smartest catch-as-catch-can wrestler in this country has never thought of.

'And all the while his wrestling is clean. There is no violent exercise of his strength when having forced an adversary into a particular decision which suggests that if the victim does not move something will be broken. There are no strangles, no foot twists, no bridging or head spinning, the latter for the very simple reason that the Indian wrestler has no use at all for ground wrestling. His wrestling is done on his feet. If forced to the ground, or to ease himself he goes down, his object is not to sit there and seek defence, but to get up as quickly as he can and resume the struggle afoot, and the opponent who does try ground wrestling against Gama will very quickly find that he has made an unlucky choice.'

It is the most detailed and vivid account of Gama's wrestling that we have.

On the afternoon of 8 August 1910, Gama and Doc Roller met at the baroque Alhambra Theatre, which loomed over Leicester Square.

The massive hall was 'packed to the point of suffocation': 'The large and Cosmopolitan crowd at the Alhambra, this afternoon, to witness the contest between Gama, "Lion of The Punjaub", and the American, Dr Roller, was sufficient testimony to the fascination of wrestling, for both men were newcomers to London,' said the *Western Daily Press Bristol*.[132] Hundreds were turned away from the door. Roller, at 6′1″ weighed in at 234 pounds, Gama, a half inch below 5′8″, at 200 pounds.

One street down, Sir Arthur Conan Doyle's dramatized version of 'The Speckled Band' got its own dedicated crowd as it opened for its first show after moving to the newly built Globe.[133]

Gama came out to fight in his langot. 'Gama boasted nothing but a pair of red tights not worth the name of bathing drawers'. Roller wore long, dark blue trunks. Gama did a few rapid squat jumps, 'stooping, a la Jap, and bounding in the air like a ball', before the bell for the bout rang.[134]

The first fall was quick, and brutal. 'Gama sprang in for a leg hold at once, and Roller, very slow, was pulled to his knees,' *The Sportsman* reported. 'The Yank was soon up, only to be in a body grip, and backing to the ropes put across in front of the footlights fell over, his head coming heavily in contact with the bare boards.'[135]

Shaken by the impact, and off balance, Roller had to be brought back to the centre of the mat by the referee. Here the attacks continued: Gama immediately got a waist hold, forcing a helpless Roller down on the mat with a heavy thud. First fall: one minute forty seconds. A ten-minute interval was taken.

'Gama opened the second bout with a smack on the neck, and then ducking quickly got a leg hold, which Roller broke.' After his experience in the first round, Roller was cautious and defensive, looking to get out of Gama's way.

'The men were on their feet feinting for holds for a minute and a quarter, and then the Indian again got a body grip, and after a brief struggle Roller was sent to the floor. Gama from here to the end did all the attacking.

'The end came in 9 min 9 sec, when, after worrying his man with a vicious arm hold, Gama locked the American's legs and won with a press down from the front.

'It may interest Mr Kipling to know that the gallery greeted the dusky victor as "Gunga Din".

The *Times* of London commented on the match as well, reporting that some of Roller's ribs were broken during the fight, and that Gama would beat Zbysco and Gotch if they met. All the leading European wrestlers, the *Times* said, referring perhaps to Hackenschmidt, were hiding in the Swiss mountains.

Now there was something to cheer about. Once the first match had gone down so well, and taken up with so much enthusiasm by the press, other wrestlers would find it harder to hide from Gama's challenge. Benjamin got Zbysco to agree to a fight. This would be at The Stadium, Shepherd's Bush, in September.

The *Daily Mail* wrote in August 1910 that Gama had gone to see the venue, and then walked over to the massive Anglo-Japan White City Exhibition right next to the stadium.

'Clad in a smart lounge suit, surmounted by a glittering gold turban, and followed by a retinue of three Indian wrestlers and a native cook, the well-known athlete critically surveyed the stadium, which will be the scene of the encounter on the 10th of next month. After briefly expressing his satisfaction with the arena, the like of which, he observed, he had never seen before, Gama and his party made their way to the "Wiggle-Woggle". This attraction seemed to inspire a sense of fear as well as amazement in the Oriental visitors, and all attempts to persuade Gama to indulge in a trip proved futile, the wrestler seating himself upon a neighbouring chair, with squared shoulders, and resolutely shaking his head to the suggestion.'[136]

It was all too well that Gama did not board the Wiggle-Woggle—something between a roller coaster and 'the Twist', mounted on a giant wobbly platform. It left a lasting impression on those who did strap themselves to the spinning chairs. George Orwell was only six when he was put into the Wiggle-Woggle at the Exhibition. Years later, the memory came back to him during a harrowing ride in an ambulance during the First World War.

'By the evening enough sick and wounded had trickled in to make up a few ambulance-loads, and they sent us on to Barbastro,'

Orwell wrote. 'What a journey! It used to be said that in this war you got well if you were wounded in the extremities, but always died of a wound in the abdomen. I now realized why. No one who was liable to bleed internally could have survived those miles of jolting over metal roads that had been smashed to pieces by heavy lorries and never repaired since the war began. Bang, bump, wallop! It took me back to my early childhood and a dreadful thing called the Wiggle-Woggle at the White City Exhibition. They had forgotten to tie us into the stretchers. I had enough strength in my left arm to hang on, but one poor wretch was spilt on to the floor and suffered God knows what agonies.'[137]

In the lead up to the highly anticipated Gama–Zbysco fight, Imam Baksh managed to get a match with John Lemm, a superbly built Swiss strongman, and one of the contenders for the best wrestler working in the London halls along with Gotch, Zbysco and Hackenschmidt. On 5 September, the Alhambra was packed again, this time for Imam against Lemm. If Lemm was stocky and sculpted out of a boulder, Imam was a model of manly beauty: 6 feet tall, lean and statuesque, with piercing eyes and a regal nose—a newspaper described him as 'really like a great cat, wonderfully nimble and lissom, able to turn and twist with lightning-like dexterity'.[138]

At the very start, Lemm rushed in and got a hold, seizing the early advantage. Within seconds, that advantage was gone. Baksh toyed with Lemm, picking him up bodily and slamming him down, followed immediately by a full body hold executed at lightning speed. In a second over three minutes, Lemm was pinned. 'A masterly piece of work,' the *Sportsman* wrote. The second round was even shorter—Lemm pinned in one minute eight seconds.

The press was thrilled, Baksh had made Lemm, 'the hero of so many protracted battles, look quite commonplace'.

The reporter for the *Nottingham Evening News* made a telling point: 'the match was most interesting on its own merits, but, altogether apart from that, additional interest was lent to the affair by the light which the result throws on the Gama–Zbysco meeting at the Stadium on September 10th. The contention was that if Bux, presumably inferior to Gama, succeeded in pinning down Lemm, whose credentials are beyond dispute, then Gama's prestige must be enormously enhanced.'[139]

Zbysco was among those watching the stormy Lemm–Baksh bout.

23

THE GREAT GAMA,
RUSTOM-E-ZAMANA

As the day for the great Gama–Zbysco encounter approached, Percy Longhurst, who wrote some of the most celebrated manuals on wrestling and martial arts in the early twentieth century, paid a visit to Gama's training quarters.

'I shall not readily forget the day,' Longhurst wrote later.[140] 'The morning he spent in going through a few hundred repetitions of the "dip"; this was followed by several bouts (no rests between) with his fellow Indians, Imam Bux and another. A two-hour rest and a meal followed. The meal, by the way, was a quart of broth, concocted of a couple of fowls, with spices. The afternoon was given up to deep knee bending. Nude but for a loin cloth, out of doors in the warm September sunshine, Gama began his up-and-down motion. Methodically, rhythmically, his open hands on the top of a post standing about 4 feet out of the ground, Gama went on with his knee bending. There was nothing hurried about it; he started as though he meant keeping on forever; and after watching him for a long while, that, so I concluded, was his intention. I timed him by the watch for twenty minutes, and still he continued. The perspiration was streaming down him, but there was never a sign of wavering or slacking off. For how long he actually did continue I do not recall...

'One could understand how Gama had acquired the enormous bulk of solid flesh at the back of his upper arms; whence came the wonderful size of the muscles around the shoulders and the base of the neck. Smooth, solid muscle; muscle in bulk...'

Stanislaus Zbyszko, born Stanislaus Cyganiewicz in Krakow, Poland, was one of the foremost strongmen and Greco-Roman wrestlers of the first two decades of the twentieth century. Like many of his famous fellow wrestlers and strongmen, Zbyszko moved to London after establishing himself in competitions and championships in Europe.

The Polish man was known for his tremendous strength, and his ability to lift enormous weights was as celebrated as his wrestling prowess. In 1906, after winning the Greco-Roman world championship in Paris, Zbyszko was brought to London to make his debut in the world of show wrestling and strongman demonstrations. This move was not surprising. Even the very best wrestlers of the day—the most dedicated athletes—made the switch from real wrestling to pro wrestling. The reason was simple. There was little money and even less organization in competitive wrestling. Pro wrestlers made large sums of money on almost a weekly basis, working the music halls of London and the theatres in the provinces.

'After his London engagement, Zbyszko did enormous business in the provinces,' Cochrane, his manager of that time, wrote in his 1925 book *Secrets of the Showman*. 'I supplied him with a number of aggressive contestants, who always appeared to have a good chance with him—and this made for big receipts. I had learned from experience with Hack[141] that the music hall public required a show, and I had no compunction in giving them what they wanted—a show.'

In 1908, for example, when Zbyszko was appearing at the London Pavilion regularly with the promise of an open challenge, a massive Turkish wrestler—Turkish wrestlers were all the rage then—called Kara Suliman, 'The Champion of the Bosphorus', son of a wealthy carpet seller, took up the challenge. On 4 January, the two met for a 50-pounds-a-side, twenty-minute match. Neither could get a fall in the stipulated time, with Zbyszko on the defensive throughout. The crowd reacted badly, booing Zbyszko, and rioting inside the hall. Some of them pulled the electric lights off the walls and threw them on the stage. To calm the crowd, a return match was announced. The Pavilion, shaken by this incident, cancelled all wrestling at the hall, but other theatres lapped it up. The Gibbons hall signed Zbyszko for eighteen weeks, the Holborn Empire agreed to host the Zbyzko–Suliman rematch.[142]

The rematch was a more robust affair, with Zbyszko on the point of losing several times, his shoulders just millimetres off the mat, till he finally took Suliman down.

There was no Kara Suliman. The 'Champion of the Bosphorus' was actually a Bulgarian strongman called Ivan Offtharoff, who was in Zbyszko's employ. The *Sporting Life* revealed damaging details of this deception: how Offtharoff lived in a house rented by Zbyszko, and how all of the Bulgarian's bills were paid by the Polish man.

'We cannot deny that there is a certain element of humour in the situation,' the *Sporting Life* wrote. 'Here are two foreign wrestlers hoaxing the British public as it had not been hoaxed for many a long day.'

The 'deluded British public', the article said, 'were rolling up in their thousands to pay for admission to see the wrestling…Is this wrestling farce never to end?'

Zbyszko recovered from this fiasco, and a year later, when he faced the Russian Ivan Podoubny, considered throughout Europe as the best Greco-Roman wrestler of the time, the crowds came again in droves. Thousands had to be turned away from the London Pavilion, the venue, even though ticket prices were steep.

'I have never known Piccadilly Circus to be more crowded than on the day of the match,' Cochrane recalled in *Secrets of the Showman.*[143] It was a grim, violent match. Zbyszko was brutally fouled by Podoubny, but despite a bloodied face, he was unmoveable. The crowd went into a frenzy, and Podoubny was finally disqualified for repeated fouling. The match was billed as the Greco-Roman Championship of the World, so Zbyszko could now claim to be the holder of that title.

He now started touring America as well.

When his match with Gama was arranged, Zbyszko knew full well that this was not going to be a scripted bout but a real test of wrestling, and he trained accordingly, spending hours at a gym in Rottingdean as well as swimming, wrestling, boxing and hill-walking every day.

A popular tabloid called *John Bull*, owned and run by the well-known raconteur, rabble-rouser, member of Parliament and soon-to-be-convicted fraudster Horatio William Bottomley, sponsored the Zbyszko–Gama fight (*John Bull* had also backed the Gama–Roller match). It was fixed at 250 pounds a side, and an honorary trophy, the John Bull Belt.

On the afternoon of 10 September 1910, a 12,000-strong crowd descended on The Stadium, Shepherd's Bush. Gama was on the attack from the very beginning. Within a minute, he had Zbyszko down on the mat. Bewildered by this frenzied opening, Zbyszko immediately went down to a defensive position—on all four on the mat, and sliding down on to his stomach at the slightest sign of danger that he would be turned on his back.

A couple of months after the match, in a letter to the editor of *Health & Strength* Zbyszko said: '...as I had expected, I found Gama to be a remarkably good wrestler. It has always been acknowledged on the Continent that I am a good wrestler when in an upstanding position, and that I have improved in this during the last few months as my victories over Dr. Roller, Antonitch, Steinbach, etc. will show, and I am willing to prove my capabilities at upstanding wrestling at any moment; in spite of this, however, I found that I could not stand on my feet for two minutes against

Gama…as soon as there was any space between us he brought me to the mat with one of his swings which I really cannot yet understand.'[144]

With Zbyszko clinging on to the mat, Gama tried hold after hold to get him to turn. A quarter of an hour later, the two men were still stuck in the same position.

At the half-hour mark, Zbyszko felt confident enough to get on his feet. A flurry of attacks followed, described in some reports as a 'rugby scrimmage', and he went back to his defensive position, and the whole futile scene played out again on loop. It went on like this for two hours, and the crowd got increasingly agitated.

After two hours and thirty-five minutes of this, the match was stopped due to fading light. The crowd, upset at the Polish wrestler's defensive tactics, surged forward riotously, and he had to be escorted under the protection of the police.

'Gama, who appeared to be fully a stone the lighter man, did most of the attacking, and, in fact, during the whole of the time the contest took place Zbyszko only gained his feet on three occasions,' wrote the *Western Daily Press Bristol* in its report.[145]

A rematch was announced for the next Saturday to decide the winner.

'Fiasco at the Stadium', ran the headline in the *Sporting Life*.

'A more miserable, more disappointing match than this, the first professional out-of-door match of any consequence that has taken place in London of recent years, has fortunately seldom if ever taken place,' the report said. 'It was disgraceful, a mockery of wrestling; and by it the game, which, it had been hoped, had received a healthy stimulus and recommendation to the public interest, has received one more bad shock.'

Almost all of the ire was directed at Zbyszko. The editor of *Health & Strength* called him 'a figure of ponderous, gawky, clumsy cowardice'—though Gama too 'evinced a woeful ignorance of the technicalities of ground wrestling'.

Some wrestlers, though, took a different view. Baron Helmuth von Knobelsdorf-Brenkenhoff, a German wrestler plying his trade in London at the time, pointed out that this in fact was what real wrestling was like.

'When I bought my ticket,' he wrote, 'I expected to see no "wrestling" as I knew that it was a straight match. People who know only a little of wrestling know too well that they can never expect exciting bouts in straight heavyweight wrestling. Certainly in fake wrestling and exhibition bouts both competitors try to bring themselves into most impossible positions and come out of even more impossible ones, thanks to the previous "arrangement". I do not want to mention names, but I have witnessed two well known champions wrestling for three-quarters of an hour and going six times over the footlights among the audience, taking the referee with them on one occasion. The audience took this game as most serious.'[146]

A few days later, *Health & Strength* carried the comments of the two wrestlers themselves. The editor went to see Gama at his training quarters at the Oak Hotel, Surbiton, and talked to him through an interpreter. Gama, he noted, had taken to wearing a bowler hat occasionally, 'and very handsome and dignified he certainly looks'. The Indian champion said he was sorry he had to win in such a way, but it was very difficult to deal with someone who just wouldn't wrestle—and here he compared Zbyszko very unfavourably with John Lemm—and he was sure that he would have beaten Zbyszko if the contest had been continued on 17 September. He felt that Zbyszko knew this, and that was why he had fled London.

In his interview to the editor, Gama revealed another reason why his ground wrestling was so limited: 'You have no idea how handicapped I was in my match with Zbyszko by my ignorance of the English language. The referee spoke to me several times. I knew that certain holds were barred, but I had a very hazy idea as to what they were, and I fancied every time the referee spoke he was cautioning me. For instance, when I had hold of Zbyszko by the foot he said something to me, and, believing that I was doing what was not allowed, I relinquished my hold, and thereby lost a decided advantage. I have since learnt that he merely meant to point out that I mustn't put on a toe-hold. His caution was really a friendly one, but, unfortunately for me, I misunderstood it.'

In effect, what Gama was saying was that he would have been better prepared for a rematch. When the date came around, Gama and his entourage reached The Stadium. Zbyszko's name was called out several times, but he had already left England. Gama was declared the winner, and Horatio Bottomley, the editor of *John Bull* presented him with the John Bull Belt, saying he was glad to find that a *British subject* had won.

Where was the strike against colonial arrogance at the heart of the Empire? This fight wasn't the flag of indigenous physical culture flying against the imperial idea of Indian weakness; not the bold and brave statement against racism, against the propaganda that Indians were inferior to their British overlords.

That fight was fought by the black American boxer Jack Johnson, who arrived in England, on the run from Jim Crow and his violently racist ways, a year after Gama.

The British searched desperately for the 'Great White Hope' who would beat the 'unruly negro' and show him his proper place of subservience.[147] A match with 'Bombardier' Billy Wells (an India-returned British army man, the perfect candidate for the 'Great White Hope') sparked incredible racial tension in London. Just the idea that such a match was to happen created such a tsunami that everyone from the British Home Office—Winston Churchill was the home secretary then—to the ecclesiastical leaders of England got involved. If Johnson was allowed to fight in London, Reverend J.H. Shakespeare of the British Baptist Union said, 'White and Black will be pitted against each other in anger, revenge, and murder, especially in lands like America in which the negro is the gravest of all problems.'[148]

This then is what nationalists in India would have wanted

for Gama—this debate, this fear among the colonizers about the hidden strengths of its subjects. Instead, Gama and his men were at best good wrestlers and 'British subjects' who had done the Empire proud by beating those arrogant wrestlers from the continent. At worst they were a circus act in a city full of wonderful and exotic curiosities from all over the world.

Count Vivian Hollender, a major in the British Army, summed it up: 'Many people who swear by, and even applauded Hackenschmidt and other foreign wrestlers, will not even bestow a welcome to a British subject even if it is not a Britisher,' he said. 'I refer to the Indians. It is an extraordinary thing that an American negro, as a boxer [Jack Johnson], should be more popular than an Indian, who is not only a British subject, but an entirely different class of man.'[149]

If there were anti-imperialist undercurrents to Gama's stay in London, it was quickly subdued. The editor of *Health & Strength* wrote just before the Gama–Zbyszko fight that 'I actually received letters from readers in India pointing out that if they [the Indian wrestlers] kept on winning, their victories would give a dangerous fillip to the seditions amongst our dusky subjects that menace the integrity of our Indian Empire. But that is another story, upon which I do not propose to enter.'

Gama's time in England had come to an end. In the winter of 1910, the troupe made their way back home. They went as quietly as they had come.

In India, though, the story had acquired a different momentum. Gama was hailed as a hero, and his fame spread ever wider. He was feted as the world champion of wrestling, a title that Gama believed he had earned. Among many nationalists and physical culture enthusiasts, he became the symbol of India's suppressed strength, a glorious, wholly indigenous icon of masculinity.

The maharaja of Patiala gave him land and showered him with gifts. He was invited to the twenty-fifth session of the Indian

National Congress at Allahabad in December 1910, where an Indian wrestling championship was held along with the United Provinces' Exhibition. About 10,000 people gathered to see Gama, reported the *Aberdeen Daily Journal*, and 'so far, Gama, the famous Indian wrestler, has not been defeated'.[150]

At Allahabad, Gama fought his old nemesis, the giant Rahim Sultaniwala. S.C. Muzumdar, a physical culture historian who wrote the book *Strong Men Over the Years* (1942), witnessed that fight. Sultaniwala swaggered towards the arena covered in red ochre, shouting out his battle cry, 'Deen, Deen Elahi'—'a red fury let loose from the underworld', Muzumdar wrote. Gama was calm, regal, patient, 'a veritable Apollo'. It was a breathless, furious battle. Sultaniwala retired hurt.

Gama was undefeated. He was Rustom-e-Zamana, champion of the world.

24

Pioneer Gobar

It could lead to a riot.

It had happened before, much to Lou Daro's glee, though he was arrested for it.

Here he was, the former circus strongman, in his sharply cut suit, his floral-print tie, a red carnation on his lapel—a big man with a big voice.

Here he was, Mr Daro, smiling his jowly smile, doing his last-minute round inside the brand new Grand Olympic Auditorium, which had opened just a couple of weeks before.

What an opening! Rudolph Valentino, pomaded and ravishing, was there. Jack Dempsey, mean and massive, but melting hearts with his angel smile, was there. Bejewelled matrons, spangly gowns, blonde curls, long legs, politicians and businessmen—the grand opening of the grand auditorium, Newsboy Brown and Sammy Shack on the fight card.[151]

Back when he was arrested, Daro had played a little publicity stunt for his wrestling show, giving away 50,000 free passes for a match to be held at the Philharmonic Auditorium, which had a seating capacity of 5,000. When the hall filled up, and thousands more were stranded outside threatening to pull the venue down, the police had to be called. This was much better—more than 15,000 seats at the Grand Olympic, the first auditorium in America built for boxing and wrestling.[152]

This was where he belonged—he was not Daro here, but Carnation Lou, wrestling impresario, the man with the 'greatest chest expansion' in the world.

Los Angeles, 22 August 1925. Showbiz!

The crowd gathered outside the solid, boxy stadium, the art deco flair on its façade embellished further with posters for the show. They came in streetcars and Ford Model Ts, and placed wild illicit wagers on the wrestling. The newspapers too had drummed up the event, Carnation Lou's second big wrestling show in as many weeks.

'Lou Daro, the circus luminary of a decade ago, breaks into the limelight at the Olympic Auditorium again tomorrow night with a pair of new performers for his mammoth mat show,' said a splashy article in the *LA Times*.[153] 'The rotund rasslin promoter, showmanship oozing from every pore of his torso, has added two of the most colorful stars in the wrestling game.'

One of the stars headlining Daro's show was well known in Los Angeles; Joe Stecher, a Nebraska farmboy who had been a wrestling sensation for a decade now, and holder of the 'world heavyweight championship'. Stecher was a long-limbed, preternaturally good-looking man with radiant blue eyes, a smile that could light up stadiums, a cleft chin and 'legs so strong they could crack the ribs of an elephant'.

The challenger for Stecher's title was unknown to the good people of LA—exotic, mysterious and foreign—a prince from India, no less. The newsmen had a field day with him. He had been sent by the raja of Egypt, and he had come with six slaves as training partners, said one.[154]

'Coming from India, he naturally has many habits that seem nothing less than freakish to the American public,' declared another. 'In the first place his favourite food is gold fish and it is not served with a dash of applesauce either. In India, the natives dine almost exclusively on gold fish and rice. The richer you are the more gold fish you are able to buy as they bring a fancy price.'[155]

The giant Hindu wrestler, the article concluded, 'being a nobleman, is naturally able to dine on the fish to his heart's content'.

Yet another article offered a different perspective. It was not goldfish, but actual gold that the prince ate. 'The Hindu, three times a day, swallows a small gold leaf. His slogan is "Have you had your gold today?" It takes the place of a stimulant and puts him in the right physical state for a tough match'.[156]

He had been 'wrestling ever since he was old enough to wiggle his ears', the newspapers said; back home, he keeps a stable of '200 wrestlers'. 'The mat game being the great national sport of India, the Hindu noblemen look upon a fine stable of wrestlers in the same light as an American or Englishman does a splendid collection of racing horses.'

'Massive Hindu Tops Mat Card' screamed the headlines.

People streamed into the Grand Olympic. The outlandish mystery man against the all-American hunk. Irresistible.

The wrestling ring was ready and glowing in the centre of the Grand Olympic, the floor sloping away in tiered octagonal lines from it, and then the enormous balcony, ever steeper as it swept upwards in every direction towards the roof.

The fans were in their place. The giant Hindu, his imposing height peaked by an elaborate turban, wrapped in an ornate shawl and sporting a dignified moustache, came out of his tight little dressing room. He had travelled down a long, strange road to be here. He had not been sent by the raja of Egypt, if such a thing even existed, and he had no taste for goldfish. He was not a prince, and had no stable of wrestlers. He had come from Calcutta from a well-known business family, which was turning rapidly into a well-known wrestling family, with the expected accompaniment of a slide in fortunes. He was a musician and a patron of music. He had left his young wife back home.

He was ready.

Stecher was ready.

The announcer crooned his name into the microphone, stretching each syllable for maximum effect: GO-BAR—like crowbar—GO-HO.

The overcrowded auditorium roared.

After he returned home, leaving Gama and his band of wrestlers back in England, Gobar grew increasingly more restless. What was he to do now? His predicament had not got any better. He was still barred from fighting in India. In 1911, while R.B. Benjamin took yet another set of Indian wrestlers to England, Gobar made a second attempt to go.

In London, wrestling had fallen on even harder times. Real matches were almost impossible to come by, and even the pro wrestlers had left the hostile environment of the city and gone to the more lucrative shores of America, where the public was less concerned about authenticity. Gobar struggled to find opponents. There is little information about what exactly he was doing in Europe at this time, but some of his contemporaries say that he was attending university as well. Then, in 1913, newspapers carried reports of 'another wonderful wrestler', an 'Indian called Gobar, who stands 6ft. 1in., is 20 years of age, and has a chest measurement of 50in'.

The reports carried a challenge: 'Gobar is open to wrestle any man in the world for 50pound a side Graeco-Roman or catch-as-catch-can.'

A few months later, Gobar fought and beat Jim Campbell, one of the foremost pro wrestlers in Glasgow at that time, on 29 August 1913 at the Coliseum in Glasgow.[157]

The next wrestler to lose to Gobar was Jim Esson, at the time the top pro in Scotland, at the Olympic Theatre in Edinburgh. Esson, a lean, long-limbed man, was one of the few people of the time who could lay claim to a legitimate wrestling title as well—he

won the first world freestyle heavyweight championship, held in
London in 1908 by the National Sporting Club.

There is little else to report about Gobar's trip to Europe,
except that he was fond of telling his friends the story about how he
met Jack Johnson. The great heavyweight boxing world champion
was by then in exile in Europe, hounded out of the US by Jim
Crow laws, and then out of England after the controversy over his
match with Billy Wells (which was banned by the government).
Johnson too was finding it hard to get any legitimate matches,
and had been reduced to fighting 'open' challenges and scripted
bouts at cheap music halls in Paris. In December 1913, Esson had
travelled to Paris for one such bout with Johnson.[158]

In 1914, a catch-as-catch-can wrestling tournament organized
by the Swiss wrestler and strongman Maurice Deriaz brought
together wrestlers from across Europe to Paris. It was probably
held to influence the Olympic Congress—which was being
conducted in Paris at the same time—to include catch or freestyle
wrestling as a permanent Olympic sport.[159]

Gobar too travelled to Paris for the tournament, fighting three
bouts or so, including a victory over Belgian wrestler and future
Olympian Poul Hansen. It was here that Gobar met Johnson.
Gobar would later recount to novelist Hemendrakumar Roy and
other friends how Johnson asked him to demonstrate some Indian
wrestling moves backstage at the tournament. He asked Gobar
to hit him on the neck—a common opening move in wrestling.
When Gobar did so, the boxer was unfazed. The wrestler hit
him repeatedly—Johnson laughed off the blows. He then asked
Gobar to hit him with a boxing punch while he stood in a small,
restrictive space. Not one punch connected with the fleet-footed
Johnson, Gobar would later recall with great fondness.[160]

Then in 1915, as the First World War consumed Europe,
Gobar returned to India.

Like Gama, the accepted narrative about Gobar is deeply
entwined with the myth of the fall and resurgence of physical

valour in India. In biographies, hagiographies, newspaper profiles and reports, and even in more scholarly works, he is remembered as a wrestling pioneer who was one of the first Indians to conquer the world of international wrestling. All these accounts claim that Gobar was the first Asian to win the 'world light-heavyweight wrestling championship', defeating a German wrestler called Ad Santel at the Coliseum in Chicago.

Gobar spent six years in the US in the 1920s, a time hailed by both his contemporaries and later writers as a watershed event for Indian wrestling.

The truth is that 'world light-heavyweight wrestling championship' was merely a part of the pioneer years of 'wrestling entertainment' in the US. There were hundreds of world champions doing the pro wrestling rounds. Zbyszko, was a world champion, but so were Frank Gotch, John Lemm, Joe Stecher and any number of wrestlers.

'It really does not matter much who is champion, anyway, a fact which the customers are unwilling to admit as to pugilism, although in wrestling they are quite willing to divide the title three ways,' ran an article in the *Chicago Daily Tribune* in 1919.[161] 'There are three heavyweight wrestlers in the United States alone who claim to be the heavyweight champion. Each has his own territorial rights. Jim Londos is champion in New York and its vicinity; Don George, the ex-collegian, is champion of a large practice elsewhere, and John Pesek of Nebraska seems to be the heavyweight champion of the world in Columbus, O., Cincinnati and certain counties in West Virginia.'

The article goes on to elucidate on what 'wrestling' in the US really was like.

'The earnest desire of the wrestlers to entertain the patrons is a rebuke to the cultivated indifference of the heavyweight pugilists. They heave one another in long spinning flights to three-point landings in the aisles…

'They squeal, they whinney and utter strange animal cries,

which, naturally, suggest that a group of wrestlers should be called a herd, and when one heavyweight starts knocking another one's skull upon the floor like a babboon banging a cocoanut on a rock, the patrons understand that whatever else may be said of all this, it is entertainment.'

The correspondent reported that he sat next to 'Mr Mulrooney, the commissioner of police' at ringside, and the director of the prize fight 'hitched and twisted in his chair' in excitement and joy as the 'long exhibition' thrown together by Jack Curley, one of the most successful pioneers of make-believe wrestling in the US, drew to a conclusion.

'And now,' he said at the end, turning to well-known local cynic, 'and now I want to ask one favour of you. If this was a fake, please don't tell me anything about it.'

Gobar's six years in the US was spent right in these heady early days of pro wrestling. Many of the names in the article above were people Gobar knew well. He fought Jim Londos and John Pesek and Ed 'Strangler' Lewis many times, and was part of Jack Curley's 'herd' at one point.

In many ways, Gobar was a pioneer. One of the first foreign wrestlers, certainly the first from India, to be a part of what has now become a multi-billion-dollar industry.

Yet, in Indian articles and writings on Gobar, this is completely glossed over. Like the *Chicago Daily Tribune* reporter, if it was fake, they wanted nothing to do with it.

Perhaps it is difficult to reconcile the notion that the most successful wrestler from a rich, 'elite' family—one that had played such a strong role in the early years of the physical culture revolution in Bengal and India, and known for its patronage of music—would spend years as a make-believe wrestler in a carnivalesque business.

Perhaps Gobar himself allowed this deception to take root, since even his friends and contemporaries speak of his time in the US as one where he competed as a genuine wrestler, and won a legitimate world title.

This is a disservice to his legacy.

In his grand adventure in the US, Gobar was joined by the most famous strongmen and pro wrestlers from Europe, many of them legitimate wrestlers who had won serious championships—Zbyszko himself, and his brother Wladek, Adolf Santel, John Lemm, and many others. There was really little else to do if you wanted to make money as a wrestler. The controversies about fixed matches in Europe and the audience's apathy towards real wrestling (which was either too slow and ponderous for them, like the Gama–Zbyszko fight, or too fast and incomprehensible, like the Imam–Lemm fight) had dried up most of the earnings a wrestler could make. Neither were there very many real contests that wrestlers could enter—the sport was simply not organized in the way modern wrestling is. For the giants of Europe, America was the new land of hope, and Gobar too followed that trail.

25

LOST IN WICHITA

Gobar arrived in New York on board a ship in January 1921. Almost immediately, the press, which was in the pay of pro wrestling's managerial hustlers, began spinning colourful stories of this exotic foreign fighter.

'Jatindra Charab Goho is now in this fair country,' announced the *Brooklyn Daily Eagle* on their Sunday pages on 16 January. 'A tall, smiling, agile, swarthy person is Jatindra.'

A series of crafted inaccuracies followed—Gobar is an 'Oxford graduate', is under the patronage of the 'Maharaja of Indore' for whom he won a 'monster carnival in Calcutta'.

Gobar fought his first match just a little over a week later, against a journeyman pro called Tommy Draak in Brooklyn. It was not the best of starts for the 'hefty Hindoo' as newspapers would christen him.

'Having seen the hefty hindoo in 18 minutes and 50 seconds of most masterful inactivity against Tom Draak, the big Hollander, Gobar might well have been named the "Nirvana Kid",' wrote a disgruntled Brooklyn reporter, while making snide remarks about Gobar's weight.

'Maybe the ballast was what enabled Gobar to remain down so firmly when Draak got behind him,' he wrote. 'A couple of more matches with the Hindoo and Draak would be better qualified as a weightlifter than a wrestler.'

Gobar had yet to learn the nuances of pro wrestling; yet to master the 'flying' moves, the theatrical expressions and the outrageous tumbles that it demanded.

By the end of summer though, he had switched coasts, and could be found in San Francisco, fighting Ad Santel in the match for which he later came to be so famously known as the 'light heavyweight world champion'.

'Jatindra Gobar, chewing gum and all, had too much beef and strength last night for Ad Santel,' reported the *San Francisco Chronicle* on 31 August. Gobar won one fall in one hour and three minutes with a crotch hold, and Santel had nothing in reply. 'Santel used every pet hold that he ever possessed in his efforts to throw Gobar. But Crowbar or whatever his name is, bided his time, broke holds when he was ready, and won the honors with an ease that was somewhat astonishing.'

Gobar flowered after this match, as the wrestling circus moved out of the big cities and shifted focus towards smaller towns. In Wichita, Kansas, his arrival in October sent the press into a tizzy, and a flurry of whimsical articles appeared in the papers about the 'hefty Hindoo'.

Part of the excitement was that he was matched with Ed 'Strangler' Lewis, then the most popular and the most fearsome of the pro wrestlers in the US. One article described him as an 'exceptionally intelligent Hindoo', and a 'Mohameddan not allowed to touch the food of non-believers' in the same breath.

The *Wichita Beacon* noted Gobar's 'clean record' against Americans: 'won over Mort Henderson, masked marvel, Tommy Draak, Ad Santel, light heavyweight champion…'—and concluded that if Gobar succeeds in throwing Lewis, 'it will place him in a position to demand a match with Zbyszko and, a chance at the world's heavyweight title…'

His match with Lewis was a huge success. The papers were full of praise for Gobar, who got the first fall against Lewis but eventually lost the match. He was quick 'like a fourteen toed bearcat'; he was strong, 'never before had the fans here seen such a wonderful pair of legs as Gobar possessed and his arms and his back were much stronger than Lewis'; and his defence was 'tricky', 'he would drop to the mat from a standing position and come up behind Lewis'.

Most importantly, he had won a fall against a man who had not suffered one since he lost his 'world championship' title to Zbyszko a few months earlier, despite having fought, since then, Joe Stecher, Earl Caddock, Dick Daviscourt and Wladek Zbyszko—'the most surprised man in America at 10:30 Saturday night was Ed "Strangler" Lewis…he lost a fall to an "unknown"', ran one story.

In between the frenzied press and the interminable screwball matches, charming slices of Gobar's life revealed themselves.

On 30 October, a Sunday, he went on a hike around the Wichita countryside. Walking for miles through forested paths, Gobar soon realized that he had lost his bearings. When he made his way back to the motorway, he found himself at a crossroads. Confused, and with no sense of how far he had gone from the city, Gobar took a few steps down one road. To his relief, he found a poster tacked to a telephone pole—it was an advertisement of his match against Dick Daviscourt, scheduled for the next day. Gobar began walking down the road towards Wichita when a car with four women came to a halt next to him. Gobar and the women spoke, and he soon found out that they were missionaries who had worked in India. The missionaries gave him a lift back to the city.[162]

'The missionaries won't tell me their names,' Gobar told reporters on the eve of the match, 'but you can say for me that I feel great gratitude and appreciation for their having rescued me when I was lost on the country roads.'

For the next year, he cut a lonesome path through the vast American plains. He fought in Fulton, Missouri; Alton, Illinois; Appleton, Wisconsin, where he was described as a 'grand looking Prince' who came to the fight wearing a 'gorgeous pink brocaded bathrobe lined with blue', with a black-and-red wrestling outfit underneath; then Milwaukee, Wisconsin; Springfield, Massachusetts; and Odgen, Utah.

By 1924, Gobar had acquired enough fame to be turned into the subject of a long satirical poem that appeared alongside the daily strips of a Pennsylvania paper:[163]

> 'The outlook wasn't pleasant for the Mudville fans that night;
>
> The matmen couldn't do their stuff, their antics were a sight;' it begun.

Soon, the crowd is clamouring for one 'Casey' to take the ring— presumably a local amateur who was in the audience:

> 'If only Casey in the ring would toss his hat,
>
> They'd bet their socks and overcoats with Casey on the mat.'

And then, as a 'mighty yell' that 'shattered forty skylights' went up from the 'maddened mat fans', Casey, 'tin-eared Casey' advanced to the mat.

> 'Ten thousand eyes were on him, as he soaked his hands in oil,
>
> Five thousand tongues applauded as he rubbed his favorite boil.
>
> Then, when the greasy Gobar gave him the beeg, strong grip,
>
> Defiance gleamed in Casey's eyes, a sneer curled Casey's lip.
>
> And now the swarthy Gobar came hurtling through the air,
>
> Caught Casey by the ankles, a trick that was a bear.
>
> Right through the ropes flew Casey, and landed on his head.

"It serves me right," said Casey. "Old stuff," the judges
said.'

Gobar was unique. At a time when even European wrestlers were
considered exotic, he was an Asian plying the pro trade in the
US. It was only a matter of time before Lou Daro—Carnation
Lou—who managed 'Strangler' Lewis, and was fast becoming
the most successful of all the wrestling promoters in the country,
signed Gobar on.

Daro ran a pro wrestling monopoly in California, jealously
guarded through influence and generous payouts to politicians,
law enforcers and the press. On 12 December 1924, an *LA Times*
headline shouted 'Daro Signs Gobar for First Bout'.

Gobar, though, became the exotic fall guy in Daro's circus—
always the 'foreign menace' who would pose a serious threat to
one of the 'great' American wrestlers, but would inevitably end
up losing the match to the American.

Writing later in 1954, at a time when foreign wrestlers
(including many from India) had flooded the US pro trade, the
journalist A.J. Liebling explained the concept in an article in the
New Yorker: 'A Foreign Menace, in most cases a real wrestler,
would be imported. He would meet all the challengers for the
title whom [reigning champion Jim] Londos has defeated in any
city larger than New Haven, and beat them. After that, he and
Londos would wrestle for the world's championship in Madison
Square Garden. The Foreign Menace would oppress Londos
unmercifully for about forty minutes, and then Londos…would
whirl the current Menace around his head, dash him to the mat
three times, no more and no less…'

Despite the soul-sapping nature of his work, there are curious
glimpses of Gobar as a different man from the one that appeared
on the mat as the fall guy known as the 'hefty Hindoo'.

On 3 April 1922, for example, Gobar delivered a lecture at the
Modern Arts and Letters Club in New York titled 'Rabindranath
Tagore—His Life and Teachings'. Around the same time, in

an interview to the *San Francisco Call*, Gobar spoke about his favourite writers—Bernard Shaw, Oscar Wilde, Jerome K. Jerome—and said: 'I belong to that newer race of thinkers in India that is against caste. The caste system must go. It is blinding India. And yet even free America is not so free in some ways as caste ridden India. In America, I notice, money makes the castes.'

Four years later, we hear of Gobar attending a lecture by one Dr Charles Sissons of London University at the Tabernacle, a gorgeous theatre in Queens, New York. The lecture was titled 'The New Democracy in India'. The *Standard Examiner* reported that Gobar got into an argument with Sissons, objecting to some of the things the professor said. Following this, he wrote a letter to the *Examiner*[164]—a lucidly argued indictment of British rule in India, and the imperial mode as a whole:

> Dr Sissons said it is hard to introduce self-government in India on account of numerous castes, religions, and India never had self-government. India had village self-government with full facilities of education for boys and girls in 500 BC, [and] until the advent of British rule. They ruthlessly destroyed the village industry, and with it went all the old Indian custom, tradition and chance for education…
>
> England never kept her promises in India, since the proclamation of the late Queen Victoria, right after what is known as the Sepoy Mutiny in 1857, down to the latest promises of Lloyd George in 1917. King George repeated it when England begged India to help her, which she did, hoping England would keep her promise. India gave many men and vast sums of money, the exact amount I can't tell right now, and what did she get? As soon as the peace was declared came the Rouellate act [Rowlatt Act], and later a massacre of innocent men, women and children by General Dyer in Gallianwallah [Jallianwala] Bagh in Punjab. The much vaunted British democracy

let that general go free and I believe he is still drawing a pension from India.

England will stay in India and exploit her as the educated Indians do not get rid of their slavish mentality. I do not blame England a bit for it. I dare say if India had the same chance she would be liable to do the same. But what I object to is that anyone tries to prove that England is in India because she has such a big moral responsibility, and as soon as India will be able to take care of herself she will leave India.

Has the British parliament, which is called the mother of parliaments and symbol of democracy, given freedom to any nation up until now? Even you Americans, who were supposed to be their kith and kin, had to take it from them.

I had no intention to get into any argument at the lecture in the tabernacle last Sunday, but I was stopped several times when I tried to ask questions. One question I asked the learned doctor was: 'How much money was drained from India since the British advent?' He said he did not know, and he was speaking on the Indian problem, and the obstacle to poor British democracy in India. According to William Digby, an Englishman, 1000,000,000 pounds sterling was taken out from India without any return. Anyone can find it out if they care to by looking into his book, called 'Prosperous British India'.

I was pained to find out that a cultured audience, as last Sunday night's was, was not in a mood to listen to truth.

Please allow me to correct a mistake in your paper, and that is that I am not a philosopher, but I hope to be one some day and also a true internationalist.

Yours truly,
J.C. Goho (Gobar)

26

THE END OF THE GOLDEN AGE

By 1927, Gobar's American adventure had come to an end, and he was back in Calcutta. The family business was slowly disintegrating. As the Goho family became more involved with the nationalist ideals of the time, working with the British was getting more and more untenable. Anyway, Gobar was neither interested nor trained for business. He was content to keep the family akhada running.

In 1928, Zbyszko travelled to India for a rematch with Gama organized by the maharaja of Patiala. It was a strange match. Thousands of people turned up for it, and there were plenty of royalty in attendance, but the match was over in forty seconds.

With his very first move, an ageing Gama took an equally old Zbyszko down. It was the end of their careers as active fighters. Gama was put in charge of the maharaja's akhada in Patiala.

Zbyszko moved to the US, where he settled down in a farm in Savannah, Missouri, with his brother Wladek. The two started a pro wrestling school here, and trained future pro stars.

Carnation Lou's career as a wrestling promoter too came to an abrupt halt in 1939 when a special state investigative committee in California found that he had an illegal monopoly in the business and had paid more than $200,000 over four years to sportswriters, radio announcers, politicians and public relations firms to endorse his business.

'Strangler' Lewis emerged as the new king of pro wrestling promoters along with Billy Sandow and Joseph 'Toots' Mondt, who together formed what later came to be known as the 'Gold Dust Trio'. Mondt would go on to form the wildly popular World Wrestling Federation (now known as World Wrestling Entertainment) with Vince McMahon Sr, whose son still owns WWE.

For all that he was running a pro wrestling school, Zbyszko was scathing about that world in the handful of interviews he gave. 'If the public would refuse to be cheated, the promoters would be compelled to turn to useful work,' he told *New York Times*.

In another, a lengthy correspondence with a wrestling writer in 1957, he said, 'Worlds Champion nickel a bushel. That's the downfall of this noble sport of wrestling, just to be like rotten apple a rotten apple for rest of the sports.'[165]

In this letter, Zbyszko spoke at length about Gama, 'the magnificent athlete from far-off India, the tiger of Punjab'.

The Indians, he said, 'are superbly trained their system is attack furious with abandon attack charging—they never think of serious opposition never are pressured properly [even] if they find themselves in real danger...danger is unknown to them'.

Zbyszko died in 1967, eighty-eight years old, and broke. No one could tell why one of the most successful pro wrestlers in history lived his last years in poverty.

As for Gama's sad end, more was chronicled.

The 'tiger of Punjab' had five sons and four daughters. All of his sons died young. Jalaluddin, his last son, died aged thirteen in 1945, and it was said to have sapped Gama of his will to live. Two years later, in the murderous Partition of India and Pakistan, Gama and his family were forced to move to Lahore. They lost all their land, and most of their wealth. He established an akhada in Lahore, but in 1951, he took out a loan in Karachi from the Refugee Rehabilitation Finance Corporation. With this loan, he bought a bus and started the 'Gama Transport Service'. Within two years, the company folded, and Gama returned to Lahore.

In 1955, Gama issued a final, lonely challenge to a world that had forgotten him—he would wrestle anyone, anywhere, at any time.

No one came.

Gama had a series of heart attacks, and slid further into poverty.

At this point, the Birlas, the family who had financed Guru Hanuman's akhada in Delhi, heard of Gama's troubles and gave him a grant of Rs 2,000 and a monthly pension of Rs 300 for a year. The West Pakistan health minister intervened too, admitting Gama to the Mayo Hospital in Lahore at public expense.

In 1960, wrestling fan Walter Steinhilber travelled to Pakistan to meet the Great Gama. He wrote about that meeting in *Health & Strength*: The chief physician at the Mayo Hospital, a military attache, and other VIPs 'led the way through what seemed miles of antiseptic-reeking corridors—ward after ward. At last we were ushered into a cold, dark and dank cot-crowded room. And here, wrapped in a blanket, squatting on his high hospital bed, I found the Great Gama in the flesh. What flesh there was left was arthritis-racked.

'In the hospital wardrobe and a woollen scarf wrapped as a turban, there was little to remind one that here, as a fact, was one of the giants of all time.'[166]

On 22 May 1960, Gama died.

'Oh he was a strange one, the old man,' says the thin and hoary former wrestler, peering through thick glasses, and smiling warmly. 'A strange, wonderful man, the old man!' He slams his fists on the large table in front of him with startling verve.

Biswanath Dutta is one of the last living students of Gobar Goho. He is eighty-four, and every morning, without fail, he comes to Gobar's akhada. It is not an easy trip to make—from his apartment in the suburbs, he walks a little over a kilometre, with fast, long strides, to a bus stop. Here he hops on to a crowded bus, standing and swaying through the bumpy twenty-minute ride. Then there's another kilometre to walk, and one of the busiest and biggest streets in Kolkata to cross, before he arrives at the akhada on a thin lane in the older part of the city.

The lane is called Gobor Guha Sarani. Here, a small old door leads into the akhada that Gobar called home for the last thirty-six years of his life. It's built like most akhadas are—the raised wrestling pit in the middle of a courtyard, surrounded on all four sides by a series of rooms.

'This was the old man's room,' Biswanath says from across the table. 'And he slept here,' he points to a low bed in one corner of the room, on top of which are displayed framed photographs of Gobar, some newspaper clippings and some of his exercise equipment. The walls of this small room, lit by two windows opening out to the street outside, are filled with framed black-and-white photographs of various members of Gobar's family, students of his akhada and the great wrestlers of the past—Gama, Imam, Gulam.

Biswanath was born in a village near Chittagong, now in Bangladesh, and his family moved to Calcutta in 1942.

'When we came here,' he says, 'we had nothing to call our own. Nineteen of us lived in three small rooms in Sealdah.'

His father started working in a tailoring shop, and this is where he met Gobar, who had come in to get measured for a three-piece suit. When Biswanath's father realized who the man was, he encouraged his son, who was already spending most of his time playing football, to join the akhada. Biswanath took to wrestling quickly, and in 1944, won his first state championship. But his family continued to struggle with poverty, and in 1949, with his school-leaving exams looming, Biswanath's father went to Gobar to tell him that the young boy did not even have a corner in their house in Sealdah where he could sit and prepare for his exams peacefully.

'Send him here, let him stay here,' the old man told my father immediately, Biswanath says. 'That's what he was like, he did not wait to think it through—he had space, I needed a place to stay, for him it was that simple.'

By then, the Goho family's fortunes had dwindled to almost nothing. They had sold most of their property (twenty houses, according to Biswanath), and all the patriarchs were dead. Gobar did not enter the family business, and moved into one of the last remaining houses of the Gohos, and opened his akhada a few metres down the road. In 1949, when Biswanath began to live in the akhada, it was already in a slightly dilapidated state.

In 1952, Gobar's wife died. A few days later, Gobar left the family house to his five sons and four daughters, and took refuge in the akhada. Here, he cut all his ties to the past splendour of his life, and settled into a monastic routine.

Somewhere in the 1950s, the novelist Hemendrakumar Roy met Gobar at a social evening in the house of a common friend.

In that house at the far end of Masjidbari Street belonging to a 'rich and art-loving' friend, the same street where the Gohos had a house as well, Roy was to meet the wrestler many times. On Saturdays, a musical session was held at the house, and Gobar would not miss a single one, Roy recalls. 'You could see from the expression of his face, that he was drinking deep the beauty of the music, with his heart and soul and ears.'[167]

Soon, Roy found himself visiting Gobar at his akhada. A small nucleus of journalists, writers, poets and teachers had begun gathering there regularly.

'The old man slept on the bed, and I slept on the floor,' Biswanath recalls. 'In the morning, before sunrise, the old man would get up and start doing squats and push-ups, and at the same time, there was another fellow who lived here, another poor boy called Shabitullah who was training in music, and he would start practising on his sitar. Then the other boys would come to wrestle, and the old man would sit on the bench outside his room and give instructions. He spoke very little. Just a "hmmm" or an "yes" or a "no, not like that"…mostly, he spoke in gestures. At eight, practice was over, and he would go outside and sit and smoke his cheroots.'

My grandmother, who walked down this same street on her way to school, remembers seeing Gobar sitting and smoking every morning. 'All of us girls knew who he was, the great wrestler, and seeing him in the morning was something we always looked forward to,' she told me. 'Every day, it was the same. He sat outside his house, in a white kurta and pyjama, with a Gandhi topi on his head, smoking his cigar.'

One day, the electric supply to Gobar's house was cut off after a skirmish over unpaid bills.

'A few months after that, Satyen Babu (the scientist Satyendranath Bose) was sitting in this room talking to the old man,' Biswanath says, 'and the conversation veered towards this lack of electricity. Satyen Babu told Gobar Babu, "Listen, enough is enough, get the electricity restored." The old man looked at Satyen Babu, and said, very calmly, "But I have got used to living without it, I don't need electricity." I remember it so clearly that even thinking about it makes me want to cry.'

Biswanath is silent for a moment after saying this. He looks blankly at the wall. Outside, a small street market has sprung to life. There is the clucking and crowing of chicken, a fishmonger shouting out his wares, two women quarrelling in shrill voices and the squeek-squeek of a rusty bicycle passing by.

'The old man used to tell me in his last years, he would tell me, "Bishu, get me adh pau [around 125 gm] of meat,"' Biswanath says. 'Who will tell him that you can't get adh pau meat any more? I used to stand there at the shop embarrassed, and the shopkeeper would tell me, "If you want adh pau meat, you will have to wait for it." So I would wait.'

Then one morning in 1972, Gobar woke up and felt a pain in his chest. Biswanath remembers him asking another student of his:

'If you have a heart attack, which side of your chest hurts?' The student did not know, but everyone advised him not to exercise, to lie down and take it easy. The pain did not go. Sometime in the afternoon, he had a heart attack. A doctor came and stayed with Gobar for most of the day. It seemed like the danger had passed. Late at night, Gobar had another heart attack.

'It was a good way to go,' Biswanath says. 'He suffered very little. He was doing everything he did the day before he had his heart attack, he was perfectly fine…Listen, that old man, he was…I did not understand then what he was, what I was in touch with. I did not understand that he would give me everything I got in my life. That because of him I would live my life with happiness. The old man, he was a saint. I still miss him.'

Biswanath laughs. 'What a man,' he says again, and again, he slams his fist on the table. He gets up quickly, as if remembering something suddenly. 'It's time to go home,' he says.

27

THE AKHADA

The akhada exists in an illusion. The most urban of wrestlers believe, with no trace of irony, that they are deeply rural. The akhada is built within the bubbles of this deception. In the cities, even the largest of them are hidden from view in plain sight. You walk down a chaotic traffic-snarled street, horns blaring with full gusto all around you, choked by the smoke and dust, metro lines soaring above you, shop lights blazing all around, and there will be a wall, an insignificant yellowing thing, not especially high, not much in span, and there will be a little door, you may have walked past it a hundred times without really noticing it, but this time you walk through it, and...

The noise ceases. The air clears up (this too is an illusion), and there is the smell of rich earth. There's a well-muscled man, skin glistening with oil and sweat, ploughing the earth. There are large, shady trees, their broad leaves dappling the ground with shadows. There is a deep well, and a pulley with a bucket to draw the water out. After the fifth or sixth time this happens to you, you are less puzzled, but the depth of the mirage becomes more tangible. The akhada, in a few broad masterly strokes, can recreate a slice of village life—not some Disney display of it—but the real thing, in the lost nooks of crammed concrete. The wrestler may own smartphones, wear Levi's and drive SUVs, but his soul is locked inside the akhada walls.

The Varanasi pahalwan Kallu once wistfully told me about a student of his who had gone to train in Russia before the 1984 Olympics. 'They lived in a village meant only for pahalwans! And what a village it was. It had rows of tangerine and orange trees, and they would drink the juice of the fruit straight after plucking. A river ran through it, and its waters were so clean it could cure all skin problems. There were trees everywhere, and the air was pure oxygen. The cows were big and smooth and full of milk—you drank a glass of that milk and you would be full all day. There were apple trees, and wonderful almonds. Not just your body, but your soul would be cured in a place like that.'

It reminded me immediately of a hilarious song that I first heard in a film called *O Brother Where Art Thou*. It's an old American 'hobo' song, written by a folk singer called Harry 'Haywire Mac' McClintock at the turn of the twentieth century, and it goes something like this:

> In the Big Rock Candy Mountains
> There's a land that's fair and bright,
> Where the handouts grow on bushes
> And you sleep out every night.
> Where the boxcars all are empty
> And the sun shines every day
> And the birds and the bees
> And the cigarette trees
> The lemonade springs
> Where the bluebird sings
> In the Big Rock Candy Mountains.

Like Haywire Mac, Kallu dreamt of a village that never was.

Sushil Kumar's father dreams of a time that has slipped away. He owned six buffaloes once, now he has none. There is no space to keep them. All the farmland of his village, and the next village, and the next, they are all gone, replaced by residential buildings and small factories. There is no earth to be seen, no shady tree to sit under. Sushil's family sold all their land and now own only the ground on which their house stands. They made a lot of money from it, more than they could have made from a lifetime of farming, and Sushil's brother is a real-estate manager.

Yet, for them, the urban colonies are the root of all that is wrong. When Sushil comes home, or his father goes to Chhatrasal, the talk inevitably veers towards this theme.

'Now that the colonies have been built, everything has gone bad,' Diwan says. 'There are all kinds of people, no one knows any one, and there are criminals and gundas. It has fucked everything up.'

'Yes,' Sushil agrees. 'The boys from the village have all this money that they have done nothing to earn, except that their father sold their land, and they are driving huge, powerful cars they don't know how to drive. And all day they hang around, do nothing, drink, look at girls, go to a mall in Delhi.'

Diwan's house recently acquired furniture—sofas and wooden chairs and tables—instead of the all-purpose string charpoy. He does not use any of it unless there are guests. He sits on the floor when he wants to sit, and eats his meals sitting on the ground. He takes his afternoon siesta outside in the courtyard, in blazing hot afternoons or cold wintry ones, sleeping on his charpoy with a white scarf covering his eyes. The rumble of passing buses and trucks do not disturb him. Flies settle on him.

The rest of the family is outside too. Sushil's mother Kamala, her brother-in-law and his wife sit on plastic chairs just outside the gate of the house, chatting amiably. They talk about electricity theft in their village, and raids by the police: whose house was raided when, who got their lines cut off, who is scrambling around to get a meter installed to legalize their connection. Then they discuss refilling their quilts with cotton for the coming winter. How much cotton do they need? 2.5 kg? The brother-in-law goes in to get a sample quilt. Do we have to put all new cotton, or just some to bolster the old cotton and then blend it together?

'Just don't touch the old man's quilt,' Kamala says. 'He likes it the way it is—in tatters—let it stay like that. Let's get the rest done nicely. We must get the covers done in colours that don't show too much dirt. That shop in Panipat has good ones for 250.'

They ask the wife, Sushil's aunt who had seen visions of him winning at the 2008 Olympics, to make one more round of tea. 'Put less sugar in his'—they point to me—'he is from the city.'

'See, in the cities people thought wrestlers are gundas,' Kamala says. 'If a city person saw a wrestler on the street, they would cross to the other side. If I told someone my son is a pahalwan, they thought I was saying that my son is a hired strongman for a politician!' She laughs heartily. 'After 2008, that thought changed completely. The whole country suddenly rediscovered wrestling.'

Just the other day, Sushil had attended a dangal sporting a T-shirt with the legend 'Hugs for Thugs' emblazoned across his chest.

The wrestler's world fits itself in a curious interstice, where it can meet everything halfway, moulding what it can, adapting when it has to, rejecting what it must. Wrestling is monastic with the option of a family life; anti-materialist while making comfortable sums of money; it is an escape from the drudgery of the village to an idealized rural life in an urban space; it is somatic but not sexual; spiritual without being overtly religious; it is a little socialist, a little communist, a little capitalist, and it is none of those.

The Chhatrasal akhada, where Sushil trains, is different from most akhadas. Unlike other akhadas, that are more concerned with upholding a wrestling way of life, Chhatrasal is more focused on the competitive, athletic side of wrestling; with training its students for international competitions as well as local dangals.

Yet daily life in Chhatrasal too has the calm rhythm of a village.

I watch Sushil as he trains in a strange compound. It is in the bowels of Chhatrasal, down a large ramp that disappears into the vast underground parking lot built in 2010 for the Commonwealth Games in Delhi. It has no cars now, but one section of the whitewashed catacomb structure with its low ceilings, rows of pillars and flat white light has been turned into a vast training zone. It has three Olympic mats laid side by side, a black square of cheaper warm-up mats next to it, and a rectangular embankment of raised earth for mitti ki kushti in one corner.

This makeshift arrangement was necessary: after Sushil's 2008 Olympic medal, Chhatrasal was flooded with new trainees. The single-mat wrestling hall above ground could hardly contain thirty wrestlers, let alone five hundred.

Sushil, his training partner Pradeep, and a handful of other wrestlers are squeezing out the last bits of energy out of their muscles, practising a new move again and again. The rest of the trainees are done, and most of them have gathered around the two to watch. Sushil, sweat pouring out of him in a river, is breathlessly exhorting Pradeep to get it right. 'Jerk the hip hard to the left, raise it, raise it, bring it on, come on. Now get your left foot in, get it in, get it in, there, shabash!'

'Put all your effort behind the move only if you see that you can go somewhere with it,' Sushil tells the gathered wrestlers. 'Or else, let it go, conserve your energy, think of an alternative. Use your brain first—the muscles will tire easily. Wrestling is in the mind.' He taps the side of his head hard with his index finger, making pearls of sweat fly.

The wrestlers troop out of the basement. Now they bathe in an open area behind the overground hall, using garden hosepipes, and mill around in various stages of undress outside their rooms. There's Sushil again, a towel wrapped around his waist, and vigorously massaging his hair with another one, while chewing a twig of neem. Some of the younger boys have started pounding almonds in large wooden mortars. Others have gone to help in the open kitchen. For lunch, there is dal; large, thick rotis; a salad of tomatoes, onions, chillies and cucumber dressed simply with lime juice and salt; and milk. They eat this with large helpings of ghee—on an average, six to eight tablespoons of it per person. This diet almost never varies. Along with some fruits—bananas, apples, oranges and guavas—and paneer three or four times a week, they eat this meal for lunch and dinner every single day. I love food with a passion and I eat everything, and the first few meals of hot dal and thick roti loaded with pure ghee was delicious. But when it was repeated for the tenth, or twentieth, or thirtieth time, my mind screamed silently for mercy even as I smiled a thin smile at Sushil, telling me yet again how much he loves dal-roti.

The Hariyanvi wrestlers are vegetarian food tyrants. They are obsessed with their difficulties in eating abroad, or really, anywhere else in India where they don't easily get dal-roti. They discuss with horror a training camp once in Goa where they were served fish and rice.

Sushil laughs and recalls how a friend of his, a Bulgarian wrestler with whom he has often trained, came to visit him just before the 2012 Olympics, when the Indian team was in training in Bulgaria. 'He gave me this tin, and he said, "Eat this, it will give you a lot of strength. This is the best food you can get here. It is very special." So I asked him what it was, and he says, "Fish eggs." Fish eggs!' Sushil laughs loudly. 'I told him, brother, I am a vegetarian! I still have the tin with me somewhere.'

It has been two weeks since Sushil won his Olympic silver in London, and after a break with his wife and newborn twins, he is back in the familiar embrace of the akhada. Now he has it all—two Olympic medals, a world championship, numerous Commonwealth and Asian Games titles. Well, almost. He still does not have an Olympic gold. It kills him. Four more years! And all this time, he gets older, the body gets slower, weaker. And what if everything has gone perfectly, and a week before the 2016 Olympics, his ankle twists? Or there is a tear in his shoulder muscle? Or his back cramps? God, no, no. Such thoughts must not be entertained, spoken of, or discussed. There will be no other chances. 2016, if he makes it there, will be his last Olympics. Perhaps his last competition of any kind.[168]

Little has changed in Sushil's room since he first came here as a child. Yes, there is also a small AC now that groans on all day; and a rickety refrigerator, balanced on bricks, in one corner. But the paint peeling off the walls is still a pale green, burnished with dirt stains. The dingy mattresses still line the floors. The wrestler's belongings are still stuffed inside duffel bags stacked on one side of the room. There are still shoes and clothes and singlets in claustrophobic piles. One wall is a shrine—Hanuman the god, Guru Hanuman the coach, and a framed photo of Sushil's grandfather. Another is a shrine to Sushil: numerous photographs of him and cut-outs of articles stuck helter-skelter with glue. There is a rough placard on top of the fridge in India colours with the legend 'Sr Sushil Kumar World Champion' written in a childish hand. These are all gifts from young wrestlers.

The room is cramped, and smells of sweat, ammonia and old socks.

Six wrestlers live here with Sushil. When he was a child, he lived in a room the same size, just a few doors down, with twenty-five other boys of the same age. 'Now that's cramped,' he exclaims.

Before his meal, Sushil goes and inspects the other rooms, pointing out cobwebs, or messy piles of clothes, or unwashed utensils. In one room of senior wrestlers, all the curtains are drawn and the lights are off and in the semi-darkness, six or seven men are collapsed on the floor in their langots in various stages of recline. The room is a mess.

'Get up, you,' Sushil says to one of them, and then looks around. 'You look like bricks lying around on a construction site. Get up and clean—it takes ten minutes—then sleep.'

'When I first came here, it was like a dream for me,' Sushil says. 'I could hardly sleep the first few days because of the excitement. All those huge men with huge muscles! I dreamt only of becoming like them, a big, heavyweight wrestler who could take on anybody.'

Like most wrestlers here—make that all—Sushil more or less gave up on school when he was about thirteen. He continued to be enrolled, and appeared for exams, but effectively, his education was centred on wrestling.

He has little interest in anything else—he's a bit romantic about big cars, but only slightly so, and has a teenager's fleeting fascination with guns and the armed forces. He hums a couple of popular tunes through the day, but has no real interest in music. He does not watch films, or TV for that matter, and reads no books.

Yet his brain is sharp; it's just that he does not allow his mind to wander to anything that is not wrestling. He watches training videos on YouTube on his phone to while away time. He can disappear into his mind mid-conversation—make that mid-anything—and his eyes glaze over. For the next fifteen or twenty seconds, he performs a series of abbreviated wrestling sequences with minute movements of his hands and his body with a faraway, frowning look. Then he will come out of the reverie as abruptly as he went into it, and join the conversation again. He does it all the time, in all kinds of situations, quite unselfconscious.

Wrestling is in the mind, and Sushil is always in training.

'I have no special love for anything except wrestling,' he says. 'I am not even very religious. I believe in god, and spend a few minutes in prayer twice a day. In the morning I pray that the day goes well, in the evening I say thank you for another day. I go to temples and mosques. I don't handle my money—it goes to my father, who does what he thinks fit. If I want or need something, I get it. My assigned role is to be an athlete, a wrestler, and I'm fulfilling that role, and beyond that I don't really bother myself with anything or keep track of anything.'

Sushil is a millionaire. But the money has no place here. Inside the confines of Chhatrasal, he is one of the boys, maybe just a bit more, only because he is the country's most decorated wrestler, and his experience is invaluable.

Why do they come here? All these boys, leaving their villages, their families, forsaking school, living the hardest of lives? There are the sons of farmers, labourers, bus drivers, policemen, electricians, shop owners, tailors and milkmen. There are orphans at Chhatrasal, and boys who cannot afford their own clothes or their own food. What lures them to a sport that asks for everything but guarantees no return? Is it the money? It is true that a national-level wrestler can easily get a government job, the great dream of the vast rural population. An international medal winner can make millions from government awards. Even the local mitti pahalwan, if he is moderately successful, will make more money than his farmer or labourer parents can make. But many of these boys will never taste even that much success, and they will leave the akhada with little education and no practical skills.

Yet they come, they keep on coming. Because kushti offers not just the distant dream of riches, but also a way of life that wrenches them out of a substratum of social anxieties. Wrestler boys pay little attention to school because, for them and their parents, it is a waste of time. A place where the teacher sleeps in the classroom, or worse, is so unqualified that he or she teaches the wrong things. The school is where, under the eyes of the uncaring teacher, the boys go bad. Better the strict confines of the akhada, whose morals and teaching methods are well known, and accessible—any parent can walk into an akhada and watch a class in progress, or spend the leisure time with their children.

'In school, every question I asked was met with hostility,' Sushil says. 'Every question was dumb, to be laughed at or rebuked. The teachers' main lesson was: keep your mouth shut.'

Is it this that turned Sushil into such a manic teacher? He is very open with his knowledge, and all his training sessions are also lessons—he absorbs into the session anyone within his radius. No question is too dumb for him, no one too young, too thin, too fat, too poor, or too rich for him to call on the mat.

The boys come because wrestling does not care for bribes or nepotism or influence. It strips you, it puts you in full public glare, and you either have it or you don't. It lets merit shine in a simple, pure way that anyone can understand. So different from life outside the akhada, where nothing moves without a bribe, and nothing gets done without appealing to undue influence. You cannot get an electricity connection, you cannot get a death certificate or a birth certificate, you most definitely cannot get land registered, bought, or sold; you cannot get a job, and you cannot get your children enrolled in school if you don't know the right people, or grease the right palms. That's the wrestlers' view of the India they live in.

In wrestling, you can go from a small village to being the champion of the world without ever having to do any of this (or just a little bit of it). On mitti or on the mat, your only identity is your wrestling skill—you are caste-less, you have no history, you are not judged by your economic might. Or at least, that's what wrestlers like to believe.

The akhada is a silent revolution against a world gone awry.

'Being strong, that is most important,' Captain Chand Roop had once told me. 'But what does it mean to be strong? If the body is powerful but poverty makes you powerless, are you strong? If the body has muscles but the mind is empty, are you strong? If the mind and body are both powerful, but society strips you of power, are you strong?'

28

THE DANGAL

It has been a year since I last met Satbir, but even in that short space of time, much has changed in his life. When I called him, I was surprised to find that he was no longer in Rohtak, but in Delhi, and was leaving that very night for a dangal in a village near Varanasi.

'Why don't you come with me,' he asked.

'I don't have a ticket.'

'So what? I don't have a ticket either.'

So we met, late at night, at the Old Delhi railway station. Satbir was carrying a heavy, cheap duffel bag. The train was late, so we sat on the platform, backs against a wall, and my eyes closed. I was awoken by a rat sniffing my shoes. Satbir too had gone to sleep, stretched out fully on the platform with no regard for the dirt, his head on the duffel bag. Everywhere I looked, there were people sleeping.

The train was three hours late, and arrived at two in the morning with a great clatter. The air-conditioned coaches, behind the glazed windows, were dark, but the other coaches were lit brightly and people were squeezed in so tight that the ones at the windows had their faces helplessly pressed against the bars.

My heart sank. Satbir led the way, barging through the crowd to enter one of the compartments, and immediately proceeded to block the way for others by sitting down near the door and placing his large bag next to him. I did the same, buffeted by knees and shoes. There was no point trying to enter the compartments—we could see that even before we boarded—so the next best thing was to make the narrow space near the door our own.

When the train started moving, Satbir brought out old newspapers from his bag and spread them on the floor, and resumed his sleep. I stayed awake. It was hot. There were two others on the floor with us, a shrivelled old couple who were now forced to sit with their knees drawn to their chests because of the amount of space Satbir had commanded. I felt guilty. The toilet was right next to us and stank terribly. It was only when the train made its way out of Delhi that a cool breeze through the open door lulled me to sleep.

To reach the dangal, we used almost every mode of transport possible. From Mughal Sarai junction, we took a bus to Varanasi. From the Varanasi bus depot, we took an autorickshaw to another depot, and then another bus to the village where the dangal was taking place. That bus dropped us at a crossroads, from where we walked for a kilometre, farmland all around us, till a man on a bike gave us a precarious lift. He dropped us off at his village, five kilometres from the dangal, and we resumed walking.

Soon, a tractor packed with people stopped for us. I stood on the metal frame of the hull at the back, the only space that was left on the tractor. The frame swung from side to side, and I held on tightly to a handrail, my back and shoulders tiring with each passing moment. Satbir and some of the other passengers sat squeezed together high on the buff above the rear wheels, having a conversation.

'Where are you from?'
'Rohtak.'
'Which akhada?'
'Mehr Singh's.'
'You came alone?'

'Yes.'

'That is a fair distance to travel, brother. Many good wrestlers are coming to this dangal.'

'Oh yes.'

'There is a Bharat Kesri from Delhi.'

'Yes.'

'And our own Baiju pahalwan. Beware of him, he is a big, strong wrestler. His ears are as mangled as yours.'

Part of this conversation was a lie. Satbir was not with Mehr Singh's akhada any more. In fact, he wasn't with any akhada. He couldn't find a good one willing to take him. The reason for this, I learnt partly from Satbir, partly from others later, was that Satbir attacked a coach during a dangal.

He was fighting against another wrestler from a well-known akhada near Rohtak, and was upset that he was losing. He blamed the referee for this. Time and again, Satbir interrupted the fight to remonstrate with the referee. Each time he did so, the coach of the other wrestler, and the owner of that akhada, screamed at him. 'Obscenely,' Satbir said.

'His face looked like a deranged monkey's. He was probably drunk. He kept saying, "Just finish this fight, let this coward go home. He moves as slowly as a grandmother! Send him home!"'

Whatever the truth of that maybe, at one such flashpoint, Satbir lost his cool entirely and rushed at the coach and slammed him to the ground with a flying tackle. Chaos ensued. Satbir and his brother, taking advantage of the delirium, slipped away. The coach had a heart attack and was hospitalized. Satbir did not even try to go back to his akhada. He went to his brother's house on the outskirts of Delhi. Since then, he has heard from his wrestling friends that the news of the incident has reached all the major akhadas in Delhi and Haryana, and that he will not be welcome at any of them. So Satbir is flying solo. He is picking dangals outside the two states and fighting there.

When we finally arrived at the village, a large crowd had

already gathered there. The atmosphere was carnivalesque. There were all sorts of food carts with people calling out their wares.

One thin, dark man, wearing a straw top hat which had real sunflowers stuck on it, sang a ditty about the ice creams he was selling. The children flocked to him. The sun was high above our head, and the air thick with dust as more and more people arrived—in tractors, bikes and cars. When the wrestling began, I was already defeated by the heat, and found it hard to retain any interest in it. Satbir lost after three matches, just two steps from the final.

For the next week, we travelled to various villages in the area, by foot and hitching rides, as Satbir fought in dangals. In most villages, Satbir and I were given a sleeping space by the organizers. They were mostly rooms meant for the storage of grains. There were usually ten or so wrestlers (and me) crammed into a space just enough for us to lie down fully. The rooms smelled so sharply of sweat and muscle spray that I often sneaked out at night and slept outside.

Most of these villages were in the throes of an ugly transformation. Construction dust hung over them like smoke; highways and scarred roads wound around them in strangle-knots; cars and bikes rode roughshod over the chaos; and plastic and garbage choked every open field, sewer and waterbody.

I pined throughout for the simple pleasure of sitting on one of the ghats in Varanasi, cooled by the evening breeze, watching the river flow past in dark ripples.

Satbir is tired of his life as a wrestler. We sit near a canal cutting through farmlands in eastern Uttar Pradesh.

'This is a good place, fertile land,' he says, squinting at the horizon.

'I love this,' I tell him. 'It's so beautiful. I wish I could live here, run around among the trees, swim in the canal when I want.'

He looks amused and disgusted at the same time.

'And wrestled.'

'Yes.'

'But if you were any good as a wrestler you would have run away from the village fast, left all this that you think is beautiful.'

'And gone to Rohtak?'

But no, even Rohtak, once a sleepy university town now growing rapidly into a busy city, is too suburban for Satbir. He wants to escape Rohtak as well. He wants to be in Delhi. Or Australia.

'How is the wrestling in Australia,' he asks me. 'I heard they are no good at it and they want people to go there and become wrestlers for them.'

All these hundreds of wrestlers I see at dangals, Satbir says, are just waiting for their chance to move to a city.

'That's why they work so hard, put their bodies through so much pain,' he says. 'To run away from their villages, get to a city, make some real money. If you are from a village, you will remain a fool all your life. You will make no money, work till your bones grind down to nothing, and talk about the same old nonsense every day.' He slaps a palm on his thigh. ' I'll be getting out of this mess.'

Satbir wants to fight only on mats. He cares little for tradition. There is only one thing he says he will miss if he makes it to Australia.

'You know after training, there is nothing like lying on the akhada mitti. It gives you good dreams.'

Later, Satbir tells me about the village in Haryana he comes from, Mandothi. It is less than 20 kilometres from Sushil's house in Baprola, and boasts a robust crime rate. The village even lends its name to one of the most prolific criminal outfits operating in Haryana and Delhi: the Kartar Singh Mandothi gang, involved in everything from drug trafficking and gunrunning to contract killing.

People in the village, Satbir says, are constantly engaged in blood vendetta. And murders, as Satbir's brother put it so eloquently at some other time, are more common than marriages.

Satbir tells me about a dispute during a dangal in Mandothi where one wrestler was refusing to fight a tie-breaker after a drawn match. 'And the guy says, "You can't do this to me, I'm a DSP in Haryana Police"—and the organizer tells him, "You may be a DSP, SP, or just P, who cares? If you don't fight, we will bury you alive right here and you will become fertilizer." Fertilizer!' Satbir laughs.

'That's what we are like,' he says with a smirk. 'We left the village six years ago. They burned our older brother alive while he was sleeping. Our whole house went up in flames.'

Suddenly, he looks tired, older.

'All the time it was like this. Someone was out to kill someone. People were beaten to death in front of us. Boom, boom, people would take out guns and shoot at any time of the day. My brother was a wrestler. He could not make any money, gave it up and started running booze. Pick up from Haryana, drop in Delhi. Then they made him threaten people. He was a big, strong guy, perfect for that kind of thing. We needed the money. We were making nothing from farming, crops don't do so well there. And anyway, half the land in the village is blocked up in disputes and wasting away, and there's no water either! It's hell. Father and mother were always ill. That's why I went away.'

He loses the thread here. 'What was I saying? Yes, my brother. So anyway, it was bound to happen. He got into arguments with others in the gang. They said he stole money, he shot someone. That fucker lived. He shot him in the leg anyway—right here, on the knee—I don't know what he was thinking. He should have killed him, or not shot at all. Anyway, he shot him in the knee, and then he ran away for a while. I think two or three months, and every day someone came to the house looking for him. They threatened to kill me instead. They stopped us from going to the fields. And then one day my brother came back, and he said everything is sorted, and it will be alright. A few days later, they threw litres of petrol into his room at night, blocked off the exits, and set it on fire. I wasn't there. I was already at the akhada.

'My parents died soon after.'

We travel to one last dangal, Satbir and I, to a village called Tungaheri in Punjab. It is a beautiful place, the air clear and sweet. We arrive a day before the dangal, and live with the family of a former wrestler who knows Satbir well. The house is large, with a sprawling courtyard, a barnyard and a big, loopy German shepherd dog who rubs her head and ears against my legs for long periods of time.

The pahalwan's mother waddles around the house, smiling toothlessly and arranging food for us.

The dangal will take place only a hundred metres or so from the house along narrow thickly hedged paths, on the edge of a large pond. A temporary tent with seats and a dais has been set up in one corner of the akhada.

The wrestling begins. There are some big names on the mat, pahalwans who have travelled here from Uttar Pradesh, Madhya Pradesh and Delhi, some from as far as Bihar, and close to Rs 3 lakh is on offer for the winner.

Satbir has wrangled some ice off a juice hawker and is rubbing it on his left knee, an old injury that is inflamed. I wander around, and enter the 'VIP' tent. The guests of the day include a group of sadhus from a nearby temple, passing around a chillum. There is the sharp, sweet smell of hashish, trapped by the sticky heat inside the tent.

When I find Satbir again, he is sitting at a most envious resting place—a luxuriously shady tree next to the pond. He sits there chewing on a stalk of grass.

'Better to sit here than see the kushti,' he says, looking out at the water. 'I do it for the money, and nothing else. If I could make good money some other way, I would do it and leave this. I have started asking around with former pahalwans in Delhi who run real estate businesses.'

'But what about becoming an international wrestler, going to Australia?' I ask.

'I don't care about it. It is over. I loved it for sometime, but now it's over.'

Satbir looks on wistfully at a gang of children frolicking in the pond. 'I'd rather swim here than fight.'

A herd of buffaloes are being led to the pond by athletic women, tall and lean and beautiful. Satbir and I stare. The buffaloes buck and bellow in ecstasy as they approach the water, but become somnolent as soon as they are in the water. The women scrub them down.

A pair of kingfishers take turns diving into the pond. Dragonflies, deep gold and red, hover on the surface.

Later, when Satbir has already left to warm up and prepare for his fight, the buffaloes are herded back. One of them sneaks away and remains submerged in the middle of the pond with only her snout held in the air. Her eyes are closed in bliss. A small, lean man comes to the bank and calls out to the buffalo, who opens her eyes to look but disregards him. The man lets loose a string of weird noises, alternately berating her for her rebelliousness and appealing to her to come out. After a few minutes, she decides she has had enough, and turns her back to the man and walks deeper into the pond, craftily glancing back. She knows she is a bad cow. The man leaves in a huff.

The buffalo spots the group of children playing in the water near the other bank and makes her way quickly to them. She wades right into their play, the black monster, and begins to roll on her side while the children whoop with delight and splash her with water.

I hear Satbir's name being announced and leave my paradise reluctantly.

Satbir has lost his listlessness, and looks all fired up. He is doing quick squats on the side, while another match is on. It is a hilarious bout. A fat wrestler from Guru Hanuman akhada, a hopeless fighter, is being thrown around by a far better wrestler. The commentator is having a field day.

'Maybe pahalwanji should have come running here from Delhi, lost some weight on the way,' he says.

'Oh no, no,' the other commentator quips. 'Can't you see he is feeling weak today? Someone get him a kilo of jalebi, quick! There's a mithai shop right here. The great pahalwan from the great Guru Hanuman akhada, no pahalwan like him.'

Satbir is unmoved, lost in his world. When the fight ends, he swaggers into the arena.

The wrestlers smear each other with earth. They lock.

They move quickly. Their limbs cut through the air, trailing swirls of dust that glow orange in the setting sun. They coil and uncoil, they stumble and turn, their muscles and veins bulge and shine, sweat drips in muddy rivulets down their dust-covered faces.

Satbir, after two rounds of tussling, holds his opponent in the third with both arms locked around the man's waist.

He looks tired, eyes closed, and he is leaning into the other wrestler, who, spotting an opening, transfers all his weight on to Satbir, his feet leaving the ground with the effort.

Satbir does not resist, no, just the opposite. As he feels his opponent leave the ground, he flings himself backward, so that they are both in the air in a deadly embrace for one dreamlike moment.

Then, in a flash of pure magic, Satbir torques himself and his opponent around in the air, spinning weightlessly. When they land, Satbir on top of his man, the thud makes my heart leap into my mouth. The crowd erupts.

The wrestlers disappear in a cloud of red earth.

NOTES

1. This was narrated to me by a wrestler in Varanasi called Sohan Lal Yadav. A version of the story also appears in Joseph S. Alter, *The Wrestler's Body: Identity and Ideology in North India*, University of California Press, Berkeley, ebook, Kindle edition. Another, more elaborate version can be found in Flora Annie Webster Steel, *Tales of the Punjab: Told by the People*, Macmillan, London, 1917, pp. 211–12.

2. 'There was this American wrestler, remember? He was so fat he could hardly walk.' Sushil is referring to Rulon Gardner, the son of a dairy farmer from Wyoming, who beat the Russian wrestling legend Karelin at the 2000 Olympics to win the USA's first gold medal in Greco-Roman wrestling. Karelin was undefeated for thirteen years before this match.

3. Rohit Brijnath, 'A Shocking Mess', *India Today*, 15 August 1994.

4. 'A daunting prospect', Shekhar Gupta and David Devadas with Amarnath K. Menon, *India Today*, 30 September 1988.

5. Abhinav Bindra with Rohit Brijnath, *A Shot at History: My Obsessive Journey to Olympic Gold*, HarperCollins India, Delhi, 2013.

6. Mark McClusky, 'One One-Hundredth of a Second Faster: Building Better Olympic Athletes', *Wired* magazine, 25 June 2012.

7. David Epstein, *The Sports Gene*, Yellow Jersey Press, London, 2013, p. 6.

8. In standard kushti parlance, a move.

9. See Joseph S. Alter, *The Wrestler's Body*, op. cit., for a very detailed analysis of the connection between body and mind (and soul) in kushti's philosophy, and its connection to religion and caste.

10. Joyce Carol Oates, *On Boxing*, HarperCollins Publishers, New York, 2009, e-book, Kindle edition.

11. The word for kushti training in north India.

12. 'I too am a student of Indore's Vijay Bahadur Ustad!', *Don*, 1978.

13. Greco-Roman wrestling. Olympic wrestling is divided into two styles, Freestyle and Greco-Roman.

14. Thomas Duer Broughton, 'Letters Written in a Mahratta Camp During the Year 1809', *Constable's Oriental Miscellany of Original and Selected Publications*, Vol. IV, Archibald Constable And Company, Westminster, 1813, pp. 163–65.

15. From the Arabic 'Khalifa', 'successor', used to denote the head of a religious order (caliphate) or a teacher.

16. Dirk H.A. Kolff, *Naukar, Rajput & Sepoy: The Ethnohistory of the Military Labour Market in Hindustan, 1450–1850*, Cambridge University Press, Cambridge, 1990.

17. Ibid., pp. 3–6.

18. Ibid., p. 2.

19. *From Sepoy to Subedar – Being the Life and Adventures of Subedar Sita Ram, a Native Officer of the Bengal Army Written and Related by Himself*, Translated and first published by Lieutenant-Colonel Norgate, Bengal Staff Corps at Lahore, 1873, Vikas Publications, 1970, pp. 6–11.

20. Dirk H.A. Kolff, op. cit., p. 20. Here, he is quoting from J.N. Sarkar, *The Military Despatches of a Seventeenth Century Indian General*, Scientific Book Agency, Calcutta, 1969.

21. Nilkanth Sadashiv Takakhav, *The Life of Shivaji Maharaj, Founder of the Maratha Empire*, Manoranjan Press, Bombay, 1921, p. 849.

22. For a detailed discussion of this see, Rosalind O'Hanlon, 'Military Sports and the History of the Martial Body in India', *Journal of the Economic and Social History of the Orient*, Vol. 50, No. 4, 2007.

23. Ramachandrapat Amatiya (tr. by S.V. Puntambekar), 'The Ajnapatra or Royal Edict Relating to the Principals of Maratha State Policy', *Journal of Indian History*, Vol. 8, 1929, Madras, pp. 104–05.

24. D.C. Majumdar, *Encyclopedia of Indian Physical Culture*, Good Companions, Baroda, 1951, p. 21.

25. Rosalind O'Hanlon, op. cit., pp. 510–11.

26. Ibid., quoting from 'Selections from the Peshwa Daftar', a selection of letters and official documents of the Maratha Empire edited by Jadunath Sarkar and published by Government Central Press, Bombay, 1930.

27. Thomas Duer Broughton, op. cit., p. 165.

28. A. Rogers and H. Beveridge (tr. and ed. by), *The Tuzuk-i-Jahangiri or Memoirs of Jahangir*, Royal Asiatic Society, London, 1909, p. 335.

29. Ibid., p. 19.

30. My account is based on Emma Flatt, 'Young Manliness: Ethical Culture in the Gymnasiums of the Medieval Deccan', *Ethical Life in South Asia*, edited by Anand Pandian and Daud Ali, Indiana University Press, Bloomington, 2010, pp. 161–64. Flatt's account is from *Tazkirat al-Mulūk* by Rafi'al-din Shirazi, Hermann Ethe No. 2838, MS 'I.O. Islamic' from the Library of India office.

31. For a detailed analysis of this, see Emma Flatt, op. cit. The narrative here is based on her analysis.

32. 'Futuwwat' is the Arabic word for the Persian 'jawanmardi' and was used interchangeably. *The Futuwwat of Kashifi* was one of the most influential books in medieval India on the proper conduct of the nobility, and was a distillation of the many thoughts and written treatises on jawanmardi. The reference here is taken from Emma Flatt, op. cit.

33. H. Beveridge (tr. from the Persian by), *The Akbarnama of Abu-l-Faz'l*, Asiatic Society of Bengal, Calcutta, 1897, Vol. 1, p. 455.

34. H. Blochmann (tr. from the Persian by), *Ain-i-Akbari by Abu-al-Fazl 'Allami*, Asiatic Society of Bengal, Calcutta, 1873, p. 253.

35. Arthur George Warner and Edmond Warner (trs), *The Shahnama of Firdausi*, Trubner's Oriental Series, London, 1912, Vol. 3, p. 261.

36. Emma Flatt, op. cit., p. 159.

37. Ibid., p. 157.

38. Ibid., p. 159.

39. Ali-Mohamed Amirtash, 'Zoorkhaneh and Varzesh-E-Bastani', *Journal of Movement Sciences and Sports*, Special Issue, No.1, 2008, p. 65; Lloyd Ridgeon, *The Zurkhana Between Tradition and Change*, *Iran*, Vol. 45, British Institute of Persian Studies, London, 2007, p. 245.

40. From a discussion initiated by the author on Language Log (www.languagelog.ldc.upenn.edu), a linguistics blog and research forum run by Geoff Pullum, professor of general linguistics, School of Philosophy, Psychology and Language Sciences, University of Edinburgh, and Mark Liberman, Christopher H. Browne distinguished professor of linguistics, University of Pennsylvania. For a full list of works consulted for the origins of these words, please see http://languagelog.ldc.upenn.edu/nll/?p=24257, last accessed 29 May 2016.

41. The act of girdling the waist has deep connotations in wrestling. 'Belt wrestling', which loosely denotes any form of wrestling where a

fighter is allowed to grab the clothing around the waist of his opponent, is as widespread and ancient as wrestling where the grabbing of clothes is not allowed.

For most of this book I make no distinction between the two forms, since they are heavily intertwined, and their techniques are more or less the same (with the critical exception of the kind of grip you can get on your opponent). Also, in India, kushti has included 'belt-grabbing' for its entire history, and only very recently – beginning slowly from the 1970s – was this practice discouraged to bring kushti more in line with the two Olympic wrestling styles (Freestyle and Greco-Roman), neither of which allows a grip on the clothes. The cloth that is girded around the waist, and in turn, contains the genitalia, also has great ritual significance. See the chapter on Hanuman.

42. Rosalind O'Hanlon, op. cit., p. 197.

43. Robert Sewell (tr. from the original Portuguese by Robert Sewell), *A Forgotten Empire*, e-text by Project Gutenberg, http://www.gutenberg.org/ebooks/3310, last accessed 29 May 2016.

44. Ibid.

45. From the introduction by the author, G.K. Srigondekar (editor), *Manasollasa*, Gaekwad's Oriental Series, Baroda, 1925.

46. Clearly, a reference to the Jyesthimallas.

47. Robert Sewell, op. cit.

48. Rosalind O'Hanlon, op. cit., p. 508.

49. They still do. Though their numbers have dwindled and their importance as a community almost forgotten, in some parts of Rajasthan and Gujarat, the Jyesthimallas still run akhadas.

50. Rosalind O'Hanlon, op. cit., p. 504.

51. From the introduction by the authors: B.J. Sandesara and R.N. Mehta (eds), *Mallapurana*, Gaekwad's Oriental Series, Baroda, 1964.

52. Edwin Bryant (ed.), *Krishna: A Sourcebook*, Oxford University Press, New York, 2007, p. 5.

53. First century CE, or at least fifth century CE. Hindu tradition says that the *Harivamsa* was written by Vyasa. Ekkehard Lorenz, 'The Harivamsa: The Dynasty of Krishna', in Edwin Bryant (ed.), op. cit., pp. 95–97.

54. Benjamin Preciado-Solis, *The Krsna Cycle in the Puranas*, Motilal Banarsidass, Delhi, 1984. The quotes from *Harivamsa* are taken from this book, which translates it directly from the Sanskrit.

55. Joseph S. Alter, *The Wrestler's Body*, op. cit.

56. Ibid. The wrestlers interviewed for this book all characterized butter in this fashion.

57. Another name for Balarama.

58. *Harivamsa*, translation from Benjamin Preciado-Solis, *The Krsna Cycle in the Puranas*, op. cit., p. 79.

59. Ibid., p. 80

60. Benjamin Preciado-Solis, op. cit., p. 82.

61. D.D. Kosambi, *The Culture and Civilization of Ancient India in Historical Outline*, Vikas Publishing House Pvt. Ltd, Delhi, 1997, p. 107.

62. Buddhist tradition holds that the Buddha died in Kusinara, which was a Malla town.

63. For a discussion on the various gods, demons and historical kings in India whose names featured the word 'Malla' – wrestler – see Gunther D Sontheimer, 'The Mallari/Khandoba Myth as Reflected in Folk Art and Ritual', *Anthropos*, Vol. 79, 1984.

64. Edwin Bryant, op. cit.

65. David J. Lunt, 'The Heroic Athlete in Ancient Greece', *Journal of Sport History*, Vol. 36, No. 3. 2009, p. 379.

66. The Games at Olympia, Delphi, Isthmus of Corinth and Nemea.

67. David Lunt, op. cit. p. 381.

68. Stephen Hodkinson, 'An Agonistic Culture? Athletic Competition in Archaic and Classical Spartan Society', Stephen Hodkinson and Anton Powell (eds), *Sparta: New Perspectives*, Classical Press of Wales, Swansea, 2009, p. 158.

69. E. Norman Gardiner, *Athletics in the Ancient World*, Dover Publications, Inc., Mineola, New York, 2002.

70. Robert Brophy and Mary Brophy, 'Deaths in the Pan-Hellenic Games II: All Combative Sports', *The American Journal of Philology*, Vol. 106, No. 2, 1985, p. 174.

71. Ancient Greek wrestling consisted of only standing moves. No ground wrestling was allowed. The first combatant to touch the ground thrice with any other part of the body except the feet was the loser. For more on the sports of ancient Greece, see Stephen G. Miller, *Ancient Greek Athletics*, Yale University Press, New Haven, 2004.

72. E. Norman Gardiner, op. cit., p. 182.

73. E. Norman Gardiner, op. cit., p. 8.

74. Phillip Lutgendorf, *The Life of a Text: Performing the Ramcaritmanas of Tulsidas*, University of California Press, Berkeley, 1991, p. 9.

75. By 'people', I mean the people of the Hindi-speaking regions of India. Major vernacular versions of the Ramayana in Tamil, Bengali, Telugu, etc., had been produced much before the *Ramcharitmanas*.

76. M.K. Gandhi, *The Story of My Experiments with Truth*, http://www. columbia.edu/itc/mealac/pritchett/00litlinks/gandhi/, last accessed 29 May 2016.

77. Phillip Lutgendorf, *Hanuman's Tale: The Messages of a Divine Monkey*, Oxford University Press, New York, 2007, p. v.

78. Ibid., p. 11.

79. For more details on this, see Phillip Lutgendorf, *The Life of a Text*, op. cit., passim.

80. Phillip Lutgendorf, *Hanuman's Tale*, op. cit., p. 31.

81. Prabhu Bapu, *Hindu Mahasabha in Colonial North India, 1915–1930: Constructing Nation and History*, Routledge, New York, 2013, p. 98.

82. Joseph Alter, op. cit.

83. Ibid.

84. Philip Lutgendorf, *Hanuman's Tale*, op. cit., p. 31.

85. Joyce Carol Oates, op. cit.

86. For a detailed work on this, see: Joseph Alter, 'The Body of One Colour: Indian Wrestling, the Indian State, and Utopian Somatics', *Cultural Anthropology*, Vol. 8, No.1, 1993.

87. Philip Lutgendorf, *Hanuman's Tale*, op. cit., p. 186–88.

88. Ibid., pp. 187.

89. Thomas Hubbard, 'Pindar's Tenth Olympian and Athlete–Trainer Pederasty', *Journal of Homosexuality*, Vol. 49, Nos 3–4, 2005, p. 137.

90. Christopher Jaffrelot, *India's Silent Revolution: The Rise of the Lower Castes in Northern India*, Columbia University Press, New York, pp. 157–61.

91. Mark Palmer, 'InterMat Rewind: 1960 Olympics', https:// intermatwrestle.com/articles/7241, last accessed 23 May 2016.

92. Mark Palmer, 'Interview with Ed Dewitt', https://intermatwrestle. com/articles/7241, last accessed 23 May 2016.

93. At least its first competitive wrestler. There have been women wrestlers before, but they were more of a circus act than actual wrestlers.

94. A shorter version of this chapter appeared in 'Lounge', *Mint*, 20 September 2014.

95. Two of the sisters did qualify for the 2012 Olympics, Babita and Vinesh.

96. The training centres run by the Sports Authority of India offer wrestling for both women and men, of course.

97. Captain Godfrey Charles Mundy, *Pen and Pencil Sketches: The Journal of a Tour in India*, Volume II, John Murray, London, 1832, pp. 279–85.

98. Robert Orme, *History of the Military Transactions of the British Nation in Indostan*, J. Nourse, 1763, quoted in Pramod K. Nayar, *Colonial Voices: The Discourses of Empire*, Wiley-Blackwell, Sussex, 2012.

99. William Dalrymple, *The Last Mughal*, Penguin Books, New Delhi, 2007, p. 58.

100. John Rosselli, 'The Self Image of Effeteness: Physical Education and Nationalism in Nineteenth Century Bengal', *Past & Present*, No. 86, Oxford University Press, 1980, p. 121.

101. Ibid., p. 123.

102. Rajnarayan Basu, *Ekal O Sekal*, Chirayat Publishing, Kolkata, 2008, pp. 41–48. First printed as a pamphlet in 1874 and as a book in 1875. Trans. author's own.

103. Ibid., p. 43.

104. Abhijit Gupta, 'Cultures of the Body in Colonial Bengal: The Career of Gobor Guha', *The International Journal of the History of Sport*, Vol. 29, No. 12, 2012, pp. 1687–700.

105. Jogesh Chandra Bagal, *Hindu Melar Itibritta*, Talpata, Kolkata, 2009, p. 25.

106. Rabindranath Tagore, from 'Chhelebela', *Rabindra-Rachanabali*, Vol. 13, Visva-Bharati, Santiniketan, p. 722. Trans. author's own.

107. Now Jessore, Bangladesh.

108. Details from the biography of Gobar Goho. See, Samar Basu, *Deshpremik Mallaveer Gobor*, Ratna Publishers, Calcutta, 1996. Also based on interviews with former students of Gobar.

109. Jogesh Chandra Bagal, op. cit., p. 28. Trans. author's own.

110. Joseph Alter, *The Wrestler's Body*, op. cit.

111. His granddaughter spoke of it with pride later. 'Speech by H.E. Mrs. Indira Gandhi: 1983: The Prime Minister Shrimati Indira Gandhi made the following speech here today after receiving the "Olympic Order Gold" from H.E. Mr. Juan Antonio Samaranch, President, International Olympic Committee. "Our Indian tradition in games, as in many other areas, is an ancient one. It is celebrated in our epics and in our legends. In my own family, my grandfather, Motilal Nehru, did a great deal

to promote wrestling and even took Indian wrestlers to various cities in Europe.'" *Olympic Review*, Official Publication of the Olympic Movement, No. 183, Lausanne, 1983.

112. Graham Noble, 'The Lion of the Punjab – Gama in England, 1910', *The Journal of Alternative Perspective on Martial Arts and Sciences*, Vols I-IV, 2002, http://ejmas.com/jalt/jaltframe.htm, last accessed 29 May 2016. He quotes from Edmond Desbonnet, *Les Rois de la Lutte*, Berger-Levrault, Paris, 1910.

113. Samar Basu, op. cit., p. 9.

114. The foundation of the physical movement in India relied heavily on Muslim wrestlers – they were by far the best in the country, and formed the backbone of the teaching community – but they were neither glorified nor named by the patrons of the Hindu Mela. The 'Hindu Mela', by definition, did not have anything to say about Muslims. This was made explicit by Nabagopal Mitra. When the *Ananda Bazar Patrika* criticized of the Mela's Hindu bent, Mitra wrote in an editorial in the *National Paper*, 'We do not understand why our correspondent takes exception to the Hindoos who certainly form a nation by themselves...'

115. Peter Heehs, *The Bomb in Bengal: The Rise of Revolutionary Terrorism in India 1900-1910*, Oxford University Press, New York, 1993, p. 42.

116. Sarala Debi Chowdhurani, *Jibaner Jharapata*, Dey's Publishing, Kolkata, 2012, pp. 94–96. Translation author's own.

117. Ibid., p. 119.

118. Ibid., p. 121.

119. Ibid.

120. Graham Noble, op. cit., p. 14.

121. Ibid.

122. Joseph S. Alter, 'Gama the World Champion: Wrestling and Physical Culture in Colonial India', *Iron Game History*, Vol. 4, No. 2, 1995, p. 5.

123. Graham Noble, op. cit.

124. Abhijit Gupta, op. cit., p. 1693.

125. During the second Olympics in 1904 in St Louis, USA, Greco-Roman was made a permanent Olympic sport, and 'catch-as-catch-can' was introduced as an 'optional' event. The French, who controlled the world wrestling body, tweaked the rules of catch-as-catch-can in 1921, and called it La Lutte Libre, literally, 'freestyle wrestling'. Till the early 1950s, Americans, Britons and Scandinavian countries dominated the event. Since then, eastern Europeans, Iranians, Turkish and

Japanese wrestlers, who began to tailor their training specifically with the Olympic rules of freestyle wrestling in mind, have become the major wrestling nations.

126. Graham Noble, op.cit.

127. Ibid.

128. At that time, a 'pro-wrestler' was simply someone who wrestled for money. Whether they actually engaged in competitive bouts or put on pre-scripted shows was for the audience to decide. Now, 'pro wrestler' expressly means an entertainer who engages in show bouts. Competitive athletes, like Olympic wrestlers, are 'amateurs'.

129. *Health & Strength* as quoted in Graham Noble, op. cit.

130. In wrestling, 'working' refers to a pre-scripted match, not a real contest.

131. *The Sporting Life* as quoted in Graham Noble, op. cit.

132. 9 August 1910.

133. *Western Daily Press Bristol*, 8 August 1910.

134. Graham Noble, op. cit.

135. Ibid.

136. *The Daily Mail*, 18 August 1910.

137. George Orwell, *Homage to Catalonia*, https://ebooks.adelaide.edu.au/o/orwell/george/o79h/chapter12.html, last accessed 29 May 2016.

138. Graham Noble, op. cit.

139. Ibid.

140. Ibid.

141. 'Hack' refers to George Hackenschmidt.

142. Graeme Kent, *The Strongest Men on Earth: When the Muscle Men Ruled Show Business*, Robson Press, London, 2012, ebook.

143. *Secrets of the Showman* as quoted in Graham Noble, op. cit.

144. Ibid.

145. 11 September 1910.

146. Graham Noble, op. cit.

147. Theresa Runstedtler, 'White Anglo-Saxon Hopes and Black Americans' Atlantic Dreams: Jack Johnson and the British Boxing Colour Bar', *Journal of World History*, Vol. 21, No. 4, 2011, pp. 657–89.

148. Ibid., p. 679.

149. Graham Noble, op. cit.

150. 31 December 1910.

151. Based on an *LA Times* report, 23 August 1925.

152. Cecilia Rasmussen, 'In LA, He Was King of the Ring', *LA Times*, 3 June 1996. The details of the events, places and people come from

this article, photographs from the time, and various *LA Times* articles from the 1920s and '30s were accessed through www.newspapers.com, last accessed 29 May 2016.

153. 'Prince Go-Ho Gobar Meets Champ in Main Event at Auditorium Tomorrow Night, *LA Times*, 23 August 1925.

154. *LA Times*, 12 December 1924.

155. Ibid., 16 August 1925.

156. Ibid.

157. www.prowrestlinghistoricalsociety.com

158. Abhijit Gupta, op. cit., p. 1694.

159. Ibid.

160. Hemendrakumar Roy, 'Ekhon Jaader Dekchhi', *Hemendrakumar Roy Rachanabali: 2*, Asia Publishing Company, Calcutta, 1976, p. 134

161. Westbrook Pegler, 'Wrestling, be it fake or on up and up, provides action', *Chicago Daily Tribune*, 28 January 1931.

162. *The Wichita Daily Eagle*, 31 October 1921.

163. *The Evening News*, Harrisburg, Penn., 3 November 1924.

164. *Standard Examiner*, 30 June 1926.

165. Graham Noble, op. cit.

166. Ibid.

167. Hemendrakumar Roy, op. cit., p. 132. Trans. author's own.

168. Sushil Kumar failed to participate in Olympics qualifying tournaments due to injuries and did not make it to Rio 2016.

ACKNOWLEDGEMENTS

MY DEEPEST LOVE and gratitude to my parents, and Neelam and Shekhar for their love and support; Sanjit Basu for tea, conversations, patience and guidance; Devalina Mookerjee for being such a wonderful friend and for being my proto-editor and reading those terrible first drafts; Sujoy Chakravarty for letting me work in his beautiful house and for all the music; Abhijit Gupta for the original spark; Priya Ramani, who made me write and pushed me into the world of wrestling; my editor Ajitha, without whom, of course, this book would not have been possible; and all the wrestlers who gave me access to their lives so freely and warmly.